The End of the Third Reich

Third Reich

Reich

Defeat, Denazification & Nuremberg,
January 1944 – November 1946

We maintain that war is simply a continuation of political intercourse, with the addition of other means. We deliberately use the phrase 'with the addition of other means' because we also want to make it clear that war in itself does not suspend political intercourse or change it into something entirely different. In essentials that intercourse continues, irrespective of the means it employs. The main lines along which events progress, and to which they are restricted, are political lines that continue throughout the war into the subsequent peace. How could it be otherwise? Do political relations between peoples and their governments stop when diplomatic notes are no longer exchanged? Is war not just another expression of their thoughts, another form of speech or writing? Its grammar, indeed, may be its own, but not its logic.

Carl von Clausewitz, *On War* (1832)

Throughout this war, we have all been facing the distant problem of dealing with Germany after the victory we anticipate. To-day the hour is nearer. It is not easy to bring vividly before our eyes the landscape of wreckage and chaos into which our armies will march, nor to imagine the temper in which the defeated nation will receive them. It is harder still to clear our own minds of the passions which this cruel war has engendered. [...] Year after year we have met this enemy only in one capacity, as the conqueror who was reducing the manhood of Europe to slavery. Our memories are heavy with the recollection of his barbarous crimes. It needs a formidable effort to recall what he was before the plague of Nazi corruption affected him, and a still more difficult act of faith to imagine what he may again become, when the Dictator falls.

H.N. Brailsford, *Our Settlement with Germany* (1944)

The End of the Third Reich

Defeat, Denazification & Nuremberg, January 1944 – November 1946

TOBY THACKER

TEMPUS

First published 2006

Tempus Publishing Limited
The Mill, Brimscombe Port,
Stroud, Gloucestershire, GL5 2QG
www.tempus-publishing.com

British Library Cataloguing in Publication Data.
A catalogue record for this book is available from the British Library.

ISBN 0 7524 3939 1

Typesetting and origination by Tempus Publishing Limited
Printed in Great Britain

CONTENTS

LIST OF ILLUSTRATIONS

All illustrations are from the author's collection unless otherwise stated.

production continued to rise until the end of 1944.

13 Armaments Minister Speer and senior German industrialists enjoy a sociable evening.

14 A propaganda image shows a fashionable lady at a German newspaper kiosk, surrounded by newspapers for foreign workers.

15 The Allied invasion of Italy in 1943 did not bring an early end to the war.

16 Hitler, before the bomb plot of 20 July 1944, which left him physically weakened.

17 Many photographs like this, showing Nazi atrocities in the Soviet Union, were published in Britain and America during the war.

18 Seventeen-year-old German boys doing labour service in 1943.

19 In 1943, the Germans began a long retreat through Ukraine.

20 German grenadiers on the Eastern Front, with Tiger tanks.

21 German rocket artillery on the Eastern Front.

22 Winter on the Eastern Front.

23 Message from Montgomery to his troops before D-Day.

24 The artificial breakwaters used to create a harbour around the D-Day landing beaches at Arromanches.

25 The town of Villers-Bocage in Normandy, on 25 May 1944.

26 Villers-Bocage on 18 July 1944 after Allied bombing.

27 The entrance to the concentration camp at Natzweiler in Alsace.

28 After the failed attack on Arnhem in September 1944, it was not until April 1945 that British troops liberated the town.

29 A British tank equipped with chains for mine clearing moves through burning streets in Arnhem, April 1945.

30 German prisoners are marched past a British tank in April 1945.

31 Tracked amphibious vehicles in the mist near the Rhine.

32 British troops relaxing during the final stages of the campaign in Germany.

33 A propaganda leaflet announces that the Allies are coming to restore law and to punish war criminals.

34 Montgomery's order of March 1945.

35 In the order, Montgomery urged his men not to repeat the mistakes of 1919.

36 Montgomery allowed his men to speak to, and to play with little German children only after the first six weeks of occupation.

LIST OF MAPS

ACKNOWLEDGEMENTS

This book arises from a course on 'Defeat, Denazification, and Division: Germany 1944–1949', which I taught as a Special Subject at the University of Wales, Swansea, from 2003–2006. My thanks go in the first place to the then Head of Department, Noel Thompson, who encouraged me to develop the course, and to the students who took it. Much of the research for the book was undertaken earlier, and I am grateful to the many archivists and librarians in Britain, Germany, and France who have helped with the location of obscure but relevant materials.

A number of individuals have helped particularly with ideas, information, and inspiration. I wish to express my thanks to Gareth Pritchard, now of Canterbury University, New Zealand, who shares my interest in the transition from war to peace in Germany in 1945; to Dirk Deissler, of the Université de Haute Alsace in Mulhouse, who alerted me to some of the intricacies of language reform in Germany after 1945, and generously provided hospitality during visits to Germany and to France; to my former student Gemma Denslow, who kindly lent me copies of some of the papers of Robert Birley; to Cliff Rogers of the West Point Military Academy for his thoughtful leadership of the Clausewitz study group in Swansea University in 2005–2006; and to my former colleague Graham Gordon, who helped with the provision of photographs and documents from the Soldiers of Gloucestershire Museum in Gloucester. Thanks also to Jonathan Reeve, my editor at Tempus, who encouraged me to write the book.

Finally, I am grateful for the support of Susan, and our daughters Amy and Phoebe, in tolerating my absent-mindedness while writing this book, and for helping with the numerous computer problems that confront an author today.

Toby Thacker
Gloucester, 2006

INTRODUCTION

Peace does not exist merely because of a surrender. [...] Our occupation of
Germany is an act of war of which the first object is to destroy the Nazi system.
*Field-Marshal Montgomery explains to his troops what they are doing in Germany
in March 1945.*[1]

The Second World War came to a furious climax in Europe in 1945.
After years of fighting through the occupied countries of Hitler's 'New
Order', in January 1945 huge Allied armies fell upon Germany itself,
from east and west. Millions of Soviet, American, British, Canadian, and
French soldiers, supported by thousands of tanks and guns, fought pain-
fully through German towns and villages, while overhead, by day and
night, huge fleets of bombers pulverised already battered cities. Through
January, February, and March, a desperate resistance was offered by the
remaining units of the German *Wehrmacht*, stiffened by the hardened
soldiers of the *Waffen-SS*. These regular soldiers were supplemented by
hastily assembled groups of elderly men and boys, Hitler's *Volkssturm*,
or 'people's storm'. As Germany collapsed, the most modern weapons,
rockets and jet aircraft, were thrown into the struggle. With total determination, and using overwhelming force, the Allied forces pushed into
Germany. Some towns and villages which found themselves in the front
line were almost totally obliterated by the weight of firepower. Others
still behind the lines faced immolation from the skies.

Behind the lines, there was a growing tide of violence. As Germany contracted, millions of prisoners and slave labourers were moved from one place to another; in many cases, orders were issued to their guards to kill them all rather than allow them to fall into Allied hands. Malnutrition and disease took their toll. As the end approached, fanatical Nazis formed summary courts, and executed many of their own people who did not share their views. German soldiers and civilians were hanged from lamp-posts, trees, and improvised gallows. In the last weeks of the war the distinctions between soldiers and civilians, old and young, prisoners and guards, became increasingly blurred as the violence mounted. The casualties amongst the attacking Allies were great, but they were dwarfed by the numbers of Germans who were killed in the last weeks of war, and indeed by the numbers of concentration camp prisoners who died from one form of ill-treatment or another. Before the fighting stopped in May 1945, there was a level of violence, destruction, and suffering in Germany that has never been equalled before or since.

Thousands of books have been written about the end of the Second World War, and 1945 is universally recognised as a turning point in history. Films and television programmes continue to develop this theme. Very few of these accounts go beyond May 1945 to ask what became of Germany after the collapse of the 'Third Reich'.[2] All over the world, history courses in schools and universities look at Germany up to 1945, or in fewer cases start from that date. What is still known in Britain as VE Day, 8 May 1945, the day of Germany's unconditional surrender to the Allies, has become a great historical divide, encapsulated in Germany itself in the phrase *Stunde Null*, or 'Zero Hour'. This is – allegedly – when history itself stopped, and the clock started again.

Carl von Clausewitz, the great military philosopher of the early nineteenth century, characterised 'the pure concept of war' as 'a complete, untrammelled, absolute manifestation of violence'. He recognised that this was an abstract idea, and that in reality, particularly when 'whole communities' went to war, it was always 'an act of policy'. This led to his famous aphorism that 'war is merely the continuation of policy by other means'.[3] The public fascination with the untrammelled violence of the Second World War, with Nazism, and with Hitler's suicide in the bunker has obscured this insight. The start of the Cold War, even before the fighting stopped in Germany, has also strengthened the popular notion that one era of history, and of conflict, started in 1945 as another came to an end. The policy objectives of the Second World War in Europe are all too often completely overlooked, or it is assumed that with the death of Hitler and the military defeat of Germany those objectives had been fulfilled. Those who see Communism and Nazism as different forms of 'totalitarianism' may imagine that in 1945 one objective was merely replaced by another, one that was not achieved until the collapse of Communism in 1989.

The confusion stems also from the nature of the Second World War, which was fought by a coalition. Clearly, when Britain, the Soviet Union, and America became involved in war with Hitler's Germany, they initially had differing objectives. Although Britain went to war in 1939 nominally to preserve Polish sovereignty, it soon became preoccupied with a desperate struggle for mere survival. Similarly, after being attacked by Germany in 1941, survival and the recovery of occupied territory were the Soviet priorities. Hitler's declaration of war on America in December 1941 brought about a change. America had no territorial objectives in Europe, nor was it directly threatened by Germany. Its entry into the war, coupled with Germany's failure to defeat either Britain or the Soviet Union, meant that Hitler now faced a coalition, which – if it held together – could marshal an overwhelming preponderance of manpower, raw materials, and industrial strength. This coalition was able, in the middle years of the war, to determine what it was fighting for. Although initially this policy emerged in an uncoordinated way, it was subsequently firmed up and formally stated. In the public mind, then and since, it was encapsulated in the simple, if misleading phrase 'unconditional surrender'.

The Allied commitment to force the unconditional surrender of Germany first emerged in January 1943, when President Franklin Roosevelt made a statement to the press at the end of the Casablanca Conference. In a remarkably informal way, Roosevelt announced, drawing on a homely example from American Civil War history, that 'the elimination of German, Japanese and Italian war power means the unconditional surrender by Germany, Japan, and Italy'. This policy, subsequently endorsed by Churchill, and later by Stalin, was reiterated at various meetings of the Allied leaders, in Moscow in November 1943, in Quebec in September 1944, and in Yalta in February 1945. It has generated endless debate, over whether Churchill knew beforehand what Roosevelt was going to say at Casablanca, over whether Italy (and other states fighting alongside Germany like Finland, Romania, and Hungary) should have been included, and above all over whether it prolonged German resistance. According to one popular line of argument, by precluding any kind of negotiated settlement, the demand for 'unconditional surrender' was 'a gift to Goebbels' propaganda machine'.[4] Faced with no other way out, it is argued, the Germans had no chance but to fight on to the bitter end.

All this overlooks the two other significant policy objectives which accompanied the demand for unconditional surrender. In the press conference at Casablanca, Roosevelt explained the first of these: the 'total elimination' of German war power, he said, 'does not mean the destruction of the population of Germany, Italy, or Japan, but it does mean the destruction of the philosophies in those countries which are based on the conquest and the subjugation of other peoples'.[5] Leaving aside Italy and Japan, the object of the war against Germany was therefore the destruction of Nazism. In October 1943 the Allied Foreign Ministers met in Moscow, and they developed this further. At the end of the Conference, the 'Moscow Declaration' reaffirmed the determination to force the unconditional surrender of Germany, and added a new commitment: the punishment of Nazi 'war criminals'. It included a 'Statement on German Atrocities', carrying the signatures of Stalin, Churchill and Roosevelt, announcing that Germans who had taken part in 'atrocities, massacres, and executions' would be delivered to the countries in which these had had been carried out for judgment and punishment. Those who had committed atrocities in differing locations would be punished 'by joint decision of the Allied Governments'. The Declaration, which bears the unmistakeable stamp of Churchill's rhetoric, concluded with a stern warning to those Germans who had not yet carried out crimes: 'Let those who have hitherto not imbrued their hands with innocent blood beware lest they join the ranks of the guilty, for most assuredly the three Allied Powers will pursue them to the uttermost ends of the earth and will deliver them to their accusers in order that justice may be done.'[6]

At this stage in the war, these were necessarily vague declarations of intent. At subsequent meetings, they were debated further, but their essence was unchanged. The British, Soviets, and Americans remained jointly committed to forcing the unconditional surrender of Germany, in order to destroy Nazism and to punish Nazi criminals. They established a joint planning body, the European Advisory Commission, to meet in London and develop plans for the future occupation of Germany.

We know now that the post-war occupation of Germany was largely peaceful, and that it ended after only four years. It is important to bear in mind that in the final stages of the war, as the German resistance continued, and indeed became more fanatical, the Allied planners feared the worst. They imagined that they might face prolonged fighting from a 'National Redoubt' in the Alps, and assumed that there would be a guerrilla resistance, perhaps led by the Nazi Party or the SS. Cordell Hull spoke for many in September 1944 when he argued that the occupation should last for 'twenty-five to fifty years, as necessity might require'.[7] An article which now seems ludicrous was published in a French military journal in 1945: it alleged that 'at the least' 10,000 members of the Gestapo had taken on false identities in order to masquerade as 'good Germans' under occupation. Some had even had cosmetic surgery. Thus disguised, they would assume leadership roles in youth and church organisations. Weapons and money had already been secreted. These disguised Nazis would be put under the control of a 'super Gestapo', superior even to Himmler's SS; they were ready for years of resistance.[8]

The Allied occupation was, as Montgomery put it to his troops, 'an act of war'. Its object was 'to destroy the Nazi system'. This book therefore does not consider the defeat of Germany in 1944–45 as an end in itself, but as the prelude to a wide-ranging programme of denazification, and to the punishment of those Nazis alleged to have committed crimes. It treats the period between January 1944, when the Allies planned the final onslaught on Hitler's 'Fortress Europe', and November 1946, when the surviving, captured Nazi 'major war criminals' were executed in Nuremberg, as a continuum. It asks how far these Allied objectives were achieved. To answer this question, it looks not only at the major war crimes trials held after 1945 in Germany, but at the wider process of denazification. This included the abolition of the Nazi Party, the repeal of Nazi laws, and the purge of Nazis from German elites. It considers also the far-reaching efforts made to 'denazify' education, the press, and the arts. Although these processes continued beyond November 1946, the eighteen months after the German surrender which concluded with the execution of those convicted before the International Military Tribunal at Nuremberg can be considered as a decisive first phase.

This is also a story of Allied cooperation. In the shadow of the Cold War, it is understandable that many historians have seen the closing stages of the war against Germany, and the subsequent military occupation of Germany, as an unfulfilled project. According to this narrative, the high moral goals of Britain and America were compromised by their reliance on the military potential of the Soviet Union. At Yalta in February 1945, Churchill was undermined by Roosevelt, then in terminal decline, who aided and abetted Stalin's cynical plan to subjugate Eastern Europe to Communism. The subsequent meeting at Potsdam was a failure, which produced no agreement on Germany, and where the new British and American leaders, Attlee and Truman, were again outmanoeuvred by the wily Soviet dictator. The supposed 'Four-Power' government of Germany was a sham, and the subsequent division of Germany confirmed this. The establishment of a satellite Communist dictatorship in East Germany was a betrayal of the Allied commitment to restore democracy and human rights to all of Germany.

There is much that is plausible in this narrative. There was virtually no military cooperation between the western Allies and the Soviet Union in the closing stages of the war. Churchill – and many others in Britain – were bitterly disappointed by Stalin's enforced revision of Poland's frontiers; and Roosevelt was too ill to play a decisive role in standing up to Stalin at Yalta. The Allied leaders were not able to agree on a long-term future for Germany at Potsdam, and the four zones of military occupation in Germany were to a large extent separately administered afterwards. The division of the country in 1949 was unfortunate, above all for those non-communist Germans who found themselves behind the 'Iron Curtain'. This narrative, though, completely overlooks the most significant Allied cooperation in Germany after 1945, in the programme of denazification. For three years, the British, Americans, and Soviets, with the late addition of the French, administered Germany through an 'Allied Control Council' sitting in Berlin. Here they dismantled the Nazi Party and the legal framework of the 'Third Reich' and instituted the whole programme of denazification. It was under the authority of the Control Council that the International Military Tribunal was formed to try the major Nazi war criminals; and that many other war crimes trials were separately held in different parts of Germany.

The Control Council broke up in 1948, and was consigned to the dustbin of history as the blockade of Berlin started. By then, the soldiers and civilians who worked in the Control Council had grown weary of the difficulties involved in trying to secure agreement between four separate states, each with its own national interests. Perhaps because it was so unloved, the Control Council passed rapidly into oblivion, and has been neglected by posterity. German citizens at the time were more conscious of the specific military occupiers under whom they lived, and soon became far more concerned with the actions of their own politicians. Professional historians have neglected the Control Council, and most have chosen to focus on the separate zones of occupied Germany, and on the ways these were administered by individual military governments. Nonetheless, the Allied Control Council can claim much of the credit for the successful denazification of Germany. It is a testimony to the Allied cooperation in the Control Council that Nazism has not since 1945 become a significant political movement in any part of Germany.

This was a unique historical experiment, of particular interest now that under United Nations mandates, various parts of the world are under international military occupation, with the express purpose of rebuilding civil societies. Significantly, while America and Britain are attempting to reconstruct Iraq under military occupation, many of the documents published by the Control Council for Germany have been put on the Internet by American law schools to help inform this process. This book examines the role played by the Control Council for Germany in implementing the policies for which the Second World War in Europe was fought.

A NOTE ON SOURCES

More has been written on the Second World War and Nazism than on any other area of history. From every conceivable angle they have been turned over and analysed. In every literary genre, in film and television, in drama and documentary, they have been constructed and reconstructed. There is a substantial literature on almost every topic touched upon in this book, and on all key figures in its narrative. Layers of mythology have become encrusted around many areas, in historical and popular perceptions. While recognising and drawing from this huge reservoir of secondary material, I have tried at all points to go back to contemporary sources to provide a more genuinely historical narrative. Fortunately there is a huge mass of published primary material on the Second World War and on Nazism, in the form of diaries, letters, speeches, and memoirs. Many of the most important figures involved in the conflict and in the occupation of Germany published long accounts, written either at the time or very shortly afterwards. I have drawn here on the writing of Churchill, Truman, Goebbels, Speer, de Gaulle, Adenauer, Cordell Hull, Lucius Clay, and many others. I have also used the memoirs of senior German soldiers and airmen, like Guderian, Blumentritt, Mellenthin, and Galland; of the Soviet General Chuikov, and of the most important American and British commanders, Eisenhower, Brooke, and Montgomery. Some of the best memoirs have come from aides to senior commanders, working and living with them for years, and observing them from day to day. Harry Butcher's diary of 'three years with Eisenhower', and John Colville's Downing Street diaries are good examples. Airey Neave's account of the Nuremberg trial from the perspective of a junior officer involved in the prosecution is another.

All the armies in the Second World War were media conscious, and had their own historians, pressmen, and photographers. Many of these were hacks and produced writing of greater or lesser mediocrity, too much of which has become the common fare of subsequent histories. There were a few who were both engaged observers, and writers sufficiently gifted to express their insights in prose of lasting quality. The recently published English-language edition of Vasily Grossman's writings as a correspondent with the Red Army stands out from the formulaic Soviet propaganda accounts previously available from Ilya Ehrenburg, or Colonel Fedorov. Over the years, more histories of the Second World War and of Nazism have come 'from below', from ordinary people, and I have introduced many of these into my narrative. Wars appear one way to the generals and politicians planning campaigns, and another way to citizens caught up in them. In recent years, some extraordinary contemporary writing has been published, or re-published after years in obscurity, and given us fascinating new views of the central events in this book. From the German perspective, the diaries of Victor Klemperer must be mentioned. Klemperer, living always in the shadow of death as a Jew, provides, day by day, a commentary both on his immediate world in Dresden, and on the wider war news as it reached him. His awareness of his own frailties and foibles, and his intelligent scepticism, raise his writing head and shoulders above that of any other contemporary memoir. He of course provides particular insight into the fate of the Jews, a central theme of this book.

Most of the writing on the Second World War has been by men, and about men. Again this has been redressed in recent years, and many contemporary accounts by women are now available. I have sought to use these to provide a female perspective on the experience of the war and its aftermath in Germany. Sybil Bannister's account of living as an Englishwoman married to a German in the 'Third Reich' has been available since 1956, and the extraordinarily candid anonymous diary of a woman from Berlin which was first published in Germany in 1953 has now been republished in translation. Edith Hahn, a Jewish woman living disguised as an 'Aryan', has recently published a valuable memoir. The memoirs of Hitler's secretary Traudl Junge, first published in German in 2002, are now available in English, but contribute little or nothing to our understanding of Nazism; they say more about the extraordinary moral blindness of a generation. There are good published collections of interviews with German women, like that by Alison Owings. In the anthologies relating to separate aspects of this period there are numerous accounts by women, and I have tried to represent them.

There is no substitute for the individual voices of these participants and observers, and wherever possible I have quoted them in the original to illuminate particular scenes and episodes in my narrative. This has drawn in some who might be considered unworthy, like the worst SS men, perpetrators of cruelty and terror. The autobiography of Rudolf Höss, Commandant of Auschwitz, written while awaiting trial and sentence after the war, is an example. Similarly I have quoted from the testimony of the defendants at Nuremberg, as from the prosecution lawyers and witnesses. Three criteria have been used in the selection of all the sources used, and presented here in quotation. Firstly they are from people who were close to events; secondly from accounts written or recounted as near as possible to the time of those events; and thirdly they are from people who wrote, or spoke, with reflection and insight. I have therefore preferred diaries to memoirs and autobiographies; I have relied more on Eisenhower's *Report* of 1945 than his *Crusade in Europe* of 1948; more on Montgomery's *From Normandy to the Baltic* of 1946 than on his *Memoirs* of 1958.

Separately, I have relied heavily on contemporary official documents. Huge collections of these have been published, in English, German, Russian, and French, and in other languages. More are appearing almost every day on the Internet. The published collections, many dating back to the early post-war decades, are far more candid than a cynic might imagine, and contain many documents which do not cast their authors in a good light. The four-volume British official history of Bomber Command's campaign against Germany is still an indispensable starting point for any serious study of that subject, and the documents reprinted in it are an invaluable guide to the evolution of that most contentious policy, 'area bombing'. Similarly, anyone seriously interested in the Nuremberg trial, warts and all, will profit from the extensive secondary literature, notably by Bradley Smith, but will do better to start with the twenty-seven volumes containing the actual trial proceedings and related documents. The Allies wanted to legitimise their conduct in the Second World War and immediately afterwards, and all regarded it as a duty to publish relevant documents. Thus, even in the ruins of post-war Germany, they established secretariats to publish the proceedings of war crimes trials, and the legislation enacted by the Control Council. The *Official Gazette of the Control Council for Germany*, published between 1945 and 1948, is an invaluable source.

The archives of the post-war military occupations in Germany have now largely been opened to researchers, and I have used a number of these, notably those of the American and British Military Governments. Although the French zone of occupation, which was agreed to only in February 1945, was smaller and less populated than the others, it has been unjustly neglected by historians. I have tried to redress this by drawing on many official documents from the archives of the French military occupation in Germany now in Colmar. The Soviet occupation differed from the others in that they immediately put émigré German communists in key administrative positions in their zone. Extensive archives relating to these administrations are now open in Berlin, and have been used here. Most of the memoirs to emerge from the Soviet occupation are written in the Marxist-Leninist jargon of the time, and conform rigidly to the party line, but I have also used the classic account by a defector, Wolfgang Leonhardt's *Die Revolution entläßt ihre Kinder*, widely available in English translation.

Obviously all these sources must be approached with caution and scepticism. The post-war memoirs published by senior figures, to a greater or lesser extent, seek to present their authors in a good light. Some, like the best-selling books by Albert Speer, are obviously exercises in self-exculpation. Official documents published by various governments are obviously those that they are content to release. Most of the documents relating to the conduct of the war, and to the post-war occupation of Germany, are now open for consultation in various archives, but many sensitive individual documents are still classified. Many more were destroyed. In almost all cases, the memoirs and documents available are not mendacious, or blatantly inaccurate. They are, however, highly selective. If one wants to find out about the conditions of slave workers in Nazi Germany, Speer's books will not help. Churchill's huge history of the Second World War says very little about the British attack on Dresden in February 1945. The German generals who wrote their memoirs after 1945 were shamefully silent about the barbarous conduct of their armies in Eastern Europe, and saw no need to discuss the reasons why their armies invaded country after country. Vasily Grossman was shocked by the behaviour of Red Army troops in Germany at the end of the war, but even in his writing there are only brief references to their unbridled sexual violence. In almost all cases though, diarists, correspondents, and memorialists give away far more in their writing than they intended, and even those who might be considered highly untrustworthy yield surprising insights.

Many of the documents, published and unpublished, used in this book are available only in individual archives and specialist libraries. An increasing number are now available on the Internet, but again these must be approached with caution. Many of the topics discussed in this book are still highly contentious, and are subject to endless allegations of concealment, denial, and revision. Dozens of websites on military topics, on the Holocaust, and on war crimes, are run by groups or individuals with particular agendas, and are as a consequence very unreliable. There are others which are more trustworthy, particularly those run by archives and universities. The best of these – like the Eisenhower and Truman libraries – reproduce many documents in facsimile. Some, like the Avalon Law Project run by Yale University, or the excellent site on war crimes run from the University of the West of England, present many transcribed documents. The same proviso applies as with documents in hard copy. The documents presented on the Internet have been selected; they do not tell the full story. Wherever possible, I have sought to use hard copies rather than Internet sources. All translations from German and French sources, unless otherwise noted, are my own.

THE PRELUDE:
JANUARY—SEPTEMBER 1944

You will enter the continent of Europe and, in conjunction with the other
United Nations, undertake operations aimed at the heart of Germany and the
destruction of her armed forces.

From the instructions issued to Dwight Eisenhower on his appointment as Supreme
Commander, Allied Expeditionary Force, February 1945.[1]

On 1 January 1944, Victor Klemperer, a Jewish academic in Dresden,
reported in his diary a conversation about how much longer the war
might go on. He was not overly optimistic: 'Our usual discussion revolved
around whether "he" would last another four or six weeks. The always
cautious Feder thought: "till the end of October"... Today I am not at all
certain that "he" will be finished off this year.'[2] There were good reasons for
Klemperer's scepticism. At the start of 1944, the German armed forces still
controlled most of Europe. From the outskirts of Leningrad to the steppes
of Ukraine, a brutal and discriminatory rule was enforced over much of
European Russia, Belarus, Ukraine, the Baltic states, and Poland. In the
north, Denmark and Norway were occupied, and were used to provide
naval bases. Beyond the Arctic Circle, in Lapland, German and Finnish
troops shielded the vital mineral deposits of northern Sweden. In Western
Europe, France, Belgium, Holland, and Luxembourg lay under Nazi
dominion, and along the French coast forced labourers toiled to construct
Hitler's much-vaunted 'Atlantic Wall'. All of south-east Europe was either

occupied by German forces, or run by fascistic governments supported by them, as in Romania, Hungary, Bulgaria, Slovakia, and Croatia. Hitler's 'Fortress Europe' had been breached by the Allied invasions of Sicily and Italy in 1943, but the situation there had been stabilised by the rescue of Mussolini, his reinstatement as head of a puppet 'Social Republic' in northern Italy, and a tenacious German defence south of Rome.

At the heart of the Nazi empire was 'Greater Germany' itself, expanded since 1938 to include Austria, the Protectorate of Bohemia-Moravia, parts of western Poland, and the previously French provinces of Alsace and Lorraine. Millions of slave labourers from the conquered territories now eked out a miserable existence there, constituting an ever larger proportion of the workforce. The economy of all the territories controlled by Germany was subjugated to the needs of the 'Third Reich', and ruthlessly, if ineffectually exploited to feed Hitler's war machine and to maintain living standards in Germany. Despite Allied bombing, German armaments production was still rising, and new weapons were maintaining the technical advantage exploited by the *Wehrmacht* and the *Luftwaffe* since 1939.

From the perspective of the early twenty-first century, it seems obvious that Germany was facing defeat by 1944, but this was less clear to contemporaries. There had previously been serious military reverses for the Germans at Alamein, Stalingrad, and Kursk, in each case followed by enforced retreats. The Germans had been expelled from North Africa, the Caucasus, and from parts of eastern Ukraine and Russia. Ever larger fleets of British and American bombers ranged over Europe by night and day, and on all the fighting fronts the Allies enjoyed aerial superiority. Hitler's strongest ally, Italy, had been partitioned, and was now the site of a desperate battle of attrition, focused in the winter of 1943–1944 around the monastery at Monte Cassino. Above all, Hitler had provoked the creation of an unlikely but immensely strong alliance dedicated to his overthrow, composed of Britain and its empire, the Soviet Union, and the USA. This coalition, if it could overcome its ideological differences, could marshal far greater resources of manpower, industrial strength, and raw materials than Germany. It was committed by the Casablanca declaration of January 1943 to forcing the unconditional surrender of Germany, and by the Moscow declaration of October 1943 to the prosecution of Nazi criminals. The USA and Britain, also embroiled in conflict with Japan in the Pacific, had agreed to conclude the war in Europe before turning fully to the defeat of Japan.

Hitler himself was not prepared to accept defeat, or to try to undermine the Allied cause by any serious negotiation. For all the discontent
in the German officer corps, which came to a head in the unsuccessful
attempt on Hitler's life on 20 July 1944, the huge German war machine
was effectively under his sway. There was no large-scale resistance to Hitler
amongst the German population, which was increasingly harnessed to
what Goebbels had called 'total war'. The misery inflicted by British and
American bombing of German cities, and the ever increasing toll of casualties on different fronts, had not broken the will of the German people.
The heady mood of 1940, when crowds had turned out in German streets
to celebrate the fall of France, had disappeared, but had been replaced, as
far as one can generalise, by a grim and determined acceptance. Rational
discussion of likely outcomes of the war in Germany was submerged
by an avalanche of Nazi propaganda, and by a gnawing awareness that
crimes had been committed, crimes far too terrible and too extensive
to be overlooked. Richard Overy, surveying the reasons for the Allied
victory in the Second World War, has rightly drawn our attention to the
moral dimension of the conflict. By 1944, he has argued, there was a broad
conviction on the Allied side that they were fighting for a just cause,
matched by a corresponding uncertainty on the German and Axis side.[3]
This is certainly true of the Allies, and nothing in the last eighteen months
of the conflict seriously diminished this conviction; indeed there were
many developments which strengthened it. For the Germans, the situation
was less clear cut. Many, in the armed forces, in the security services, and
as civilians, had participated in and had direct knowledge of Nazi crimes
and cruelties. Most had heard in considerable detail about the concentration camps, about the persecution and killing of the Jews of Europe,
and about the brutal way the war had been conducted, above all on the
Eastern Front. But, they had also been subject to intense propaganda from
their own regime, to widely shared beliefs about the victimisation of
Germany after the First World War, and in many cases, to Allied bombing
which appeared to be directed against civilians. Until the final days of the
war, many either closed their eyes and ears to the horrible truth, or found
ways of justifying the conduct of the Nazi regime.

By 1944, there were many reasons why different Germans and other
European fascists still supported the war effort. Some were devoted
to Nazi ideology and believed in the final victory trumpeted by
Hitler and Goebbels, aided by the 'wonder weapons' being developed.

Mihail Sebastian, a Jewish writer still surviving in Romania, recorded in his journal a conversation overheard in a Bucharest café in June 1944 which illustrates well the sheer unreality of some of these hopes. At the next table, a group of men, 'all beaming with joy', were enthusiastically discussing the news of the deployment of the V1 flying bomb. 'At last!' one exclaimed. 'It's not enough', said another, 'Washington must be hit – Washington!'[4] Others, particularly amongst the German armed forces, believed that the Allied coalition would disintegrate, and that the Western Allies would join with the Germans in a 'crusade' against Bolshevism. This misguided notion runs like a *Leitmotif* through the post-war memoirs of German officers. F.W. von Mellenthin, a senior tank commander, spoke for many when he wrote in 1955: 'Our only real hope was a cleavage between the Soviet Union and the Anglo-Americans.' Later in his memoir, he referred to 'the cultural circle of the West', expressing the notion that somehow Nazi Germany had more in common with Britain and America than did the Soviet Union.[5] Field-Marshal Gerd von Rundstedt, portrayed by his Chief of Staff Guenther Blumentritt as the archetypal 'non-political' soldier, is quoted as writing similarly, in September 1944: 'I had, of course, always assumed that the Allies would do everything in their power to reach Berlin before the Russians out of regard for "western ideals" and to prevent the Russians from advancing too far to the west over the Oder.'[6]

The extent to which this ludicrous idea was misplaced – the idea that somehow Nazism could be seen as an acceptable part of 'Western culture' or of 'Western ideals' – can be judged from the way that Eisenhower, not a particularly bloodthirsty man, was thinking about the German General Staff at the same time. Harry Butcher records a conversation in July 1944: 'He [Eisenhower] would exterminate all of the General Staff. [...] Halifax asked Ike how many officers are on the German General Staff. Ike guessed about 3,500. He added he would include for liquidation leaders of the Nazi Party from mayors on up and all members of the Gestapo.'[7] Many Germans, in and outside the armed forces, were sustained, or felt compelled by senses of duty and patriotism. A few realised clearly that there was little place for them in a post-Nazi world. Sybil Bannister, an English woman living in Germany, recalls an interview in 1944 about the custody of her child with the chief of the Gestapo in Bromberg, in East Prussia. In the course of the interview he remarked straightforwardly that if Germany did not win the war, he would not be there to dispute matters with her.[8] Far more German people felt simply overtaken by events beyond their control and continued from day to day, clinging to routines, obeying orders, and hoping for the best. In the last eighteen months of the war in Europe, nothing is more striking than the German armed forces' desperate continuation of the unequal struggle until literally its final days and hours.

Hitler still had great hopes. By the later stages of the Second World War he controlled an enormous war machine, in certain ways very efficient and formidable, in others increasingly weak and disorganised. It has become a commonplace that the German army fought more effectively than any of the Allied armies, and that man for man, it was superior until the last weeks of the war. Likewise the better quality of German weapons, including the Tiger and Panther tanks, the all-purpose 88mm gun, the jet aircraft, the V-weapons, and even the hand-held rocket-propelled grenade launcher, the *Panzerfaust*, has often been commented upon. Less attention has been paid to the infrastructure which provisioned and supported these huge armies fighting often in distant locations, and which allowed Hitler, late in the war, to plan and execute broad strategic thrusts, involving the transport of thousands of men and vehicles. Many of the millions of people – mainly men – fighting for Germany in 1944 and 1945 had been at war for years now, and were hugely experienced.

We should not underestimate how very difficult this force was to attack and defeat, from either the Soviet or the Western perspective. Hitler, and the German elites which supported him, had by the late stages of the war become habituated to suffering and casualties on a huge scale, and thought little of losing thousands of men in any given military operation. Stalin and the Soviet leadership were, if anything, even more profligate and insensitive. In Germany and the Soviet Union, there was a prevailing ideology which minimised the importance of the individual soldier or civilian and gave priority to the collective; there were harsh leaders, and a willingness to enforce compliance with their wishes. Both these countries were prepared to punish, and to execute, large numbers of their own citizens in the prosecution of their war effort. For the Western Allies, the situation was very different. They fielded large civilian armies, were more sensitive to public opinion, and used capital punishment in the field only very rarely. In combat operations they were reluctant to countenance large losses. For Britain particularly, there could be no repetition of the losses of 1914–1918, or anything like them.

German hopes that the Allied coalition was unsustainable were not entirely unreasonable. To all intents and purposes, the British and Americans fought one war against Germany in Western Europe, and the Soviets fought a separate war in the East. There was virtually no cooperation between the Allies: they did not conduct combined operations, or try to turn their encirclement of Germany to practical advantage. In notorious cases, like the uprising of the Polish population of Warsaw in August 1944, the Germans were able to exploit this. The British and the Americans made a huge effort to supply the Soviet Union with supplies and war materials, through the Arctic convoys, and from the south through Iran, and this greatly helped the Soviets. The longer the war continued, the more mechanised and technically sophisticated the Red Army became in comparison with the *Wehrmacht*. The relationship between the Soviets and the Western Allies was characterised too much by mistrust to permit the formation of grand plans, or even to coordinate the timing of separate efforts. 'During the whole of the War', wrote Alan Brooke, Chief of the Imperial General Staff, 'I never received a Russian order of battle showing their dispositions.'[9] Suspicion between the Soviets and the Western Allies was so great that any information confided by one was treated by the other as potentially misleading. By January 1945, when both the Soviets and the Western Allies could realistically contemplate the imminent end, they were competing more than cooperating in the final defeat of Germany.

Nonetheless, Hitler and Goebbels were completely mistaken in their view that the Allies would break apart. The Allies' determination to defeat Hitler and to destroy Nazism was much greater than their mutual suspicion. The subsequent development of the Cold War has fostered an assumption that Allied cooperation ended in May 1945 with the end of the war in Europe; in fact it is striking how much cooperation there was in the early occupation of Germany, and above all in the suppression of Nazism and German militarism. The differences felt between Britain and America on the one hand, and the Soviet Union on the other, were real, and they came to the surface at the Potsdam meeting in July 1945, but during the war there was an overriding commitment to the defeat of Germany. Similarly, there were tensions between the Americans, suspicious of imperialism and the weight of European history, the British, and other Allies, like the French and the Poles. At no point did those tensions threaten to cause a serious breach between the Allies.

The contribution of other countries to the defeat of Nazism should not be underestimated. Those fighting alongside the British and the Americans gave something which was in the end more important than the huge material supremacy enjoyed by the Allies: added manpower. What are typically referred to as 'British' armed forces in the Second World War actually represented a huge world-wide coalition, with its own fault-lines. There were significant contingents from Canada, Australia, New Zealand, South Africa, and elsewhere. The British and the Americans had also armed substantial Free French and Polish forces by 1944. The longer the war continued, the more Britain and America struggled to provide sufficient numbers of the most basic and necessary type of soldier, infantrymen, and the more they relied on others alongside them. There is a telling contrast between the growing importance of smaller national contributions to the Allied war effort in 1944 and 1945, and the parallel collapse of other countries' support for Nazi Germany in the same period.

Allied military strength lay above all in their industrial potential. Although by the end of the war the American economy was assuming its post-war supremacy, enjoying a huge quantitative and qualitative growth, the British economy was still immensely productive, and was geared totally to the war effort. Together, aided by control of the world's seas and ready access to any raw materials they needed, the British and the Americans were able by June 1944 to deploy large and well-equipped armies on the European mainland. They enjoyed an increasing superiority in the air which they came to rely on heavily. The British army was numerically small, certainly in comparison with the huge force commanded by Haig between 1916 and 1918, but was by 1944 experienced and tested. The American army had undergone a brutal learning process, starting with the humiliation at the Kasserine Pass in 1943, but was better prepared in 1944 for the rigours of war in Europe. In comparison, the Soviets had greater manpower than any of the other Allies. The Red Army deployed 5,568,000 frontline soldiers in Europe on 1 January 1944, with a further 419,000 in reserve.[10] Equipped with great numbers of modern tanks and guns, closely supported by a large air force, and capably led by specialists, the Red Army contended with the greater part of Hitler's forces in a war that has become notorious for its scale and brutality. The Soviets triumphed not merely by brute strength, or by numerical superiority. By 1945 the Red Army had become a fighting force of unprecedented potential.

Modern wars are fought with machines, and are based on essential materials: iron, steel, coal, oil, rubber, and a host of others. The Second World War was accompanied by an extraordinary technological revolution, and by 1945 uranium was emerging as a new material of strategic significance. The Allies broadly enjoyed better access to these materials by the closing stages of the Second World War, and this played a central part in their victory. They had ample steel for tanks, guns, and aircraft, and the oil needed to keep their armies moving. In contrast, the German situation deteriorated sharply in 1944 and especially in 1945. Before 1939, Hitler had sought 'autarky' – economic self-sufficiency – and as a result Germany had developed large projects intended to produce synthetic raw materials like oil and rubber, but these failed completely in the last months of the war to compensate for the loss of raw materials from outside Germany. Through 1944 and into 1945, the supply of minerals for weapons production was maintained (largely with the help of neutral countries like Sweden, Spain, and Turkey), and until the last weeks of the war, German factories turned out huge quantities of high quality weapons, many of them better than their Allied counterparts. Germany had plentiful supplies of coal, and, despite Allied bombing, maintained power supplies and operated a huge transport network based on railways. The Achilles' heel of the German economy was oil. By 1944 any hope of using Caucasian oil was ended; the small oil wells in Austria and Hungary could not produce anything like enough to supply the huge German industrial economy. The only large source of oil left was from the refineries at Ploesti in Romania. The longer the war continued the less fuel there was available for German vehicles and aircraft; conversely, the Allies could count ever more on using aircraft and tanks, and on greater mobility in the field.

PLANS FOR 'D-DAY', AND THE GERMAN COLLAPSE IN THE EAST

By 1944 it was clear that the British and Americans would have to attack Germany itself in northern Europe to bring the war to an end. As in the First World War, any hope of using naval supremacy to land on the German coast or to mount a foray into the Baltic Sea was ruled out by geography. In January 1944, at Churchill's insistence, a last effort was made to reinvigorate the Italian campaign by landing behind the German

'Gustav Line' at Anzio, but the landing force here was quickly penned into a small beachhead. Realistically the only way to invade Germany was through northern France and the Low Countries. We are so used now to triumphal images of huge Allied landing fleets off Normandy in June 1944, and of overwhelming air support, that we may easily overlook the possibility that an Allied invasion of France might have failed. Churchill particularly was mindful of potential disaster. He felt that he knew the mood of the British people, and judged that they did not have an endless reserve of willpower or willingness to sacrifice. His well-known procrastination over when and where an invasion of France should take place is frequently misunderstood. He saw that an invasion which was repulsed, and ended with the ignominy of evacuation, would be a very serious blow, and that it might be impossible to mount another. His final consent to the plan for 'Overlord', given only at Tehran in November 1943, was based on a conviction that the invasion must be successful, and lead to a breakout and advance into Germany itself.

Two factors dictated the choice of the Normandy beaches for a landing. Militarily, they were judged suitable for the debarkation of sufficient men and tanks to secure a large bridgehead. The relative proximity to the ports of southern England was vital, allowing both for quick supply of an army in France, and for protection of this supply route. More problematic was the question of how to land supplies on the beaches. The 'Overlord' planners envisaged that a French port would have to be captured and used fairly swiftly to land the supplies necessary to mount a larger campaign in northern France, but intended to use prefabricated harbours – the famous 'Mulberry' structures – and a direct oil pipeline – Pluto – to overcome the problem temporarily. Many of the subsequent problems of the British and Americans in north-western Europe stemmed from this initial difficulty. 'Overlord' was planned also as a joint Allied operation, and the involvement of different national contingents in the landing forces was to set a pattern which prevailed until the conclusion of the war against Germany, with British and Canadian forces on the left flank, and Americans on the right, under the joint command of the American General Dwight Eisenhower. Eisenhower was no strategic genius, and he has been roundly criticised for his unimaginative and rather distant leadership of the Allied campaign in northern Europe. His failings at this level are less significant, though, than his great success in maintaining the cooperation of his joint Allied forces, and particularly in managing and containing the quarrels of his senior generals. The bickering between Montgomery, the British commander, and the American generals, Bradley, Patton, and Hodges, worsened during and after the Normandy campaign, and relationships between them were very poor in the final months of the war. Eisenhower, aptly described as 'the policeman of Allied unity',[11] kept his eye firmly on the greater good, and worked tirelessly to minimise these quarrels, both privately, and through careful media management. He also avoided catastrophic errors of military judgement. His leadership was not inspirational, but he did successfully conclude his assignment.

The weakness of the German military position at the start of 1944 was most apparent in the East. Since the failure of the huge Kursk offensive in July 1943, the Germans had struggled to create a stable defensive position, particularly in Ukraine. By this time they were facing an enemy fighting with intense patriotic determination, with far greater numbers, and increasingly with much greater mobility. In the winter of 1943–1944, the Red Army chased demoralised German forces out of most of Ukraine; the depopulated city of Kiev, site of some of the most gruesome Nazi crimes, was liberated in November.[12] Now that the strategic initiative had decisively passed to the Soviets, there was confusion at the highest levels of the German command structure over how to conduct the war in the East. Hitler had assumed direct control of the *Wehrmacht* in the crisis of December 1941, and was reluctant to abandon his cherished vision of a racial empire in the East. Guderian, the general he respected most, and now serving as 'Inspector General of Armoured Troops', was more realistic and advised a strategic retreat to prepared defensive lines on the Bug and Niemen rivers in Poland. Both clung to the chimerical hope that the Allied coalition would break up if Germany could prolong the conflict and repel an Allied invasion of France.

The Red Army did not observe the Western European convention of a summer campaigning season followed by a winter of rest and recuperation. On 14 January 1944 the first of a series of huge offensives was launched outside Leningrad. Overwhelmed by sheer force, Hitler's Army Group North was ejected from the positions it had occupied since 1941, and driven back towards the borders of Estonia and Latvia. The railway between Moscow and Leningrad was secured by the Red Army by the end of January. In February and March Soviet pressure was turned to the south, and, in increasing chaos, German forces were driven from Ukraine. On 30 March 1944, Hitler dismissed Manstein and Kleist, those successful proponents of *Blitzkrieg*, and put Walter Model in command of the remnants of his Army Group South. Model needed all his skills as a defensive commander over the next few weeks to extricate his forces from the Soviet offensive over the Dnestr river and to construct a continuous front along the Romanian and Hungarian frontiers with the battered and exhausted forces left to him. Odessa was liberated on 10 April, leaving the Red Army poised to threaten Romania. Further north and west, troops of Koniev's Second Ukrainian front had reached the Carpathian mountains. It was obvious that both Hungary and Romania were now wavering in their allegiance to the Nazi cause. A contingency plan, prepared in December 1943, for a German occupation of Hungary was activated, and under extreme pressure the Hungarian Regent Admiral Horthy formed a new pro-German government on 23 March 1944. Remarkably, the Hungarian Army General Staff continued to cooperate with the Germans, and Hungarian units fought effectively in defensive battles in the Carpathians in April. Hitler judged that as long as Antonescu remained in power in Romania, he would continue to support the Axis.

A further blow to this notion was struck by the loss of the Crimea. This peninsula had been isolated over the winter of 1944, and Hitler had, insanely, insisted on reinforcing the troops there by sea. When the Soviets attacked on 8 April 1944, there were 75,546 German and 45,887 Romanian soldiers trapped behind a narrow defensive line at the neck of the peninsula. Most of these were not front-line soldiers, and a number were evacuated before the defence collapsed and fell back on Sevastopol. The usual arguments between Hitler, arguing for the stubborn defence of every inch, and his generals, arguing for an orderly evacuation, were rehearsed. Orders were given and rescinded. Antonescu intervened, without effect, to call for a withdrawal. Finally an evacuation by German and Romanian ships in the Black Sea was ordered, but the ships stood off the burning city of Sevastopol as Soviet forces fought their way in. 26,700 soldiers surrendered after six weeks of indecision and chaos.[13]

The successful Soviet offensives in early 1944 displayed the characteristic features of all which followed, leading to the capture of Berlin in May 1945: overwhelming force; attacks by concentrated groups of tanks after heavy artillery and rocket bombardment; rapid advances at key points, leaving substantial groups of Germans isolated often great distances from the retreating main body. Frequently, as in the Crimea, the fate of these wretched soldiers was determined by Hitler, who forbade strategic or even tactical withdrawals, and demanded that what he regarded as key positions be held for as long as possible. Through 1944 and into 1945 Hitler again and again demanded that individual towns, typically designated as 'fortresses', regardless of whether or not they were actually fortified or had any significant defensive forces, be held to the last man, and that every inch of territory, whether or not of any strategic significance, be disputed, denying his generals opportunities for manoeuvre and for the limited initiative they might have exercised. At the same time, Stalin was giving his increasingly competent generals, Zhukov, Koniev, Chuikov, and others, more freedom to conduct operations. The Red Army became ever bolder in its deep penetrations, leaving pockets of German soldiers to be dealt with by formations moving more slowly behind the armoured spearheads.

The advancing Soviets found a wasteland in which villages had been burned, livestock carried off, cultural monuments destroyed, railway tracks pulled up, and water supplies contaminated. The destruction was organised as a systematic 'scorched earth' campaign which echoed, albeit on a much larger scale, that carried out in 1917 in France by the German army retreating to the Hindenburg Line. The surviving population liberated by the Soviets in 1944 had been subjected to indescribable brutality under German occupation. The fighting between the Red Army and the *Wehrmacht* reflected the hostility this had engendered. Both sides took few prisoners, and neither expected anything other than the harshest treatment if they had the misfortune to be captured. The casualties were enormous, those in the actual fighting added to by illness and the effects of the weather. Both sides lost men in great numbers reminiscent of the First World War. The cumulative effect of the experience of fighting on the soldiers cannot be sufficiently emphasised. Thanks to recent histories, like Anthony Beevor's *Berlin*, and the film *Der Untergang* (*Downfall*), the uncontrolled barbarism of the Red Army when it finally reached Germany has been well documented and widely discussed. Less attention has been paid to the prolonged suffering of the Soviet people under German occupation since 1941. It is hardly surprising that by the time Soviet soldiers reached the German frontier they had a demonic view of the German character, and of German soldiery. Vasily Grossman was a journalist who recorded his experiences of the war alongside the Red Army from the desperate retreats of 1941 until the last days in Berlin in 1945. In the first days of 1944 he was with the forces advancing into Ukraine, into territory which had been occupied by the Germans for two years. Documenting the atrocities committed against the local people, Grossman discovered that the Jews had been treated differently: they had been systematically exterminated. On 5 January 1944 Grossman, a Jew himself, came to Berdichev, where his mother and other close relatives had lived. He wrote to his wife:

> Dearest Lyusenka, I reached my destination today. Yesterday I was in Kiev. It's hard to express what I felt when I visited the addresses of relatives and acquaintances. There are only graves and death. I am going to Berdichev today. My comrades have already been there. They said that the city is completely devastated, and only a few people, maybe a dozen out of many thousands, tens of thousands of Jews who lived there, have survived. I have no hope of finding Mama alive.

Grossman's lack of hope was borne out. He subsequently wrote an article about the massacre of the Jews in Berdichev, but, according to the recent editors of his work, it was censored by the Soviet authorities.[14]

OVERLORD

The increasingly fragile German defence of the East followed a major strategic decision. Hitler had determined in November 1943 that an Anglo-American invasion in the West was potentially far more dangerous to Germany. In his 'Directive No. 51' he pronounced:

> In the East, the vast extent of the territory makes it possible for us to lose ground, even on a large scale, without a fatal blow being dealt to the nervous system of Germany. It is very different in the West! Should the enemy succeed in breaching our defences on a wide front here, the immediate consequences would be unpredictable.[15]

By April 1944, priority in weapons and manpower had been given for some time to building up the German defences in France and the Low Countries. American and British intelligence estimated then that

there were fifty-one German divisions deployed there, compared to
199 on the Eastern Front.[16] The German forces were commanded by
Field-Marshal von Rundstedt; under him Hitler's favourite, Rommel,
commanded Army Group B, responsible for the critical northern coast
of France. Rommel was fascinated by technical devices, and concentrated on the preparation of coastal defences of various kinds. He argued
that the Allied invasion would be best defended on the beaches, where
their troops were most vulnerable. Rundstedt, hugely experienced in the
conduct of grand strategy, believed that it was more important to keep a
mobile armoured reserve away from the coast, and use this to mount a
powerful counter-attack against a landing force. The intentions of both
were complicated by Hitler's constant interference.

The immensely thorough preparations for 'Overlord' reflect the concerns and the wisdom of Churchill and Eisenhower. The huge bomber
forces of the RAF and of the US 8th Air Force were employed to disrupt
transport facilities in France and to damage German strong points. An
elaborate campaign of deception was mounted, successfully convincing
the Germans that the main Allied invasion force would land in the Pas de
Calais, rather than in Normandy. Special weapons, including amphibious
tanks, were developed specifically to support a sea–borne invasion, and the
plan itself envisaged the use of commandos to destroy German gun positions, and airborne soldiers to seize key bridges ahead of the landing force.
Huge quantities of munitions and other supplies were assembled, and plans
made rapidly to swell an initial landing force of five divisions to an army
of thirty divisions to fight out of the Normandy beachhead. Efforts were
made, successfully, to give the impression that landings were also being
considered in other places, like southern France, Norway, or Greece.

The story of D-Day and Operation 'Overlord' has been often and
well told. At one point only, on Omaha Beach, was there on 6 June
1944 the possibility that the attackers would be thrown back into the
sea, where so many had already died. By the end of the day, and at a
great cost in life, the Allies had established a small but secure beachhead. With a well-protected supply route across the English Channel
the British and the Americans swiftly built up the initial landing force
and established a large army in what Eisenhower called a 'lodgement
area'. Charles de Gaulle managed to stage a triumphal and enormously
symbolic visit to the liberated town of Bayeux on 14 June. By 17 June,
half a million men had been landed in Normandy. It proved much more

difficult to break out of the beachhead than had been hoped, and for some six weeks this army was trapped in the hedgerows and narrow fields of the *bocage*. Given that the German troops were constantly harassed from the air, and were only able to move with great difficulty – Rommel was himself injured by a fighter on 20 June – it is remarkable how strongly they fought. Hitler and his intelligence services were still convinced that the Normandy landings were the prelude to a larger invasion in the Pas de Calais, and Hitler was slow to release forces to attack the beachhead. Nonetheless, von Rundstedt soon assembled an increasingly powerful force, including SS soldiers and the 'Hitler Youth Division', around the Allied landing area. Some of his soldiers, notably the pressed Russians, and other nationals fighting for the Germans, had only limited commitment, and were willing to surrender or to desert in the face of overwhelming Allied force. Others were absolutely devoted to the Nazi cause. John Colville, Churchill's Private Secretary, was temporarily serving as a fighter pilot, and noted in his diary this account, told to him by a nurse at a landing strip behind the line in Normandy:

> My temporary partner – I did not even ask her name, nor she mine – had been ministering that day to wounded young fanatics of an S.S. Hitler Youth brigade which had been in the forefront of battle. She told me that one boy of about sixteen had torn off the bandage with which she had dressed his serious wound, shouting that he only wanted to die for the Führer. Another had flung in her face the tray of food she brought him.[17]

The Americans took Cherbourg on 27 June, but its docks had been largely destroyed by German demolitions. It was of limited use as a supply base. On the east of the Allied beachhead, Montgomery's forces struggled to take the city of Caen, and on the west, General Omar Bradley, in command of the American 1st Army, found that his advance was 'disappointingly slow'.[18] Both resorted to the techniques which were to dominate the forthcoming campaign. Montgomery's tried and tested approach was developed. Long artillery preparation and the careful build up of superior force had been the hallmarks of his military style, and his success, since El Alamein. Now fighter bombers armed with rockets were added to the arsenal. Nonetheless, for several weeks it was difficult to progress around Caen, not least because of the superior quality of German tanks and weapons. The horrible phrase to 'brew up', used in

1944 and by some post-war writers to describe what happened to an Allied Sherman tank and its crew when it was hit by a German shell, sums this up. One can only try to imagine the feeling of Sherman crews in the vanguard of an assault on defended German positions. Not until the end of July did the ruins of Caen fall to the British and Canadian attackers. By this time many, at different levels in the American army, had become thoroughly frustrated with Montgomery's slowness.

The Americans resorted on 26 July outside St-Lô to what became known as 'carpet bombing': a huge force of 1,800 bombers was used to lay waste to a swathe of ground, five miles wide and one mile deep, in front of the attacking troops. When the bombing had finished, it was hoped that they would have only to walk into the devastated area. On this occasion, the Americans also learnt how easily the plan could miscarry. Over one hundred soldiers, including their commander General McNair, were killed by their own bombs falling short, and the projected attack was severely disrupted. Many more were wounded. After hearing the news, Eisenhower 'was visibly depressed'.[19] Nonetheless, the American attack prevailed and in the next few days, Bradley's forces inaugurated a war of movement. The American units pouring out of the beachhead were now divided into the 1st Army, under Courtney Hodges, and the 3rd Army, commanded by the newly arrived George Patton.

Eisenhower now had thirty American, British, and Canadian divisions on the ground, and was able to exploit the advantage. As the German forces in front of the Americans retreated, American tanks and lorries spilled out onto the roads of Normandy. Troops of the 3rd Army drove south to the mouth of the River Loire and sealed off the Brittany peninsula. By 6 August Nantes on the Atlantic coast had been liberated, and the US 6th Armored Division stood outside Brest. Eisenhower now used this new-found mobility to attempt a more ambitious strategic move. His 3rd Army, which now included a French armoured division, moved energetically to Le Mans and then to Argentan, well behind the main surviving German force, threatening to encircle it from the south. From the north the British and Canadians, meeting intense resistance, moved more slowly to Falaise to close the circle.

Hitler obligingly cooperated with Eisenhower's design. Instead of withdrawing from a now untenable position, he ordered the concentration of four SS and two *Wehrmacht* panzer divisions in an attack aimed towards Mortain and the Atlantic coast at Avranches. On paper this offered the prospect of cutting off the American forces which had already spilled out towards the Loire and into Brittany, and of restoring the containment of the Allied beachhead. In reality this kept the most heavily armed and effective of the German forces in France in Eisenhower's developing entrapment. Only when their doomed attack had obviously failed were they directed to try to keep open the 'gap' at Falaise and escape through it. Between 13 and 17 August the Germans conducted a relatively orderly withdrawal through the 'gap', but under constant pressure from the ground and from the air the retreat degenerated into a rout, and became a massacre. The last troops in the Falaise pocket surrendered on 22 August. Eisenhower recorded: 'Forty-eight hours after the closing of the gap I was conducted through it on foot, to encounter scenes that could be described only by Dante. It was literally possible to walk for hundreds of yards, stepping on nothing but dead and decaying flesh.'[20]

The Normandy campaign had ended in complete success for the Allies, and two German armies in France had been effectively destroyed. On 15 August, Allied forces landed on the Mediterranean coast, and commenced a rapid advance up the Rhône valley. There was far less resistance here than in Normandy, and Hitler had no reserves available to shore up this new front. In northern France the German situation was catastrophic. The German Fifteenth Army, which had been kept in the Pas de Calais to meet an imagined threat, was in full retreat along the Channel coast. Between the River Seine, Paris, and Orléans, and the Americans, there were no organised German forces. *Luftwaffe* ground personnel, the police, SS detachments, all the hangers-on of an army of occupation and the malign apparatus of Nazi terror joined in the flight. There were no prepared defensive positions, and there was no realistic hope of defending Paris, which was liberated on 25 August by French forces. De Gaulle, who had steered a difficult course between varying levels of American and British suspicion, skilfully combined his Free French movement with the communist-dominated Resistance forces, and formed a Provisional Government in France.

After the desperate fighting at Caen, the British and Canadian forces were at last able to move forward freely. The Canadian army advanced along the coast, investing the Channel ports as it went. Some were taken after heavy fighting, thus Le Havre on 12 September, Boulogne on 23 September, and Calais on 30 September; others, like Dunkirk, were besieged, and it was judged wiser to leave the German garrisons trapped there. All the ports captured had been wrecked by the Germans and were unfit for use as supply bases. Further south, Montgomery's troops advanced almost unopposed across the farmland of Flanders and Picardy which had been the site of such terrible fighting in the First World War. On 1 September, the British entered Albert, Bapaume, and Arras; on 6 September Ypres was liberated by Polish forces. Of greater contemporary importance, the port of Antwerp was captured intact by the 11th Armoured Division on 4 September. A week later, troops of the American 1st Army crossed the German frontier near Aachen.

THE END OF THE 'NEW ORDER'

The success of the Normandy campaign, and the collapse of the German defensive position in France and Belgium, which has baulked so large in the western view of the Second World War, was matched by the catastrophe which overwhelmed Hitler's forces on the Eastern Front between June and September 1944. Three days after the Allied landings in Normandy, the Red Army attacked the German and Finnish forces on the Karelian Isthmus. Within days they had reached the 1940 frontier, and the Finns sued for peace. On 22 June, an offensive was launched in Belarus which quickly took Soviet troops to the Polish frontier. South of the Pripet marshes, the Red Army thrust through Galicia, and advanced to the outskirts of Warsaw. In August the Soviets pushed into Romania, provoking the removal of the pro-German dictator Antonescu, and the formation of a new government which declared war on Germany. Mihail Sebastian recorded with mixture of elation and horror the behaviour of Red Army soldiers in Bucharest. On 1 September he wrote:

> Bewilderment, fear, doubt. Russian soldiers who rape women (Dine Cocea told me yesterday). Soldiers who stop cars in the street, order the driver and passengers out, then get behind the wheel and disappear. Looted shops. This afternoon three of them burst into Zaharia's, rummaged through the strong-box, and made off with some watches (watches are the toys they like most.)
>
> I can't treat all these incidents and accidents as too tragic. They strike me as normal – even just. It is not right that Romania should get off too lightly. In the end, this opulent, carefree, frivolous Bucharest is a provocation for an army coming from a country laid waste.

Over the next few days, Sebastian reflected further:

> Yesterday at the cinema, a film about the war in Ukraine. The horror exceeds everything. Words and gestures are no longer of any avail.
>
> These Russian soldiers who walk the streets of Bucharest, with their child-like smile and their friendly churlishness, are real angels. How do they find strength not to set everything on fire, not to kill and plunder, not to reduce to ashes this city that houses the mothers, wives, sisters, and lovers of those who killed, burned, and laid waste their country?

As a Jew, Sebastian could hardly believe that he had survived. It was not until a fortnight after the Soviet arrival that he could express his amazement: 'Germany has collapsed – and I am alive'.[21]

The whole German occupation of the Balkans was now threatened. A desperate effort to prop up the situation in Bulgaria by sending a substantial armoured force there in August failed completely. A 'patriotic front' government was formed in Sofia on 9 September, and an armistice concluded with the Soviets on 11 September. In the Greek islands and through mainland Greece and Yugoslavia, some 900,000 German soldiers now risked being cut off from their homeland, in mountainous territory with few roads and railways. In most cases these troops were already confined to towns and villages by increasingly well armed partisan groups. Slowly, preparations were set in hand for an evacuation of the whole Balkan peninsula.

Astonishingly, the unsuccessful attempt on Hitler's life on 20 July 1944 had almost no impact on the front lines, either in Normandy, in Italy, or in the East. The dramatic events of that day, Stauffenberg's success in smuggling a bomb into Hitler's daily staff conference at Rastenburg, his escape and subsequent summary execution in Berlin, were mirrored in several cities around Europe, notably in Paris. For Hitler himself, the failed plot was highly significant. It reinforced his mistrust of the German officer corps, and conversely strengthened his reliance on the SS and the Gestapo. It deepened his conviction that he was a man of destiny, fated to lead his people in their hour of crisis. In Germany itself, 20 July contributed to an increasingly poisonous atmosphere in which those suspected of treason or defeatism were likely to be arrested, brought before the 'Peoples' Court', tortured, and executed. On the front lines, it passed almost without notice, and appears to have made little difference either to the morale of German troops or to the feelings of those opposed to them. Many German front line soldiers were indeed shocked by what they regarded as treachery behind their backs. A corporal wrote about 'this vile booby-trap against the Führer [...] Thank God, once again he has survived it.' Another wrote: 'Providence has protected our Führer from everything.'[22]

As the summer of 1944 drew to a close, the military situation of the 'Third Reich' was so desperate that the end of the war appeared imminent. Mihail Sebastian, who was remarkably well-informed about the progress of the fighting on different fronts, had noted in his diary on 31 July: 'It may all be over in ten weeks.'[23] In France and Belgium, there appeared to be no German defences left at all. Mellenthin, now Chief of Staff of the Fourth Panzer Army, falling back on the Carpathians, wrote: 'At the beginning of August, 1944, the German Reich seemed to be in imminent danger of total collapse.'[24] At the same time, John Colville, now back in 10 Downing Street working as Churchill's secretary, was cautiously optimistic: 'It now begins to look as if the war will last but a few more weeks or months at the outside.' On 4 September he wrote: 'People are expecting the armistice any day now (though the Huns show no signs of offering to sue) and there have been no flying bombs for four days.'[25]

American and British forces on the ground could see little to prevent them continuing their rapid advance into Holland and Germany. Montgomery, that most cautious of generals, was similarly convinced that 'German resistance in western Europe was on the verge of collapse'. In consequence, he advocated 'one powerful thrust across the Rhine and into the heart of Germany'.[26] In Italy, after months of stalemate, Rome and Florence had been liberated. In the East, the Red Army stood outside Warsaw, and the resistance forces of the Polish 'Home Army' planned to rise up and throw off the yoke of German oppression. Along the length of the Eastern Front, the massive numerical and material superiority of the Soviets was apparent, and the Germans were in headlong retreat from the Balkans. On several fronts their allies had left them, and were trying as best they could to come to terms with erstwhile enemies. The Allied armies were growing in strength; their air forces increasingly dominated the skies over Europe, and were able to cow and intimidate German forces on the ground, to disrupt transport, and, in the case of the British and Americans, to continue their relentless attacks on German cities.

For some, the Allied successes came too late. Indeed, these successes appear to have given new impetus to Hitler and the Nazis' war against

the Jews. Nowhere is this more tragically apparent than in the fate of
the ghetto in Łódź, a large city which had been incorporated into the
expanded German Reich after the conquest of Poland in 1939, and
renamed Litzmannstadt. The Germans had established the ghetto in Łódź
in February 1940, confining some 200,000 Jews in the most rundown
area of the city. Between September and December 1941 this population
had been augmented by deportations of Jews from Prague, Vienna, and
other German cities, and from nearby places in Poland. Through 1942
the numbers in the ghetto had been greatly reduced both by calculated
starvation and by deportations to Chelmno, where the Jews arriving were immediately gassed, and their bodies burnt. The leader of the
ghetto, Chaim Rumkowski, had devoted himself to compromise with
the German authorities, and hoped that by making 'his' Jews productive
workers he could ensure at least the survival of a few. By 1944, all the
other ghettos of Poland and Eastern Europe had been destroyed by the
Germans, leaving only a few of their former inmates clinging to life in
concentration camps. But 80,000 still lived and worked in the reduced
space of the ghetto in Łódź, 'the most hermetically sealed concentration
of Jews in Europe'.[27] Like Klemperer in Dresden, they had heard the
most terrible rumours about the fate of other European Jews, and of
their former fellow ghetto inhabitants. Like Klemperer, they knew that
only the military defeat of Germany could save them.

From one anonymous diarist still living in the Łódź ghetto, we can
learn of the hopes and fears aroused by the progress of the war in the
summer of 1944. This young man was evidently well educated, sensitive and cultivated. He began his diary in May 1944, writing in Polish,
English, and Yiddish in the margins of a French novel, *Les Vrais Riches*.
After D-Day he wrote: 'It is true, the fact has been accomplished, but
will we survive? [...] God be in our help.' The Germans resumed deportations from the ghetto on 23 June 1944, prompting this entry: 'Even
though they promise that they're sending them to work, we hope they
don't do with them what they've done with so many others. It's said that
a train came back after 11 hours. Some say one thing, others another.
Every day a few hundred leave the ghetto. The hunger is getting worse.'
Over the next few days the diarist recorded the continuing deportations
and rumours of the war outside. On 10 July he noted 'news of a crushing
defeat for our enemies, which seems to have finished them for good'.
On 16 July he noted that deportations from the ghetto had stopped,

but added: 'Rumors have reached the ghetto that the Jews of Hungary, numbering 400,000 were brought to Poland and annihilated. Woe to us, impossible to describe the feelings which arise in us when we hear the news.' On 21 July he recorded news of the attempt on Hitler's life, and on 25 July he wrote: 'For five years I kept my patience, and now it's suddenly gone. One can feel the coming liberation in the air.'

On 3 August, the Germans announced that all Jews would be 'transferred' from the Łódź ghetto, pretending that work would be found for them in Germany. The diarist wrote: 'I write these lines in a terrible state of mind. All of us have to leave Litzmannstadt-Ghetto within a few days. […] When I look at my little sister, my heart is melting. Hasn't the child suffered her part? She who fought so heroically the last five years.' On 20 August he made the last dated entry in his diary:

> There are rumors we won't have much longer to wait. The Germans admit they have retreated from Lublin, Bialystok, Brisk, Dinanburg, and other places. But for the stubbornness of their leader, it would all be over. I worry terribly because despite everything the situation is still unclear. Who can predict our future? Maybe they won't kill us.

The novel with this diary written in it was found after the war at nearby Auschwitz, where virtually all surviving Jews of the Łódź ghetto, including Rumkowski, were deported in August.[28] A few hundred were left behind, in hiding, or in work gangs clearing the abandoned buildings.

GERMANY FIGHTS ON

Nothing that had occurred in 1944 had in any way inclined Hitler to do anything but fight on, and after 20 July, the armed forces and the population of Germany seem equally to have seen no other options. In this doomed and disastrous course of action Hitler was able temporarily to take advantage of several factors. Despite Allied bombing, and the loss of sources of raw materials and of production from occupied countries, the production of weapons in Germany continued to rise, peaking in September 1944. Hitler's personal architect and Armaments Minister Albert Speer recorded that 2,878 fighter aircraft were produced in that month, and that 690 tanks and 949 self-propelled guns were delivered to the armed forces, along with over 60,000 submachine guns. Most of these weapons were allocated to newly formed units.[29] The number of new tanks, aircraft, and guns produced was of course exceeded by the Allies, but it did mean that until the final weeks of the war they continued, on all fronts, to come up against German formations with considerable fighting power.

Hitler's much vaunted 'vengeance weapons' did not turn the tide of war, but the Allies did face an array of new weapons in 1944, some of which caused them great anxiety. The V1 flying bomb and the V2 rockets were almost exclusively used against civilian targets, but caused many deaths. Again they were produced in remarkable numbers: between 12 June and the end of August 1944, nearly 7,000 V1s reached England, killing 5,475 people and severely injuring a further 16,000.[30] On 8 September the first V2s fell on London. There was no defence against these rockets, and wherever they chanced to land, they caused great destruction. Over 1,000 fell in Britain before the end of the war. It is easy now to imagine these bombs and rockets as insignificant in the larger context of the war, but all the records from that time of people who were in London and the under the flight path of the weapons, which were launched from the Pas de Calais, and later from Holland, show that they were greatly feared. There was an enormous diversion of American and British effort towards the destruction and capture of these sites. Harry Butcher, who with Eisenhower and his headquarters staff was outside London on 16 June, under the flight path, grimly noted some of the consequences: 'The Bomber Command was out in strength against sites in the Pas de Calais [...] Now to bomb a new site, we have to destroy the surrounding village, which further impairs our deteriorating relationship with the French.'[31] At a more prosaic level, the German armaments industry produced over 3 million *Panzerfäuste* in the last months of the war, and these provided many soldiers with a weapon capable of destroying an enemy tank or other vehicle.[32]

Despite the enormous losses in the war so far, now amounting to millions, Germany still fielded a huge army. As the war came closer to home, their numbers were constantly augmented by new recruits, many of them very young, by pressed foreigners, and by great numbers of men who had previously not been at the front, air force ground staff, coastal forces, communication troops, instructors, anti-aircraft crews, policemen and camp guards. In adversity, the Germans developed an improvisatory tactic: from various groups of retreating men and others at hand, they formed a *Kampfgruppe*, or 'fighting group', often taking its name from its commander. These groups were used to plug gaps in the front, and to stage local counter attacks. Experienced soldiers, new recruits, and new weapons were often effectively combined. Strikingly, the German soldiers, now typically on the defensive, still fought with amazing tenacity, and this was noted by both sides. Commenting on the situation in September 1944, Blumentritt wrote:

> in complete contrast to 1918 there was no mutiny or really bad discipline. It was a miracle that these brave, battered troops showed little deterioration in their morale. It is true that the troops were tired, often exhausted, and in many cases apathetic – but they all retained the will to fight.[33]

From the other side, Eisenhower's HQ had reached a similar conclusion. Butcher summarised the position at the end of September: 'The enemy has, however, established a relatively stable and cohesive front, approximately on the German frontier except in the Low Countries. The Germans have lost a million men in France and an enormous amount of equipment, yet there are no signs of collapse in morale and in the will to defend Germany.'[34] Eisenhower himself noted how, amongst captured German officers, 'the younger ones, in whom the Nazi spirit was strongest, still proclaimed the invincibility of the German cause'. As for the senior officers, so many of whom fondly imagined they had some kind of kinship with the Americans and British, Eisenhower felt they had a reason for fighting on: 'all appeared on the list prepared by the Russians of those guilty of atrocities in the east; it was not likely that surrender would be forthcoming from such men.'[35]

The romanticised views of tough German soldiers in the final stages of the war which abound in literature and in film should be balanced with an awareness of how draconian German military discipline was at this time. Towards the end of the war, increasing numbers of German soldiers were brought before military courts, and the sentences passed became harsher. In October 1944, 44,955 soldiers were put on trial; by this time, 85 per cent of death sentences passed were actually carried out. During the First World War, forty-eight German soldiers were executed by their own army. In the Second World War, the figure was between 13,000 and 15,000. This is not something the German generals who wrote post-war memoirs chose to explore. Omer Bartov concludes that German army discipline, especially in the East, became 'positively murderous'. It was, he argues, 'the unprecedented harsh discipline of the Wehrmacht which kept the units together at the front'.[36]

The Allies in September 1944, for all their dramatic successes, faced a number of problems. Most immediately, the rapid advance of their armies had taken them hundreds of miles from their supply bases. The Soviets also had to pause and regroup. Once they had established usable roads and railways they were able to re-provision their armies on an ever greater scale. They had no problem replacing the hundreds of thousands of soldiers killed and wounded in the campaigns of 1944, and Stalin appears to have felt no compunction about losing many more. In north-western Europe, the Americans and British were still entirely dependent on supplies brought in over the Normandy beaches, or through Cherbourg, and there was insufficient petrol to fuel a constant advance by their mechanised armies on a widening front. For all the propaganda value of the celebrated 'Red Ball Express', in fact the American supply organisation, 'ComZ', was corrupt and inefficient. Max Hastings regards Eisenhower's failure to reform ComZ as a 'serious criticism'; he is even more scathing about Eisenhower's failure to prioritise the limited supplies reaching the front line troops.[37] Eisenhower in August and September 1944 faced competing demands from three subordinates: Patton, commanding the US 3rd Army in Lorraine, Hodges' 1st Army heading directly for the German 'West Wall' near Aachen, and Montgomery, commanding the British and Canadian forces rapidly approaching the Dutch frontier. All argued vociferously that they should have the largest share of the fuel available to pursue a direct attack into Germany. Eisenhower, whose headquarters was by now some distance from the front lines, refused to give any one of them clear priority, maintaining his preference for a 'broad front' approach.

At a higher level within the Allied coalition there were tensions, brought to a head by the tragic uprising in Warsaw. The military situation there was relatively straightforward: the Red Army had by August 1944 reached the east bank of the Vistula outside Warsaw, and the German administration in the city appeared on the verge of collapse. The political situation was more complicated. There was by this time a bitter hostility between the Polish government in exile in London and the Soviets, who in July 1944 established a 'National Committee of Liberation' – obviously a government in waiting – in Lublin. The resistance movement in Poland was made up of various factions, some loyal to the London government, some to the Lublin committee. On 29 July a Soviet broadcast urged the Poles in Warsaw to rise up; it was widely assumed that if they did so, the Red Army would come to their aid. In the event, the Polish 'Home Army' under the leadership of General Bor-Komorowski rose against the remaining Germans, seized key buildings in the city, and briefly felt the exultation of success. The story is well known in outline: the Red Army stood off, and Stalin refused even to help RAF aircraft refuel so they could drop supplies into the beleaguered city. SS formations, commanded by the most brutal anti-partisan specialists, were brought in to suppress the rising by whatever means they deemed necessary. After sixty-three days of bitter struggle Bor-Komorowski had to surrender; the surviving resisters were marched off to a brutal captivity, and the Germans had time to destroy much of what was left of Warsaw. Not until January 1945 did the Soviets enter the city, by then little more than 'ruins and ashes covered by snow'.[38]

On the home front, Germany finally abandoned the ideological constraints which had prevented the full mobilisation of the population for the war effort. Women had for some time been used in the labour force, and now increasing numbers were brought into service as anti-aircraft crews, as fire fighters, and as camp guards. On 1 September 1944, the Propaganda Minister Joseph Goebbels, who had emerged as Hitler's strongest and most effective supporter, decreed the closure of almost all Germany's operas, theatres, and concert halls, and the conscription for war service of all but a handful of 'God gifted' artists. Hitler ordered the formation on 25 September of a *Volkssturm* or 'people's storm'. This typical piece of Nazi bombast and racial arrogance rather inflated the military potential of hastily assembled groups of elderly men and boys. Many of these recruits, willing or unwilling, were to suffer particularly over the next few months. The German population was now thinking seriously about its future. Victor Klemperer, still observing the workings of the Nazi state, read this passage in a Dresden newspaper at this time: 'The German state is to be erased from the map, the Germans are to be dispersed over the whole globe as labour slaves.'[39]

Whether from devotion to Hitler, from Nazi ideological conviction, from patriotic sentiment, from duty to and love for family and *Heimat*, from fear of punishment, from fatalism, or from a feeling of utter powerlessness, Germany stumbled on.

2

HOPES AND FEARS:
SEPTEMBER 1944–JANUARY 1945

The *Wehrmacht* is the weapons-bearer of the German people. It protects the German Empire and Fatherland, the German *Volk* united in National Socialism, and its living space. […] The honour of the soldier lies in unconditional disposition of his person for *Volk* and Fatherland, as far as the sacrifice of his life.

From a pocket hymn book issued to all German soldiers in the Second World War. [1]

On Sunday 17 September 1944 Harry Butcher was in London visiting a fellow officer in hospital. During his visit, he noted that 'hundreds of aircraft, many towing gliders, passed overhead en route to the big jump over the Rhine at Nijmegen'. [2] Many were going further, to Arnhem, where British paratroopers were charged with capturing and holding the huge road bridge across the Lower Rhine. Thousands of the men in these aircraft would not return. This was the boldest and most imaginative strategic move of the American and British campaign in north-western Europe. If successful, it promised to turn the flank of the German fortifications along the border with France and Belgium, and to leave Allied troops poised to strike across the flat plain of north Germany, to encircle the industrial area of the Ruhr, or to advance directly towards Berlin.

The plan for this operation, 'Market Garden', was devised by Montgomery in the heady days of late August and early September. Montgomery was obsessed with the notion that Allied resources in the

West should be concentrated under his command on the left flank, and used for a direct thrust into the heart of Germany. This approach avoided the hilly terrain of the Ardennes, or the mountains of the Vosges further south, and the fortifications of the 'West Wall'. Montgomery faced instead the difficulty of crossing the intricate network of waterways in Holland which carried the waters of the Rhine and other rivers into the sea. His plan called for three large airborne landings to seize the major bridges at Eindhoven, Nijmegen, and Arnhem, and for a rapid advance by armoured forces on land to reach these bridges within three or four days. It exploited the large reserve of airborne troops still held in Britain and threatened the retreating German forces before they could construct any proper defensive line in Holland. There had indeed been a number of earlier plans in July and August to use these airborne divisions, but each had been made redundant by the rapidity of the Allied advance. From Eisenhower's perspective, the plan was attractive because of its reliance on troops to be landed and supplied from the air; it did not in his mind represent an abandonment of the 'broad front' policy. On 10 September he gave his consent to Montgomery, much to the subsequent amazement of Bradley and other American commanders.[3]

The plan was developed with great speed and secrecy. The 101st American Airborne Division was to be landed north of Eindhoven to secure the bridges over the Wilhelmina and Zuid Willemsvaart Canals; the 82nd US Airborne Division was to be landed some ten miles further north, to capture the bridges over the River Maas at Grave, and over the River Waal at Nijmegen; the 1st British Airborne Division, rapidly followed by the Polish Parachute Brigade, was to be landed near Arnhem to secure the final bridge over the Lower Rhine, some sixty-five miles ahead of the British front line. At the same time, the British Second Army, spearheaded by the Guards Armoured Division, would strike from this front line, 'with the utmost rapidity and violence, and without regard to events on the flanks'.[4] Advancing along a single road, with support from fighter bombers, the Guards would travel through Eindhoven and Nijmegen to reach the paratroopers at Arnhem. The story of how the plan unravelled has been immortalised in books and in film. The phrase 'a bridge too far', originally attributed to Frederick Browning, Deputy Commander of the airborne troops,[5] has entered the English language as shorthand for something which is a good idea, but simply too ambitious.

The initial landings on 17 September were largely successful, but far from arriving in largely undefended territory, the American and British paratroopers found themselves opposed by German forces armed with tanks and heavy weapons. The bridge at Nijmegen was strongly defended, and it took three days of heavy fighting before the Americans could seize it. The British were landed too far away from the bridge at Arnhem, and only an isolated force managed to reach and hold one end of it. The landing of the Polish brigade was delayed, and when they were dropped in, German defenders were prepared for them. The advance of the Guards towards the vital bridges was held up by tenacious defence from ditches either side of the single road being used. After great exertions, the ground forces did reach the American paratroopers in Eindhoven and in Nijmegen, but the British and Polish paratroopers in Arnhem were overwhelmed after a desperate struggle lasting nine days. Lacking heavy weapons, short of food, water, ammunition, and medical supplies, they were ground down by improvised German forces which received a steady reinforcement of fresh men and new tanks. Over 6,000 British soldiers surrendered on 26 September, and Arnhem, now largely destroyed, stayed in German hands until April 1945. The British and Americans had advanced some forty-five miles, and had crossed two major water features, but they had not made the strategic breakthrough that was intended.

Different explanations have been put forward for the failure of 'Market Garden'. With hindsight, it is possible to argue that the para-troopers should have been landed closer to the vital bridges, notably at Arnhem. There was a disastrous failure of communications within the British forces there, which left them out of touch with the outside world, and ignorant of their own dispositions around Arnhem. An American officer, in defiance of orders, carried a full plan of the operation into the battle area, and this fell into the hands of the Germans, who were thus well informed of Allied intentions from early on. The advance of the ground forces along one road was easily slowed down by anti-tank guns, and the difficulties of movement in flat terrain intersected with water-filled ditches made it almost impossible to redirect this advance when it was halted. The weather was worse than anticipated, and the Allies did not exploit their huge aerial superiority to support the beleaguered paratroopers. Nor was the local knowledge and practical assistance offered by the well-organised Dutch resistance used effectively.

On the German side, the resistance shown at Arnhem was extraordinary. Coincidentally, two SS panzer divisions were refitting nearby when the Americans and British landed, and elements of these units were skilfully combined with other available troops to mount effective, mobile counterattacks. As the fighting developed, retreating forces from further north in Holland, and reinforcements from Germany itself were thrown into the struggle at key points. Some fifty new German tanks arrived during the fighting; against these, the lightly armed paratroopers had no defence.

Curiously, from the German side, Arnhem was not seen as hugely significant. Armaments Minister Speer met in Arnhem with General Bittrich, who was 'in a state of fury' about the ill treatment of prisoners by 'party functionaries'. In spite of his orders to the contrary, these 'had taken it upon themselves to kill British and American pilots'. Speer noted, almost as an aside: 'The day before his Second Tank Corps had virtually wiped out a British airborne division.'[6] Blumentritt states that at Rundstedt's HQ, the Allied attack was anticipated from aerial photographs: 'Western Command counted upon an air landing in the corner of the Rhine between Emmerich and Arnhem, that is, on the north bank of the river.' Thus forewarned, and aided by capture of the Allied plans, the Germans were able to resist and defeat the Allies at Arnhem. Rundstedt believed that this was insignificant, and that it left the striking capacity of the Allied parachute forces largely undiminished. 'Regarded strategically', wrote Blumentritt, 'this fighting, in Rundstedt's view, brought no decision.'[7] Mellenthin was in Alsace as chief of staff to General Balck, who had been put in command of Army Group G, part of a wider reshuffle at this time, which brought Rundstedt back to command in the West, and with him, Model to command Army Group B in Holland and Belgium. Surveying the situation in the west, Mellenthin mentioned Arnhem in a few terse lines: 'he [Model] soon added to his reputation by a resolute defence of southern Holland. In late September the situation there was relieved by the victory of Arnhem.'[8] Klemperer in Dresden received the news in an entirely different way. Notwithstanding the general perception that it was insignificant, he was clear about its implications:

> Perhaps the annihilation of the English 'air landing division' at Arnhem is an
> unimportant, soon to be forgotten, episode; but it is extremely important to

me today and pushes back my hopes of an end from September '44 to Easter '45, precisely because it is proof to me of unbroken powers of resistance.[9]

Whether Klemperer was right depends on Montgomery's intentions. Eisenhower was too much of a realist to believe that if the bridge had been secured at Arnhem the Allies could have raced to Berlin. He specifically pointed out to Montgomery how vulnerable the flanks of such a drive would be: Berlin is more than 300 miles from Arnhem, and the supply lines of such a narrow thrust would have been perilously exposed. Montgomery was careful not to make explicit exactly what he thought might have been possible had 'Market Garden' succeeded. Understandably, in his post-war memoirs he played down the defeat: 'The battle of Arnhem was ninety per cent successful.' Arguing that a position of strategic advantage had been gained, he wrote: 'Full success at Arnhem was denied us for two reasons; first the weather prevented the build up of our airborne forces in the battle area; second, the enemy managed to effect a surprisingly rapid concentration of forces to oppose us.'[10] Writing ten years later, Montgomery inserted a new 'first' cause for the failure: although Eisenhower had agreed to concentrate resources on the main thrust in the north, 'in this instance his intentions were not carried out', thus implying that the American armies further south subverted the plan by diverting resources to their own fronts.[11] Eisenhower played down Arnhem in his *Report* of 1945, stressing the strategic advantages gained by crossing two of the three major rivers obstructing the route to Germany.

The greatest damage caused by Arnhem to the Allies was psychological. The Americans and the British had been growing in confidence, and their front line soldiers had, in some cases, allowed themselves to think that the end was in sight. Once again they had been taught a horrible lesson; for the British especially, the blow caused by the high losses, some 3,000 killed and missing, was augmented by the ignominious surrender of a large body of men. Too often the disaster which overcame the Polish Parachute Brigade is overlooked; in Britain the huge contribution made by American paratroopers tends likewise to be underplayed. There was not another ambitious strategic operation like that at Arnhem: after this Eisenhower's 'broad front' meant a careful, sustained offensive along the length of the Allied line.

There were numerous other signs that September of increasingly organised German resistance, but the check to the Allied advance in the

West has been attributed to failures of Allied strategic judgement. After American forces advancing from Normandy had joined hands with the troops moving up from southern France, a continuous front line ran, as it had in the First World War, from the Swiss frontier to the North Sea. Eisenhower now commanded a huge force, spread out not only along this front, but occupied in several places with strong German forces well behind the line in besieged towns. The Americans decided to capture two of these at all costs. Hundreds of miles to the west, on the Brittany coast, they attacked the port of Brest. In the wooded and hilly country of Lorraine, they determined to capture the historic fortress of Metz. It has been argued in both cases that the reasons were not purely military, and that the Americans would have been wiser to invest the garrisons in Brest and Metz and await their later surrender, as the British did with Dunkirk, or the Americans themselves with Lorient and Saint Nazaire.[12] The German forces in all these towns had great defensive firepower, but were not mobile, and were not therefore a huge threat to the Allies. Brest and Metz were in totally different geographical situations, but both cities had extensive defensive fortifications, built first by Vauban in the seventeenth century, strengthened in subsequent wars, and recently modernised by the Germans. The Americans diverted huge resources of men and firepower first to attack Brest in August 1944, and then to the complex of forts around Metz in early September. At a critical point, when the advancing armies of Patton, Hodges, and Bradley were running short of ammunition and fuel, a huge effort was turned onto Brest. Not until 20 September did the last remnants of the German garrison there surrender. Metz was even more resistant. Some 30,000 German defenders here included the staff of two training schools in the city, which since 1940 had been incorporated within the German Reich. Its defences now faced largely to the west, and although the city was largely encircled in early September, attacks on the forts around it were unsuccessful. In deteriorating weather the conditions of the First World War were replicated.

Further to the north, the Allies were belatedly realising what a huge opportunity had been lost at Antwerp. The British troops which had entered the city were exhausted, and made no immediate effort to clear the shores of the Scheldt estuary, leading to the sea. The German Fifteenth Army, in full retreat from France, might easily have been cut off here and forced to surrender. Hitler, in one the few good strategic insights he displayed at this time, realised that the extensive region of flat sandy islands and estuarial land around the Scheldt could be strongly defended, and that Allied shipping would be unable to use Antwerp unless the area was totally cleared. In early September, an improvised fleet of small vessels ferried 80,000 men of the German Fifteenth Army, with many vehicles, horses, and guns, from the south bank of the Scheldt to the north. Over the next few weeks, these experienced soldiers were used to counter-attack at Arnhem, and to add to the concentration of defensive forces on the island of Walcheren and the long Beveland peninsula.

There appears to have been a failure of communication or of leadership here. The senior British admirals, Cunningham and Ramsay, apparently made clear the need to clear the estuary, but this imperative was not impressed upon the ground troops who captured Antwerp so boldly in September 1944. According to Cunningham:

> both Ramsay and myself agreed that it must be firmly pointed out to the Army Command that Antwerp lay well inland and up a river controlled by the enemy. Before the port could be used for shipping the German defences must be cleared. Our forebodings were pretty well correct. By September 4th, Antwerp was in our hands with its port facilities practically intact. In the pæan of triumph at its capture the clearance of the approaches was not treated as a matter of urgency. For the time being one of the finest ports in Europe was of no more use to us than an oasis in the Sahara desert.

Noting the strength of subsequent German resistance in South Beveland and Walcheren, Cunningham remarked grimly that it was not until 'heavy casualties' had been suffered clearing these areas that the first Allied vessels were able to unload in Antwerp on 26 November 1944.[13]

In north-western Europe a phase of the conflict was now beginning which has been etched on the consciousness of all who took part. The weather was worsening, and the combination of cold, rain, snow, discomfort, and fear which characterised the experience of fighting in the autumn and winter of 1944 equalled in its horror some of the worst scenes of the First World War. Paul Fussell has observed how this campaign has become, for the Americans, 'the army's point of reference for its conception of war – for the way it sees itself, its doctrine, its organisation and training, its equipment, and its professional idioms'. Overcast weather largely neutralised the advantage of air power, and this was a war experienced most fully and typically by infantrymen. 'To be sure there were tanks and half-tracks and jeeps, but much of the fighting took place without heavy equipment at all, the infantry performing its role with rifles, hand grenades, machine guns, and mortars and using tactics unchanged since the First World War and even the Civil War.'[14] For the Canadians, the fighting for the flooded polders and the causeways of southern Holland was uniquely horrific. The Germans who defended these positions experienced similar hardships, and faced only the likelihood of annihilation by overwhelming force. Through September and October 1944, as the days shortened and the weather deteriorated, Eisenhower pursued his broad front policy. South of Arnhem, Hodges' Army had its first experience of fighting for a German city, Aachen. Street by street, and house by house, the defenders were forced back; the ruins of the city were surrendered only on 21 October. At the same time, Canadian and British troops inched forward to clear the Scheldt estuary. In Lorraine, Patton's assault on Metz continued.

THE 'MORGENTHAU PLAN'

The stiffening German resistance in September 1944 has often been attributed, at least partly, to the announcement there of the 'Morgenthau Plan'. Even as the American and British offensives came shuddering to a halt, Churchill and Roosevelt had met in Quebec to consider the future of Germany. There, in a surprisingly ill-considered way, they had both agreed to the plan put forward by Hans Morgenthau, the American Treasury Secretary, to impose harsh terms on a defeated Germany. The best known component of the plan was Morgenthau's idea to strip Germany of its industry and to reduce it to an agricultural economy. The plan also called for summary execution of Nazi leaders and war criminals, but this attracted less attention. Churchill and Roosevelt's acceptance of the plan was revealed to the press after the conference, and inevitably Goebbels made the most of it. Lurid visions of a future Germany reduced to medieval serfdom were presented to the German public, and, it has been argued, contributed significantly to their determination to fight on, whatever the cost.

The Morgenthau Plan did not appear that important to the British. John Colville, who attended the conference with Churchill, did not even mention it in his diary. Churchill was evidently more excited about the promise of huge American loans he had secured.[15] Roosevelt's Secretary of State, Cordell Hull, had not attended the conference, but was outraged when he heard of the plan, and that Roosevelt had accepted it. Hull's department had invested 'hundreds of hours' planning for postwar Germany, and he saw immediately that the Morgenthau Plan was entirely unworkable. Not only would it antagonise the Germans, it would cripple the wider European economy, which was dependent on German coal and steel. Hull's suspicion that Churchill had accepted the plan as a *quid pro quo* for the offer of credits 'totaling six and a half billion dollars' was a further irritation. Hull also recognised the possibility that the plan would strengthen German resistance. 'This whole development at Quebec', he wrote, 'angered me as much as anything that had happened during my career as Secretary of State.' Over the next few weeks, Hull, ably supported by Henry Stimson, the Secretary for War, mounted a determined campaign in Washington to change Roosevelt's mind. Roosevelt had a straightforward conviction that the German people as a whole shared responsibility for the war, and was inclined towards a very harsh peace. He had only days previously sent Hull a memorandum stating that although he didn't want the German people to starve to death, he did think that food served three times a day from 'Army soup kitchens' would be sufficient, and would make them hesitate before starting another war.

In heated discussions in Washington, Hull and Stimson argued for a more pragmatic course. Morgenthau fought his corner, revealing that both Churchill and Eden had been initially 'violently opposed' to his plan. Hull took it up directly with Roosevelt, telling him that 'Morgenthau's plan was out of all reason'. Roosevelt was not in good health, and clearly had only a poor grip of the details being thrust at him from different sides. He agreed to drop the idea of de-industrialising Germany, but stuck doggedly to his intention to hold down German industrial production, and to give financial support to Britain. He compromised by agreeing not to publicise any detailed plan for the occupation of Germany. Cordell Hull was also an ill man. His success in forcing Roosevelt to abandon the most draconian aspects of Morgenthau's plan was his last important act of business with the President. He resigned, on the verge of collapse.[16]

The two polarised approaches to a post-war Germany advocated by Hull and Morgenthau both remained alive in subsequent American and British planning, leaving an unresolved tension. By then the idea of destroying German industry had been widely publicised. Did it, as Hull feared, give Goebbels 'wonderful ammunition to spur the Germans on to fight to the end'? We have seen that Klemperer in Dresden was seeing lurid visions of a future Germany enslaved and destroyed in German newspapers, but these were published *before* the Quebec conference. In fact the Morgenthau plan made little difference. Nazi propaganda had for years propagated exaggerated fantasies of what might happen to Europe, and to Germany, if the Allies won. Churchill and Roosevelt had long been portrayed as Jewish-controlled plutocrats who wanted to corrupt European culture and to exploit its population. The fact that Hans Morgenthau was Jewish was grist to Goebbels' mill in September 1944, but Goebbels did not need the Morgenthau plan to scare the German people with. In any case, by 1944, the German population had become deeply sceptical about what they read in the newspapers and heard on German radio. Sensitive historians today accept that after 1942 the credibility of news issued from the Propaganda Ministry declined greatly in Germany. After that, newspapers 'were trusted by few readers'.[17] Rumours about the Morgenthau plan certainly did not stop millions of them from fleeing to the American and British Zones when the war did come to an end in 1945.[18]

While the Western Allies slogged their way, inch by inch, towards the German frontier, the Soviets made much more rapid progress. Hitler was surprisingly slow to accept the need to evacuate the Balkans, but a renewed Soviet offensive across the Danube on 22 September, supported now by Bulgarian and Romanian troops, forced his hand. On 3 October the decision was taken to evacuate all German forces from Greece, Macedonia, and Albania. As with all German withdrawals in the later stages of the war, it came too late. In this case, most of the troops on the mainland escaped, but some 30,000 were isolated on various Greek islands. Retreating units were harassed by partisans, and thrown piecemeal into action against Soviet forces as they arrived near the front. There were insufficient soldiers for Field Marshal Weichs, the Commander South-East, to create anything like a continuous front, and he was unable to prevent the Soviets from overrunning Serbia. On 13 October the Germans left Athens; on 14 October Belgrade fell to the

Soviets. By the end of the month, Weichs managed to create something like a stable defensive position holding Croatia, Bosnia, and Slovenia.

Both Stalin's and Hitler's attention was now fixed on Budapest. On 29 October, forces from Malinovsky's Second Ukrainian Front made their first assault on the city; some of his men penetrated the suburbs, but they were repulsed. For Hitler, Budapest had both a symbolic and practical importance. He declared the city a 'fortress' and demanded its reinforcement, partly to protect the small oilfields nearby, now virtually the only source of crude oil available to Germany. During November, more and more German, Hungarian and Soviet forces were sucked into the struggle for Budapest. Inside the city, the mood of the inhabitants oscillated as rumours of impending collapse came and went. It was by now clear to the Soviets that the city would not fall easily, and that a prolonged effort would be necessary to take it. Between 11 and 22 November they mounted large attacks north and south of the city to encircle it; they faced desperate counterattacks from German forces equipped with considerable numbers of new Tiger tanks. Other reinforcements were diverted from Italy and from the Western Front to try to shore up the German position. Budapest was not finally encircled until 26 December, leaving four German and two Hungarian divisions, together with other assorted units, trapped there. Hitler, astonishingly, still believed that this force could be relieved.

The collapse of the German position in the Balkans was mirrored at the northern end of the Eastern Front, where the Finnish had been observing the deterioration of the situation since early in 1944. By July, it was clear to the Finnish government that the alliance with Nazi Germany was leading to disaster: in practical terms alone, the Soviet occupation of the Baltic coast threatened to stop the import of food and military supplies from Germany. In a sequence of moves similar to those in Romania and Bulgaria, Finland came to a separate understanding with the Soviet Union. On 4 August, Marshal Mannerheim was appointed President of a new Finnish government; he was visited by Colonel-General Schörner, the most committed Nazi amongst the senior German generals, and then by Keitel, Hitler's Chief of the Armed Forces High Command, who awarded him an 'oak leaf cluster' to add to his collection of medals.[19] Their reassurances of continued German support were in vain, however, and Mannerheim opened a negotiation with the Soviets on 25 August. On 2 September the Finnish Parliament accepted the Soviet terms for an armistice, and this was signed in Moscow on 19 September.

Curiously, at this point, the Finnish experience differed from that of Romania or Bulgaria. The Soviets were not disposed to divert troops to Finland, and did not press on to occupy the country. The Finns even managed a final victory against Soviet forces on the Karelian Isthmus before the armistice. They had committed themselves to expelling all German forces from Finnish soil, and this had repercussions in the extreme north, where, since 1941, a German Mountain Army had advanced beyond the narrow Norwegian frontier to protect the nickel mines at Pechenga, and the ore fields in Sweden. In an operation which is almost unknown in the West, this Mountain Army made in October a series of staged withdrawals back to a prepared line in northern Norway; the Finns did little to impede their escape. Behind them, as with all retreats, the Germans left supplies and equipment of all kinds.[20]

The Germans had tried to convince the Finns that they would hold onto the Baltic coastline, and this became another of Hitler's fixed ideas. Again, a careful appraisal of the geography would have highlighted the difficulty here. By abandoning this largely unimportant territory, Hitler could have greatly shortened the German line, and brought this much closer to his lines of supply. His argument that the coastline must be held to secure training areas for U-boats shows that he was living in an illusory world where he imagined great powers of offensive action. In any case, despite limited successes in local counterattacks, Hitler's Army Group North in the Baltic States was too weak to maintain the four-hundred-mile front it held in September 1944. Under prolonged and heavy attack, the Germans were driven from Estonia, much of Latvia, and from Lithuania. The last German convoy left the Baltic port of Riga on 10 October. Two German armies were trapped in the Courland peninsula (in present-day Latvia); another corps was encircled in the port of Memel, one of Hitler's first acquisitions before 1939. Two further German armies were in headlong retreat towards the East Prussian frontier and the city of Königsberg. On 16 October Soviet troops crossed into Germany near Gumbinnen. The historic heartland of Prussia and of Teutonic mythology was either in Soviet hands, or directly threatened.

The Soviets did not press their advantage further in the last months of 1944. They had much to do to consolidate the occupation of the territories liberated from Nazism. For three months, along the East Prussian frontier, into Poland – still outside Warsaw – and to the Hungarian frontier, the Red Army largely refrained from further attacks. Whatever Stalin's intentions for a post-war Eastern Europe, his huge armies needed rest and replenishment. They had advanced hundreds of miles, and sustained huge losses. The battered and demoralised German forces facing them were given a welcome respite; many were drawn back to rest and to refit.

COUNTER-ATTACK IN THE ARDENNES

In Germany itself, as Allied forces surrounded the country, and while huge fleets of aircraft ranged through its skies raining death and destruction, an increasingly poisonous mood developed. Edith Hahn's husband was conscripted from his hitherto protected post at the Arado aircraft company in Brandenburg in September 1944, leaving her with their new-born baby. She observed: 'The country was falling apart. Sabotage. Desertions. And with the last of its strength, the dictatorship could think of nothing better to do than sacrifice my husband.'[21] Sybil Bannister had noted earlier in 1944 how the number of prosecutions of German women accused of having sexual relations with foreign workers was rising dramatically. Victor Klemperer in Dresden had watched the collapse of the German position in the East with some alarm. On 17 October he wrote:

> It worries me greatly that our personal situation has been so very much altered by Hungary's elimination. Now Dresden may become a transport junction behind the front which is most threatened, and that in a very short time. Then we shall get heavy air attacks. [...] Then there will be an evacuation and at the same time the mixed marriages will be separated and the Jewish parties gassed – who knows where?[22]

Rudolf Höss, who had been in command of the huge concentration camp complex around Auschwitz between 1941 and December 1943, provides an interesting commentary from this stage of the war, when he was working with the Inspectorate of Concentration Camps in Berlin. He, better than most, knew of some of the worst crimes committed by the Nazis, and could expect little from a post-Nazi world. He too picked up on the growing mood: 'Careful observation of the faces and the demeanour of the people in the public shelters or in the cellars of their homes revealed their mounting nervousness and fear of death, as the onslaught approached and the bomb-carpet came closer.' Turning to the military situation, Höss wrote:

> The Eastern Front was continuously being 'withdrawn' and the German soldier in the East no longer held firm. The Western Front, too, was being forced back.
>
> Yet the Führer spoke of holding firm at all costs. Goebbels spoke and wrote about believing in miracles. Germany will conquer!
>
> For my part I had grave doubts whether we could win the war. I had heard and seen too much. Certainly we could not win this way. But I dared not doubt our final victory, I must believe in it. Even though sturdy common-sense told me plainly and unambiguously that we must lose. My heart clung to the Führer and his ideals, for those must not perish.[23]

Hitler himself had no thoughts of a grim defensive battle, but was developing ambitious and unreal plans for grand strategy. On 12 October he confided to Speer his plan for an offensive in the West;[24] later that month, Rundstedt and Model were briefed. Heinz Guderian, who had been appointed Hitler's Chief of Staff on 21 July 1944, gives a clear description of what became the Ardennes offensive:

> The entire strength of the German Army that could be collected together during the last few months was to attack from the Eifel towards the Meuse south of Liège, with the object of breaking through the relatively thinly held Allied front in this sector; this force was then to cross the Meuse towards Brussels and Antwerp, thus achieving a strategic break-through; the enemy forces to the north of the breakthrough were finally to be encircled and destroyed.

Guderian further described how this success would, in Hitler's plan, allow him then to defeat the anticipated Soviet winter offensive, and make the Allies 'accept a negotiated peace'.[25]

Between October and December Guderian helped to build up a large reserve force – two Panzer armies – behind the left wing of the American front in the Belgian Ardennes. Hitler's plan had much in common with the successful operation of 1940, which had split the British from the bulk of the French army, and led to the evacuation from Dunkirk. In 1944 he planned again to attack the weakest point of the front line, and this time to split the British from the Americans. Once he had seized Antwerp, he intended to encircle and defeat the British and Canadian forces trapped in Holland. He hoped to use surprise, and to nullify Allied air superiority with the aid of the weather. Hitler's plan had notable strengths: it did successfully identify the weakest point of Eisenhower's front line; surprise was achieved; and the murky December weather kept the Allied air forces largely grounded. It never had any real chance of success though. It relied on the misplaced idea that the British and Americans would fall out once their armies were prised apart, and that they would not be able, separately or collectively, to contain the German attack. Hitler's plan was also fatally flawed by a lack of fuel. The Fifth and Sixth Panzer Armies, assembled for the attack, had many hundreds of tanks and other vehicles, but only sufficient petrol for a limited attack; Hitler assumed that they could rely on captured Allied stocks after the first few days of the offensive. By September 1944, German oil imports from Romania had entirely ceased; only very limited quantities of oil were still being produced from small wells in Hungary and Austria; synthetic oil production had been considerably reduced by the sustained British and American bombing of German refineries. The German military machine was literally coming to a halt.

The Ardennes offensive was launched on 16 December 1944, marking the start of what quickly became known as the Battle of the Bulge. At first, the German attack went well: American front line positions were overwhelmed and long columns of tanks pushed along the narrow, snow covered roads of the Ardennes. At its furthest point, the German offensive penetrated forty-five miles between the American and British armies, isolating pockets of bewildered Americans, many of them not front-line soldiers. Although some of these surrendered, a determined group held out at the town of Bastogne. Although there was a degree of consternation amongst the Americans and the British, reserves were swiftly moved up from both sides of the Bulge, and within a week it was clear that the offensive had been contained. Guderian had 'for the sake of my country [...] hoped that it would lead to a complete victory'. He drove to Hitler's headquarters on 23 December 'to request that the battle, which was causing us heavy casualties, be broken off and that all forces that could be spared be immediately transferred to the Eastern Front'.[26] Hitler insisted on maintaining the offensive for a few days longer, but even he could see by the end of December that it had failed.

'HERE IT IS — THE ACCURSED GERMANY'[27]

Since September, the Soviet forces along the Eastern Front from East Prussia down to the Hungarian border had carried out virtually no offensive action. They had not been inactive though. A sustained effort had built up an enormous concentration of men, vehicles, and supplies, particularly in the bridgeheads across the Vistula which had been gained in August. By January 1945, Stalin's Red Army had assembled some 3,870,000 soldiers, 7,700 tanks and self-propelled guns, and 74,000 artillery pieces of different kinds for its next offensive. Against this, Hitler could deploy only 400,000 troops, with 1,150 tanks and 4,100 guns.[28] The Red Army had huge reserves of ammunition and fuel, and thus equipped, Stalin's High Command had developed an ambitious plan. One powerful thrust, led by Zhukov, south of Warsaw, would strike towards Łódź and the German industrial area of Silesia. North of Warsaw, Rokossovsky's forces would head towards the Baltic coast to cut off East Prussia. The vacuum left as the German front was prised apart would allow a further advance directly towards Berlin itself.

The German forces facing this huge onslaught knew that an offensive was being prepared; intelligence reports prepared by General Gehlen accurately predicted both the magnitude and the objectives of the Soviet assault. On 24 December Guderian used these reports to try to convince Hitler of the need to transfer all available German troops from the Ardennes, from Alsace, and from Norway to meet this threat, but his ideas were rejected. Hitler still believed in continuing the offensive in the Ardennes, and that a subsequent thrust in northern Alsace might recapture Strasbourg. As far as the East was concerned, his fixation with the relief of Budapest was growing. Hitler was supported by General Jodl, who supported the projected attack in Alsace. An air of total unreality was developing at Hitler's headquarters, and Hitler refused to believe Gehlen's estimates. Guderian, after touring the Eastern Front, returned to the argument with Hitler on 9 January. Again, after a prolonged shouting match, he was unsuccessful. Hitler refused to sanction an evacuation of the civilian population threatened by the Soviet offensive, and was supported in this by the *Gauleiter* (the leaders of the regional branches of the Nazi Party), including Koch, the Party boss in East Prussia.

On 12 January 1945 the floodgates opened. Three hours of artillery bombardment preceded an infantry attack out of the Baranow bridgehead, south of Warsaw. On 14 and 15 January there were equally powerful attacks from the bridgeheads at Magnuszew and Pulawy. The wretched German soldiers facing these attacks were utterly overwhelmed and immediately isolated. Huge columns of Soviet tanks broke through the prepared defences, and were able to travel rapidly over the frozen landscape towards Germany. Belatedly, Hitler realised the gravity of the situation, and transferred his Headquarters to the Reich Chancellery in Berlin, where he was to stay until the end. He reorganised the command structure of the Eastern Front, putting Schörner, one of the few army officers in whom he had complete trust, in charge of Army Group A in Poland. From the remaining parts of the Nazi empire, barracks, depots, and training schools were scoured for reinforcements who could be thrown into the vortex in the East. It was to no avail. There was not the slightest chance that the weight of the Red Army could be opposed. In three weeks the Soviets pushed to the Baltic coast near Elbing, leaving pockets of German soldiers and civilians trapped in Königsberg and in the Samland Peninsula. The Soviets took the ruins of Warsaw and advanced through western Poland.

General Chuikov, leading the armoured spearhead, saw through his binoculars the factory chimneys of a large city, still smoking, on 18 January. It was Łódź, and after brief skirmishes, the city was abandoned by the Germans. Chuikov was amazed: 'Not a single building had been blown up, and both water and electricity supplies were functioning normally. Crowds of inhabitants greeted the columns of tanks, guns and lorries full of infantry as they came in. It was a general holiday. What else could it be?' Chuikov also noted with disgust the evidence of forced 'Germanisation': 'As I passed through the streets I saw with indignation how everything had been altered to the German style: there were new, German names on the enamelled plates at street corners, and German signs on the shops, and cynical notices on the door of cafés and restaurants, saying "Germans only. No Poles Admitted."' Chuikov didn't mention the Jews, or their absence.[29] Travelling with Chuikov was Vasily

Grossman. He had already been to Warsaw, where amongst the ruins he had discovered a few Jewish survivors. From them he had learnt of the destruction of the ghetto, and was therefore prepared for the absence of the Jews in Łódź. Here, he quickly established, hundreds of thousands of Jews from Poland and Germany had been concentrated; there were only 800 left alive. One, Jakob Poznanski, described the moment of liberation:

> Suddenly we heard: 'They're coming, they're coming!' At the end of Smugowa Street was a Soviet tank. It moved slowly and was greeted by the population with great enthusiasm. After a few minutes, two army cars, a mounted unit, and a group of foot soldiers appeared. Then a limousine arrived, stopping at the corner. [...] The general in the car made a short speech saying that the Polish Commonwealth now has an independent democratic government, in which all factions are represented, and with President Bierut at its head. I translated his words into Polish. Everyone applauded and cried 'Hurrah! Long Life!' The Poles gathered around us, asking how we had survived, if we had food, etc.[30]

At the southern end of the offensive, Koniev's forces pushed into Slovakia and into the mining area of Upper Silesia. By the end of January they stood outside the German towns of Breslau and Glogau. In the centre of the advance, Zhukov's forces advanced some 250 miles to cross the Oder near Küstrin, only fifty miles from Berlin. It was a military success almost without parallel. By the time a temporary thaw, and a degree of exhaustion, brought the Soviet advance to a halt in early February, the German position in the East had almost entirely collapsed, and Hitler's armies had been thrown back beyond the positions they had started from in September 1939 when they had marched into Poland.

For the Germans, it was a catastrophe. For the first time in the war, a large part of what they considered their own territory, in this case the heartland of East Prussia, and the disputed province of Silesia, had been conquered by a vengeful opponent. Since 1939, large areas of previously Polish territory now taken by the Red Army had been subject to a policy of what is now called 'ethnic cleansing': Jewish and Polish inhabitants had been forcibly deported or killed, and their land and homes given to German settlers, some from Germany, and many from areas like the Baltic states. In January 1945 virtually the whole German population of the area attacked by the Red Army abandoned its homes and fled by whatever means possible towards the west. In trains, cars, on horseback, and on foot, millions of men, women, and children struggled to escape across the flat, snow-covered land. Although in some cases they left farms and houses that had been seized from others only a few years previously, in many cases they left ancestral homes, towns and villages which had for centuries considered themselves German. Ill-prepared, undefended, and in bitter cold, many perished. Great numbers were murdered by Soviet soldiers, and many women were raped. The vivid accounts recently published by writers like Anthony Beevor and Max Hastings have brought this huge human tragedy to greater notice in the West, but earlier writers have portrayed some of the suffering involved; indeed it is clear that it was known about at the time. Propaganda literature dropped by the Americans and British in western Germany in February 1945 detailed accurately the suffering of refugees from Silesia.[31] John Colville in London reacted in the same way that many have since: 'Meanwhile, in this unusually bitter month, the Germans are fleeing from their homes in East Germany and themselves suffering the miseries which, albeit in summer, others suffered at their hands in 1940.'[32]

Those remaining in their homes were the first German civilians the advancing Soviets had encountered. A vivid description was written by Ilya Ehrenburg, the Soviet writer and journalist who has often been blamed for inciting Red Army troops to vengeful behaviour against the Germans. He was struck above all by how meek and submissive the Germans were, and by their denial of responsibility. He claims that he went to 'dozens of towns, talked to people in all walks of life'. He tried to find out what they had thought about the notion 'of a "master race", about the conquest of India, about Hitler's personality, about the Auschwitz incinerators. The reply was always the same: "We are not responsible".' Ehrenburg had seen for himself the evidence of all manner of Nazi atrocities, and was not convinced. 'In those days I had the feeling that a complicity in crime existed between the brutal SS men and placid Frau Müller from Rastenburg who had never killed anyone but had merely taken on a cheap servant – Nastya from Orel.'[33]

Sybil Bannister had been living the East Prussian town of Bromberg during 1944, far from Allied bombing and the actuality of war. Although the Soviets had in August advanced to within 130 miles, the population there had been reassured that they were not threatened. In December, news of the German offensive in the Ardennes had briefly conveyed an 'impression of unforeseen strength', and Sybil had, like others, celebrated a traditional Christmas, with an 'enormous Christmas tree', and a 'tender roast duck'. Her son Manny was delighted with a 'Hornby type' toy train set. Even after the Soviet offensive of 12 January 1945, the local authorities delayed the order to evacuate civilians, and only after fleeing refugees from nearby Thorn began streaming through the streets of Bromberg was the order to leave given. The Gestapo, army, and Nazi Party officials had all escaped, leaving railway workers and the National Socialist Welfare Organisation to get as many civilians as possible away from the town. Some of Sybil's household left with a local brewer who owned some horses. She herself managed to get onto a train with her son, together with a friend and her baby. After two days and nights in an unheated cattle truck, packed with other refugees, without any sanitary facilities, and with only the food and drink they had brought with them, they reached Berlin. Here, Sybil noted, the population still could not comprehend what was happening in the east, and was resentful at the influx of refugees. 'As we struggled up the steps from the station', she wrote, 'respectable stodgers passed us by with their noses in the air. [...] Berlin did not yet know the meaning of war.'[34] Sybil was fortunate enough to be offered temporary shelter by relatives of her husband in Hamburg.

Albert Speer, who recognised that the loss of industrial Silesia would cripple any German effort to continue the war, tried to portray some of the human suffering in the east to Hitler, showing him photographs of refugees he had taken in January. Hitler 'roughly pushed them aside. It was impossible to tell whether they no longer interested him or affected him too deeply.'[35] Rudolf Höss, ex-Commandant of Auschwitz, was also caught up in the exodus, and his involvement alerts us to another dimension of the developing tragedy, the evacuation of the concentration camps. The huge complex of camps at Auschwitz had been sited in Silesia partly so that its prisoners could work in various industrial enterprises there, including a huge synthetic rubber plant. In January 1945, as the Russians approached Auschwitz, most of its remaining prisoners were evacuated. The gas chambers and crematoria had already been blown up, and some prisoners were sent, crammed onto trains, to the concentration camp at Gross Rosen in Lower Silesia. Most were formed into long columns and forced to walk there.

The Concentration Camps Inspectorate, having ordered this evacuation, heard no further news from Auschwitz, and sent Höss to find out at first hand what was going on. He wrote:

> On all the roads and tracks in Upper Silesia west of the Oder I now met columns of prisoners, struggling through the deep snow. They had no food. Most of the non-commissioned officers in charge of these stumbling columns of corpses had no idea where they were supposed to be going. [...] The route taken by these columns was easy to follow, since every few hundred yards lay the bodies of prisoners who had collapsed or been shot.

Höss' account betrays the contradictory attitudes of senior SS men, at once brutal, but concerned also to impose order upon chaos, and to uphold a certain sense of 'honour'. He continued: 'I gave strict orders to the men in charge of all these columns that they were not to shoot prisoners incapable of further marching.' He then saw a German sergeant-major shooting a prisoner: 'I shouted at him, asking him what he thought he was doing, and what harm the prisoner had done him. He laughed impertinently in my face and asked me what I proposed to do about it. I drew my pistol and shot him forthwith.'[36]

Auschwitz was liberated on 27 January 1945 by Soviet troops of the 60th Army. They found in the huge complex of camps there some 8,000 sick and starving inmates still alive, including several hundred children. The bodies of several hundred prisoners who had been shot before the last SS guards left the camps were lying around. More shocking still was the discovery of huge piles of clothes, shoes, spectacles, artificial limbs, and human hair – a mute testimony to the vast numbers of people, mainly Jews, who had been murdered at the extermination camp of Birkenau. The Allies indeed knew in some detail about Auschwitz before the camp's liberation, but however accurate and detailed this abstract knowledge was, the stark reality of this huge camp complex was outside all previous experience.

The Auschwitz concentration camp had been founded in May 1940, near the Polish town of Oświęcim, and subsequently enlarged in successive stages. After initial experiments with poison gas in September 1941, the extermination camp at nearby Birkenau was built in 1942, and developed as the largest in German-occupied Europe. Widely varying figures are given for the number of people killed at Auschwitz-Birkenau, but there is agreement today that it was probably in the order of two million.[37] There is more certainty about the numbers incarcerated there for a longer period, as all were registered by clerical staff. In total, 400,000 people from all parts of Europe were registered as prisoners at Auschwitz. 340,000 died.[38] The number of living prisoners in Auschwitz peaked in the summer of 1944 at around 155,000.[39] The frenzy of mass killing reached a horrible peak at the same time, as trainloads of Hungarian Jews arrived at the camp. On some days over 20,000 were gassed and burnt, many in great open pits. In September 1944, the SS began to scale down the operations at Auschwitz, and to reduce the numbers of prisoners there. A revolt by the *Sonderkommando*, the Jewish prisoners who worked in the gas chambers and crematoria, seriously damaged one of the crematoria in October, and the building was demolished after this.

In November and December the gas chambers and all but one of the crematoria were also demolished. Thousands of prisoners were sent by train to other concentration camps inside Germany; more were killed, many from overwork or starvation. Between 1 December 1944 and 15 January 1945, more than 500,000 complete sets of clothing, for men, women, and children, were despatched from the camp back to Germany. At *Appell* on 17 January 67,102 prisoners were counted.[40] In the next few days, some 58,000 were driven out on the marches which Höss encountered. For the most part, only those too ill to walk were left behind. The SS men and women who worked at the camps all tried to escape, and did not carry out the widely anticipated final murder of these people.[41] The SS had good reason to be fearful. The Allies had announced publicly that major war criminals would be brought to justice, and had indeed specifically referred to those who worked at Auschwitz. In broadcasts from Radio Washington and the BBC on 31 October 1944, a number of them were listed by name and it was made clear that they faced the death sentence if convicted. Earlier broadcasts had warned that lists of German war criminals in Poland were being drawn up.[42]

Although the Soviets immediately formed a Special Commission to investigate the crimes at Auschwitz, and facilitated the work of a Polish Commission with a similar remit, the discovery made relatively little impact in the West. Victor Klemperer in Dresden recorded on 29 January 1945 a somewhat garbled story about the seizure of the camp by the Russians, and of hearing about a radio broadcast by Thomas Mann which detailed the killing of one and a half million Jews there.[43] Mann's speech was in fact broadcast on the 'Voice of America' station on 14 January 1945, and was heard by another Jew, still surviving in Germany as a 'U-boat', that is masquerading as an 'Aryan'. Edith Hahn described the impact the broadcast had on her:

> The true meaning of the term 'U-boat' came clear to me in that moment. I felt myself buried alive, in silence, under an ocean of terror. I was living amongst accomplices. No matter that they looked like housewives and shop-keepers, I knew that their acquiescence with Hitler's war against the Jewish people had led to the nightmare Thomas Mann had described.[44]

3

NEMESIS:
JANUARY—APRIL 1945

Little by little Bomber Command had been building up its strength [...]
Since the beginning of the war it has been a hammer in the hands of this
country, which is using it to batter the walls of Germany. Slowly that hammer
has grown in size and weight.

From a British Ministry of Information pamphlet published in 1942.[1]

By 1945 Victor Klemperer was one of the few Jews still living in
Germany, saved from deportation only by his marriage to an 'Aryan'
wife. He had lost his citizenship, his job, his car, and his home, and been
forced into a 'Jew's House' with other wretched survivors. He had seen
most of the Jews in Dresden deported, and knew that this meant almost
certain death. In the last few months he had became increasingly anxious about the possibility that Dresden would be bombed. His mood
fluctuated violently. On 29 January he recorded in his diary yet another
visit from the police:

While we were eating, a middle-aged police officer (two stars, probably the
most elevated lower rank) appeared in our room accompanied by Waldmann.
Very friendly 'Good evening – well we've got our little inspection to do –
don't interrupt your meal, dear!' Waldmann evidently already well acquainted
with the policeman, whom he was taking around – usually those carrying out
the inspection set up their tribunal in the hallway on the first floor, and I had

to go down to them. Waldmann said: 'The professor here is an eminent man, his name is in every reference book!' The policeman asked me sympathetically whether I got a pension. 'Not a penny since November '43.' Embarrassed silence. He then shook my hand. 'So good night, professor. Things are going to change, you will get your post back!' That in uniform, on duty, in front of witnesses! One is executed for less.

On 13 February, as rumours of the Soviet advance swept through the city, Klemperer had to take letters, door to door, to other Jewish survivors, telling them to report for 'outside work duty'. None of them had any illusions: they knew this meant death, and expected that those reprieved would also be taken within the week. At half past nine that evening he sat down, 'very weary and depressed', and heard an air raid warning. Unbeknown to Klemperer, a force of 796 British Lancaster bombers was about to arrive over Dresden, and lay waste to the virtually undefended city. Miraculously Klemperer and his wife Eva survived the attack, and he probably owed his life to this: afterwards Eva tore the yellow star from his coat with a pocket knife, and he took on a false identity.[2] The RAF attack was concentrated on the historic city centre, and caused an enormous firestorm. Immense temperatures were generated, and huge winds were sucked into the conflagration. Most of those caught in the storm were burnt to death, many asphyxiated. Thousands, including Klemperer and Eva, sought refuge by the banks of the River Elbe. The next morning, a force of over 300 American Flying Fortresses dropped another 771 tons of bombs on Dresden.

THE BRITISH AND AMERICAN BOMBING OFFENSIVE

The attack on Dresden on February 1945 was one culmination of three and a half years of British planning. As early as the summer of 1940, with Britain's ill-prepared army ignominiously ejected from Dunkirk, Churchill had determined that a huge bomber force was the only effective way to attack Germany. After the *Luftwaffe*'s 'Blitz' on British cities in the winter of 1940/41 this idea had been strengthened by a desire for vengeance. In September 1941 the British had adopted the '4,000 Plan', a programme to build a vast fleet of four-engined bombers and to train men to fly them. Bitter experience had taught the British that it was too dangerous to fly over Germany in daylight without fighter escort, and that the bombers, flying by night at high altitudes, could not hit precision targets. In February 1942, after much debate, the policy of 'area bombing' was adopted, and ruthlessly applied by the new Chief of Bomber Command, Arthur Harris.[3]

'Area bombing' meant that the British offensive was aimed at the built-up areas of German cities. In a curiously roundabout formulation, the Chief of the British Air Staff, Charles Portal, had earlier sought to make the best of the inability to hit anything more precise, arguing that 'the main weight of our air attack should be directed against objectives in Germany, so situated that bombs which miss their target will directly affect the morale of the German civilian population'.[4] The fervent advocacy of 'area bombing' by Harris and others like Hugh Trenchard reflected a British view that German civilians would not be able to withstand sustained and heavy bombing in the way that the British had. Trenchard, in a paper for the Chiefs of Staff in May 1941, had written: 'All the evidence of the last war and of this shows that the German nation is particularly susceptible to air bombing.'[5] On the night of 30 May 1942, Harris put 1,000 British bombers into the air over a German city – Cologne – for the first time, and over the next year his force was strengthened, with earlier and smaller aircraft gradually replaced by the four-engined Lancaster. From 1942 Bomber Command was joined by the American 8th Air Force in Britain. American doctrine differed in that they were committed to bombing 'precision' targets in daytime. They believed that their B-17 Flying Fortresses, in huge formations, could defend themselves from fighter attack, and deliver their bombs with sufficient accuracy to destroy individual factories or military sites. This tension between British and American ideas was to grow in the last years of the war, and contributed to a confused sense of overall strategy, and to poor coordination.

Through 1943, as plans for a 'Second Front' were debated, the RAF's Bomber Command and the US 8th Air Force took up the direct assault on Germany. As much as half of overall British war production went into the '4,000 Plan', and by mid-1943 Harris had a huge and potent force at his disposal. In a series of concentrated raids involving British and American aircraft in July and August 1943, Hamburg was devastated. On the night of 24 July, Bomber Command succeeded in concentrating its attack, and generated a huge firestorm which overwhelmed the city's already disrupted emergency services. More than 30,000 civilians were killed, many more injured, and hundreds of thousands fled the burning city.[6] Rumours spread in Germany that as many as 200,000 had been killed. This was the single most destructive RAF raid on Germany during the war, and significantly it struck fear into the hearts of the two Nazi leaders most concerned with civilian morale and with war production, Goebbels and Speer. Goebbels was aware of the waves of panic and despair that spread rapidly from Hamburg, and Speer told Hitler that similar attacks on six more German cities would halt arms production altogether.[7]

The terrible destruction in Hamburg resulted from the coincidence of a number of factors, and the British and Americans were not able to repeat this elsewhere. By this time the Germans had developed extensive and sophisticated defences against the bombers. Belts of anti-aircraft guns and searchlights ringed the larger German cities, and thousands of day and night fighters were deployed in France, Belgium, Holland, and Germany itself. British and American aircrews dreaded particularly the defences around the Ruhr and Berlin, and were of course more vulnerable the deeper their targets were in Germany. Indeed, for most of 1943 they flew only to targets closer to England, in north-western Germany and occupied France. The first American daylight raid deep into Germany, in August 1943, on the ball-bearing factory in Schweinfurt and a Messerschmitt plant in nearby Regensburg, was a disaster. An ambitious low-level attack on the oil refineries at Ploesti in Romania by aircraft flying from North Africa a few weeks previously was equally catastrophic.[8] It was clear that the unescorted bombers, flying for many hours over strongly defended territory in daylight, were terribly vulnerable. The British, flying at night, hoped for ideal conditions with plenty of cloud and no moonlight, but when these were lacking, things could go disastrously wrong. In March 1944 Harris sent his force to bomb the symbolic target of Nuremberg in southern Germany, the site of the Nazi Party rallies. There was bright moonlight, the predicted cloud cover did not materialise, and the huge stream of British bombers flying over Germany was clearly visible. Heavily laden with fuel and bombs, they were easy targets for German night fighters. Ninety-six British aircraft were lost on this one mission.[9]

Although Harris had told Churchill in November 1943 that if the British and American bombers were used in coordinated attacks on cities

Germany could be knocked out of the war,[10] by March 1944 it was clear to many that the strategy was not working. A series of sustained attacks on the Ruhr in 1943 had not stopped industrial production there, and a similar concentration on Berlin between November 1943 and March 1944, although damaging to the city, had not caused anything like the destruction or the panic in Hamburg after July 1943. From March 1944, much to Harris' disgust, the weight of American and British bombing was transferred from one set of targets to another. Thousands of sorties were flown against railway marshalling yards and bridges in France to support the D-Day invasion. In the summer and autumn of 1944 there was a considerable diversion to bomb V1 and V2 production facilities and launching sites. Both of these campaigns caused many casualties amongst the civilians of occupied countries. In the 'Pointblank Directive', which was issued after the Casablanca conference in January 1943, American and British Chiefs of Staff had identified a list of key targets in Germany, like ball-bearing factories, oil refineries, and aircraft plants; if these could be destroyed or severely damaged, they argued, German military strength as a whole could be crippled. Through the summer of 1944 priority was given to bombing Germany's oil refineries. As we have seen, once British and American land forces were engaged in northern France, the bombers were frequently used to support them directly in the field. Still the bomber fleets grew in size and in destructive power. From the spring of 1944 the introduction of the long-range Mustang fighter meant they could be escorted to targets deep inside Germany. In response, the *Luftwaffe* fielded ever more fighters, but it was increasingly hampered by a shortage of trained pilots, and of aviation fuel.

By September this onslaught on selected targets was beginning to have a decisive impact. German oil production had been dramatically reduced, and this had a material effect on the mobility of German armed forces, becoming increasingly significant until the end of the war. By the time the Soviets occupied Ploesti in August 1944, the refineries there had entirely ceased production. The destruction of railway lines and bridges seriously hampered the German campaign in Normandy, and was one reason their retreating armies suffered so greatly in northern France. All the bridges over the River Seine, for example, were destroyed, and the retreating German forces ended up clustering desperately around a number of improvised ferries. The resulting concentrations of men, horses, and vehicles were easy targets for fighter-bombers. The one aspect of the bombing campaign which had failed to produce the desired result was the attack on civilians in German cities. Although many thousands of them had been killed – including women, children, and the elderly in disproportionately great numbers – and many more bombed out of their homes, like civilians in Britain in 1940–41 their resolve had not been broken. There were many who despaired; there were those who cursed their leaders; and evidently not a few who saw in the bombing a deserved retribution for the ill-treatment of the Jews and the crimes committed in the occupied territories.[11] But most of the survivors just carried on. They displayed great industry in clearing the ruins, rebuilding houses, shops, and industrial buildings. Nazi Party welfare organisations led relief efforts, providing food, temporary housing, clothing, blankets, and facilities for contacting relatives. Municipal administrations supervised the fire and rescue services, and attended to the identification and burial of the dead. Public services were maintained in the most heavily bombed cities. Sybil Bannister, after fleeing from the Soviet advance in January 1945, ended up with relatives of her husband in Hamburg. She was amazed on her arrival there to find whole areas of the city totally ruined, but discovered that families were living in cellars, in reconstructed shacks, and in sheds on allotments. Shops had rebuilt their frontages but were surmounted by ruins.[12] In the centre of Essen, after Berlin the most heavily bombed of all German cities, the central administration building of the Krupp industrial empire was still standing, and functioning. The largest Krupp steel plant, at nearby Rheinhausen, had astonishingly hardly been attacked, and was still producing material for tanks, guns, and ships.[13] A significant factor in the maintenance of German production was the ever greater number of slave labourers used in this reconstruction work. Beaten, starved, and humiliated, thousands were forced to clear rubble and move materials. They were used in the relocation of industry from the bombed cities to underground sites in the countryside and in the construction of huge air-raid shelters. Inevitably they suffered grievously in the actual bombing; in Essen, as elsewhere, they were denied access to the shelters used by the Germans.[14]

Harris, despite the reservations of other senior Allied leaders, returned to the bombing of German cities in September 1944, his force now at the strength envisaged in the '4,000 Plan'.[15] He could deploy roughly 1,000 Lancasters, supported by a small number of Mosquitoes. These twin-engined aircraft were fast enough to evade German fighters, but could carry a considerable bomb load. They were used to fly nuisance raids, the reckoning being that small numbers of Mosquitoes could keep much of a city awake and on edge all night with a carefully timed succession of attacks. They were also used as 'Pathfinders', the advanced group of bombers used to mark a target area with flares and to light fires with incendiary bombs. The 'bomber stream' was then directed over the target, dropping combinations of incendiary and high explosive devices. These included mines with delayed action fuses, intended to explode later, when rescue crews were at work. The RAF attacks were most deadly when the bombing was concentrated on a small area and generated a single huge firestorm. Medieval buildings of wooden construction burned particularly well. Most of the larger German cities suffered terribly from bombs falling in a large area in and around them, but apart from Hamburg in July 1943, and Dresden in February 1945, it was smaller towns which suffered proportionately most in individual attacks. The provincial town of Darmstadt was raided on the night of 11 September 1944 by 218 Lancasters and fourteen Mosquitoes. The old town was completely destroyed in the resulting firestorm, and roughly half of the city's housing stock was lost. Around 10,000 people, ten per cent of the population, were killed. According to Max Hastings, who has written in detail about this raid, 'it is impossible to determine exactly why Darmstadt was selected for attack on 25 August and finally destroyed on 11 September in preference to the scores of other area targets of far greater industrial and military significance'.[16]

Only one large German city had not been severely damaged by 1945, the Saxon capital of Dresden. Unlike cities further to the north and west, it had only limited anti-aircraft defences. All of the larger guns around Dresden had been sent to other cities or deployed as anti-tank guns further east by February, and the British attack was almost unopposed, a welcome relief for the crews, many of which had survived terrifying missions on targets where they had to fly through a veritable storm of steel.[17] Although from photographic intelligence it was immediately clear in Britain that the attack on Dresden had been very concentrated and destructive, it was not initially seen as particularly different from any number of others. John Colville, a pilot himself, tersely noted in his diary on 14 February: 'Blue skies and sunshine which enabled the air forces to destroy Dresden.'[18] Chemnitz was attacked the next night,

Duisburg and Worms on 21 February, Pforzheim on 23 February, Mainz on 27 February, and Dessau on 7 March. In February and March 1945 Bomber Command flew more sorties than in any other two months of the war.[19] City after city was subjected to terrible damage. The regular targets, Berlin, Essen, Dortmund, and Cologne, were hit again and again. As Germany's defences crumbled, the RAF flew more often in daylight, joining the American aerial fleets ranging over Germany.

In a final convulsion of the flawed British and American strategy, the two combined in February 1945 for Operation 'Clarion'. This was intended to blanket all of Germany with aircraft of different types, attacking transportation targets, therefore railway junctions, bridges, canals, roads, and anything on them, locomotives, boats, and road vehicles. Nine thousand aircraft were deployed. To the Germans this appeared an indiscriminate attack on anything that moved. Hans Rumpf, an early historian of the bombing, wrote with studied outrage: 'The fighter-bomber offensive quickly developed into a cruel and brutal sport, and anything that moved – farm carts, human beings, anything – was attacked.'[20]

By this time, there were few undamaged targets left in Germany. Bombs were falling into the ruins, churning up the debris. 'Targets of opportunity' were chosen, often with little apparent purpose, and huge assaults were made which seem shockingly pointless today. The baroque town of Würzburg was largely destroyed on 17/18 March 1945, medieval Hildesheim on 22 March, and Nordhausen on 3/4 April. There was no longer a clear distinction between the strategy of the British and American forces, both of which were becoming uncomfortably aware of how disproportionate their attacks now were. The attack on Dresden (in which both had participated) provoked public discussion in Britain and America, and slowly led to a change of direction. The notion that this was 'terror bombing' (long the term used in Germany) was publicly rebutted by the air chiefs, and Churchill, who had called for attacks on Dresden and other eastern German cities in January 1945, distanced himself in late March from further bombing 'simply for the sake of increasing terror'. On 1 April he called for a review of policy,[21] but nonetheless Hamburg was bombed again on 13 April, and Potsdam on the following night. A Directive ending 'area bombing' was drawn up by the Combined Chiefs of Staff on 16 April, but bizarrely, and tragically, 'not however issued to Bomber Command or the American Strategic Air Forces in Europe' until 5 May 1945.[22]

Why did the British and the Americans pursue the bomber offensive so relentlessly into the last days of the war? In Britain particularly, this question, and the moral issues around it, have been intensively debated. Undoubtedly Churchill, Harris, and others overestimated the potential of 'area bombing': it did not provoke a German collapse. There was also a strong element of vengeance in the British bomber offensive. Harris had famously declared: 'They have sown the wind. They shall reap the whirlwind', and this was often repeated in Britain. In the last months of the war the desire for vengeance was compounded with frustration and anger that Germany would not surrender, but fought on so stubbornly. It appears perfectly clear to most people now that the war was won in early 1945, and that further attacks on German cities would not hasten its end. Angus Calder, writing in the 1960s, declared that the contin-ued bombing was 'manifest insanity'.[23] Unlike the debate on the use, later in 1945, of the two atomic bombs on Japanese cities, the proposi-tion has not been advanced that the bombing of Dresden, of Würzburg, Hildesheim, or Nordhausen led directly to unconditional surrender. The British and American bomber offensive grew out of perceived military and strategic imperatives, but the huge machinery created ran out of control. It is unfair to blame Harris alone. He was allowed by the British and American governments to behave almost as a maverick, to pursue a course which was morally and militarily wrong.

From the time of Harris' appointment in February 1942, his instruc-tions from the British Air Ministry and the combined Chiefs of Staff were confused, typically stressing an overall objective of attacking 'enemy morale' by bombing industrial areas, but then listing individual precision targets like capital ships, submarine pens, or aircraft factories. Thus on 5 May 1942 he was told:

> Whilst the primary aim of your operations must remain the lowering of the morale of the enemy civil population and in particular that of the workers in industrial areas vital to the enemy's war effort, every effort consistent with this aim should be made to reduce the output of aircraft factories, and par-ticularly those producing fighter aircraft.[24]

The 'Pointblank Directive' in January 1943 replicated this confusion. It stated:

> Your primary object will be the progressive destruction and dislocation of the
> German military, industrial and economic system, and the undermining of
> the morale of the German people to a point where their capacity for armed
> resistance is fatally weakened.

The Directive then listed six 'primary objectives', including submarine
construction yards, transportation, and oil plants, to be attacked 'within
that general concept'.[25]

This confusion was reflected in the attack on Dresden in February
1945. Was it aimed at 'lowering morale', destroying communications, or
selected industrial targets? Was it intended to hinder the German military
effort on the nearby Eastern Front? The Chief of Air Staff, Sir Norman
Bottomley, wrote to Harris on 27 January 1945:

> subject to the overriding claims of oil and the other approved targets systems
> within the current directive, we should use available effort in one big attack
> on Berlin and related attacks on Dresden, Lepizig, Chemnitz or any other cit-
> ies where a severe blitz will not only cause confusion in the evacuation from
> the East but will also hamper the movement of troops from the West.[26]

Harris was at least consistent, and constantly exploited qualifications
about weather and 'tactical considerations' in his orders to focus wherever possible on 'area attacks.'

There was also potential for confusion in the euphemistic wording of
the Bombing Directives. They referred constantly to 'lowering morale',
to causing 'confusion', 'chaos', 'disruption', or 'dislocation'. They almost
never spelt out the truth, that area bombing was intended to kill as many
Germans as possible, and thereby to 'lower morale', or cause 'confusion'.
Many historians of the air war have recycled the same euphemisms.
Much was said about reducing hours worked, or of 'de-housing' people. In a rare exception, an Air Ministry document of September 1941
defensively stated: 'It must be realised that the attack on morale is not
a matter of pure killing'.[27] Harris argued after the war that his primary
objective had been the reduction of German capacity to produce, but
during the war did not shrink from the reality of what he was doing.
Indeed, according to Max Hastings, Harris 'never took the precaution of
cloaking what he was doing in the formal dress of circumspection and
manners that the English traditionally cherish in peace and in war. [...]

He seemed to delight in assaulting social convention, in expressing the realities of the bomber offensive in the most brutally literal language.'[28] John Colville recorded a chance meeting he had with Harris on 23 February 1945 at Chequers: 'Before dinner, while waiting in the Great Hall for the P.M. to come down, I asked Sir Arthur Harris what the effect of the raid on Dresden had been. "Dresden?" he said. "There is no such place as Dresden."'[29]

This calculated bluntness has led to the accusation that Harris 'liked destruction for its own sake, and was thus in perfect sympathy with the innermost principle of every war, which is to aim for as whole-sale an annihilation of the enemy with his dwellings, his history, and his natural environment as can possibly be achieved'.[30] Although Harris was consistent in his advocacy of 'area bombing', he shared the larger uncertainty about precisely how his campaign was intended to end the war. Famously, he had responded shortly after his appointment to the proposition that bombing could not win the war: 'My reply to that is that it has never been tried yet. We shall see.'[31] This does not enlighten us. The Directives issued to him did not make clear how lowered enemy 'morale' would lead to surrender: no clear relationship was drawn between civilian morale and the will of Hitler and his senior leaders to fight on. In 1942 Harris argued passionately that bombing alone could win the war, and would prevent the need to deploy a land army in northern Europe; by 1943 the Combined Chiefs of Staff had accepted that a land campaign would be necessary and that the job of the air forces was to prepare the way for this. After September 1944 both American and British commanders clutched again at the idea that an overwhelming air attack would somehow knock Germany out of the war. The Chief of the American army, George Marshall, argued while on a visit to Europe in October 1944 that 'full pressure had not been put in the right places', and he suggested that 'long-range objec-tives of strategic bombardment be abandoned for an all out effort to force an early victory.'[32] This notion was picked up in London, and com-municated to Harris in the previously quoted instruction for 'one big attack', but nobody explained precisely how this would 'force an early victory'.

As the American bomber force in Europe was built up in 1942 and 1943, its leaders had strenuously rejected the idea of using it for 'area bombing'. Notwithstanding the mythology presented in feature films like *Memphis Belle* (1990) – where American bombers make a second run over their target to avoid hitting a school – in practice the Americans found that they frequently had to bomb through cloud, or in conditions where precision was not attainable. Increasingly they accepted that whole areas around their 'precision targets' were blanketed. David MacIsaac wrote: 'the American air forces drifted away from their intended precision attack, and came to meld their efforts with those of RAF Bomber Command.' He noted that as late as 17 April 1945, after Bomber Command had stopped 'area bombing', 572 American aircraft attacked the marshalling yards in Dresden, and questioned why the seven-volume official American history made 'no mention at all of this attack'.[33] American wartime propaganda reflected a bloody-minded determination to pursue bombing at all costs, which fully matched that of Harris. The official account of the first year's operations of the 8th Air Force stated: 'Aerial assault is directed both at the enemy's will to resist and his means to resist. One may collapse before the other; either eventuality is desirable. Bombing will be carried out to the fullest extent in any case.'[34]

To Germans and others on the ground it made no difference whether the bombers were British or American, or whether they intended to attack factories or schools. They knew only that the attacks grew ever larger and more destructive, and the defences against them ever weaker. The generals at the fighting fronts wrung their hands over the destruction of the cities, although in many cases their own families lived on country estates, or had been evacuated to relatively safe places. The Nazi leaders reacted in different ways. Hitler distanced himself ever more from the reality of the bombing. He did not tour the damaged cities or visit the homeless and wounded. In the final months of the war, he stayed deep underground in Berlin, immune from the heaviest attacks. Other leading Nazis were shocked by the destruction, and bemoaned the loss of Germany's architectural treasures. A few, typically the most nihilistic and revolutionary, tried to turn the destruction to their advantage. Robert Ley, leader of the Labour Front, wrote in a newspaper: 'After the destruction of beautiful Dresden... we march toward the German victory without any superfluous ballast and without the heavy and material bourgeois baggage'.[35] Goebbels was greatly annoyed by Ley's article; he was undoubtedly affected by the loss of beautiful buildings and cultural treasures. Like Ley though, he tried see a positive in this. Commenting on the destruction of

Würzburg, he wrote sententiously: 'Thus we say a melancholy farewell to a world which will not return. A world is going down but we all retain a firm faith that a new world will rise from its ashes.'[36] The indiscriminate bombing was also used to justify Nazi crimes. Understandably, British and American aircrew who parachuted into or crashed in German territory during the raids were often subjected to vengeance. Many were killed or beaten.[37] After the war, the Americans prosecuted Germans responsible for killing over 1,200 of their downed airmen.[38]

It has been argued that the strategic bombing was militarily ineffective. After 1945, the Americans particularly went to great lengths to assess scientifically the effect of the bombing. Symptomatically, the British were less keen on this, Churchill dismissing it as a 'sterile task'.[39] Whatever the moral arguments, it is clear now that the bombing, considered as a whole, had an enormous impact, particularly in 1944 and 1945. The greatest tragedy is that the huge attacks on 'civilian morale' had the least military impact. The tactical support of ground forces, the attacks on oil refineries, and the disruption of transportation, greatly weakened the German military effort, and this was recognised, then and since, by many of the Germans most affected. Speer, who was keen after the surrender to cooperate with American investigations, provided detailed testimony about this. German generals writing after the war recognised the effect at the fighting fronts, noting the huge difference between operating in the west in the face of British and American aerial superiority, and in the east, where Soviet aircraft, until the last days of the war, rarely appeared any distance behind the front lines. We should give the last word to the powerless civilians. Sybil Bannister was trying to work and live in Hamburg in early 1945. The city had now been bombed for four years. Trying to find someone, she was directed to look in one of the huge shelters which had been constructed:

It was the oblong sort, above ground, cleverly constructed to resist bomb explosions. As a shelter against air-raids it was admirably equipped. As a communal home for hundreds of people for which it was now being used, it was totally inadequate and they lived under deplorable conditions. There was no daylight of course and, as far as I could make out, very little fresh air. The little cubicles, originally intended as rest rooms, were occupied by families, at least four people in each one. There was only just enough room for four bunks, one on top of the other on each side, with a narrow gangway in between. There were rows and rows of these cubicles. The partitions between them did not reach to the ceiling and there were only curtains in front of the entrances. The place stank of human bodies and used-up air. [...]

In spite of these drawbacks, the inhabitants were cheerful in a passive way because they felt safe. No bombs had yet been known to damage this type of shelter. Each night, therefore, they could enjoy the luxury of undisturbed sleep. They were provided with a hot vegetable broth once a day and otherwise eked out their rations as best they could in cold foods. None of them had anything more to lose now. That their lives had been spared was a miracle for which they were profoundly thankful. They were all struck down to the same level and after the war was over they hoped to make a new start.[40]

There is no sense in her account that continuing attacks might hasten the end that these wretched survivors longed for. Let us finish where we started, with Victor Klemperer, and a selection of his diary entries. After the attack on Dresden he and Eva had been evacuated to the nearby airbase at Klotzsche. For a few days they stayed there, shocked and dazed by the sudden change in their circumstances. Like everyone there, they lived in terror lest the attack be repeated. One night 'the sound of aircraft was uninterrupted'. They resolved to go to a nearby village to seek greater safety and anonymity. Klemperer was living under what he called a 'double danger':

The danger of the bombs and the Russians I share with everyone else; that of the star is my own and the much greater one. It began during the terror night; at first I covered the star with the blanket. In the morning Eisenmann said to me: 'You must remove it, *I* have already done so.' I took it from my coat. Waldemann reassured me: in this chaos and with the destruction of all offices and lists... Besides I did not have any choice; with the star I would immediately be picked out and killed.

Even after reaching the comparative safety and anonymity of the village, Klemperer wrote, 'I have death constantly before me'.

A week or so after the 'terror night', he met another survivor and recorded her description of Dresden:

There was a dreadful smell of corpses, the authorities estimated 200,000 dead, there was a weak supply of water, no gas, there were no newspapers, instead a leaflet from the *Freiheitskampf* which threatens shooting for 'everything', narrow alleyways had been cleared through the rubble, one sees slips of paper put up: I am safe... The woman was incensed, there were no bounds to her reviling of the murderous government, repeatedly interrupted, however by outbreaks of fear and entreaties not to betray her.

Later that day, Klemperer got hold of some newspapers:

The military bulletins gave us no encouragement whatsoever: the enemy is making no progress either in the West or the East. There is no question at any rate of panic on the German side. *Like this* it can go on for months... The brief items on Dresden are shameless. Nothing but the irreplaceable works of art, not a word about the 200,000 dead.[41]

YALTA

While the bombing of Germany rose to a furious crescendo, the Allied leaders were meeting at Yalta in the Crimea. Between 5 and 11 February 1945, Churchill, Roosevelt, and Stalin, accompanied by their senior colleagues and a mass of officials, translators, clerks and servicemen, held talks to discuss the future of Europe, and indeed much of the world. Much of their time was taken up with disagreements over the future of Poland, but our concern here is with their plans for Germany. The Allied leaders were agreed that the war in Europe was now effectively decided, and that Germany should be defeated at the latest by December 1945, and possibly by July 1945. Even though they had the recommendations of the European Advisory Commission for the treatment of post-war Germany, they were only able to agree on broad outlines: Austria would be separated from Germany, and a slice of German territory in the East would be given to Poland. The precise details of this transfer of territory, and of the fate of German and Polish populations there, were postponed for future consideration. What remained of Germany would be divided into zones of occupation, and governed by an 'Allied Control Council' meeting in Berlin. At Churchill's insistence, the earlier plan for three occupation zones was modified to allow for a French Zone, and, reluctantly, Stalin accepted that the French should be represented on the Control Council. There was discussion about the dismemberment of Germany, but, largely at Churchill's insistence, decisions on this were postponed. Churchill also argued that the details of future Allied policy in Germany should not be publicised, but only a broad outline. Despite the deep disagreements over Poland the Allies maintained their unanimity of purpose in prosecuting the war against Germany, and confirmed again the demand for unconditional surrender.

At the end of the conference, a 'communiqué' was issued, for public consumption all over the world, not least in Germany itself. It reaffirmed earlier assurances:

> It is our inflexible purpose to destroy German militarism and Nazism and to ensure that Germany will never again be able to disturb the peace of the world. We are determined to disarm and disband all German armed forces; break up for all time the German general staff that has repeatedly contrived the resurgence of German militarism; remove or destroy all German military equipment; eliminate or control all German industry that could be used for military production; bring all war criminals to just and swift punishment and exact reparation in kind for the destruction wrought by the Germans; wipe out the Nazi party, Nazi laws, organizations and institutions, remove all Nazi and militarist influences from public office and from the cultural and economic life of the German people; and take in harmony such other measures in Germany as may be necessary to the future peace and safety of the world. It is not our purpose to destroy the people of Germany, but only when Nazism and Militarism have been extirpated will there be hope for a decent life for Germans, and a place for them in the comity of nations.[42]

There was a considerable, if guarded, exchange of military information at Yalta, with both Soviets and the western Allies eager to glean what they could of one another's intentions and potential. Amid renewed expressions of goodwill, agreements were made to coordinate the final offensives against Germany, to demarcate 'bomb-lines' and to plan British and American aerial operations in advance of the Red Army. The stage was set for the final onslaught.

THE BATTLE FOR THE RHINELAND

In the harsh winter of 1944 the British and Americans had lost the strategic initiative in the west. Many individual units in the front line had been roughly handled, and were exhausted. The Americans particularly had suffered from their efforts to maintain the offensive on the borders of Germany, and from the battles to take Brest and Metz. Many of their divisions were desperately short of frontline infantrymen, as well as of supplies and ammunition. In January 1945, as the 'bulge' in the Ardennes was reduced, extensive preparations were made to resume the offensive, now with the aim of striking at the heart of Germany and ending the war. Two factors dominated the thinking of Eisenhower and his generals. The first was the difficulty of crossing the Rhine, a huge barrier running from the Swiss frontier to the flooded polders of Holland; the second was the industrial area of the Ruhr, lying on the opposite side of the Rhine. If this could be captured or isolated, German war production could be largely ended. Eisenhower was now firmly committed to his 'broad front' approach, and intended therefore to close up to the Rhine along its whole length before striking across it. Even at this late stage, he was preoccupied by the idea of a possible German offensive, and intended to use the Rhine as a defensive barrier. Once the west bank of the river had been secured, he planned crossings north and south of the Ruhr basin, from which armoured thrusts could be made to encircle the industrial area. After this, his armies would be free to strike across Germany in whatever direction seemed best.

Not only did Eisenhower still have an exaggerated sense of German offensive capacity, he was falling under the sway of the myth of the 'National Redoubt'. His headquarters and intelligence staff had picked up from many sources the idea that fanatical Nazis would concentrate in the mountains running from the south of Germany through Austria. At its most inflated this redoubt would supposedly contain not only the best Nazi fighting units, but would include underground industrial plants making the newest weapons, huge concealed caches of ammunition, and be defended by extensive fortifications. Hitler and the leadership corps of the Party and SS would escape there to direct the struggle. In the overheated imagination of some, it might take years of prolonged and costly fighting to take the 'National Redoubt'.

In fact the Americans had no hard evidence of real fortifications, nor were there any. There were some modern industrial facilities which had been located to southern Germany and Austria, away from Allied bombing, but they could not operate in isolation, without fuel or raw materials. There was no concentration of the best surviving fighting units in southern Germany. Although many leading Nazis fled to the south in the last weeks of the war, there was no coordinated movement of the Party, of military command structures, or of the security apparatus, to Bavaria or Austria. In fact, the successor government to Hitler's was set up in the flat country near Denmark, and other leading Nazis who escaped from Berlin also fled to the north. The Americans failed to assess the intelligence material reaching them as critically as they should have done, and allowed the myth of the 'National Redoubt' to divert them from more obvious and more genuine objectives.

On the German side, there was less belief in the Rhine as a defensive barrier. Von Rundstedt, still in overall command of the German forces in the west, had pleaded in vain with Hitler to abandon Holland, and to allow a flexible defence of the Rhineland. Hitler, still dreaming of great strategic moves, had transferred the SS Sixth Panzer Army under Sepp Dietrich, which had spearheaded the Ardennes offensive, to Hungary, thus depriving Rundstedt of his only potential mobile reserve. Hitler also insisted that Holland be held, not least as a potential area from which to stage a counter attack, and that the area west of the Rhine be defended to the last man. The call-up of reserves over the winter had provided a number of new, if ill-trained German units, and huge numbers of mines had been laid to strengthen the defences of the 'West Wall'. Nature came to the aid of the Germans: heavy rain and a thaw in January meant that the rivers were full, and by releasing water from dams they still controlled, the Germans were able to flood large areas of land in front of their defences. The overcast weather also hampered aerial operations in support of the British and American forces.

On 8 February, after extensive preparations, the Allied offensive was opened by the Canadian 1st Army in the area of the Reichswald. Conditions could hardly have been worse. As the battle progressed, more and more land became inundated. If the roads and paths were not flooded, they were blocked by ruins. Both sides had amassed enormous numbers of guns, and there was an unparalleled concentration of artillery fire on both attackers and defenders. Montgomery's plan of feeding in replacement units to keep up a constant pressure on a narrow front foundered in the mud and water, and only extensive use of amphibious vehicles and boats permitted any advance at all. The troops of the German First Parachute Army fought with amazing determination. In Eisenhower's words, this was 'some of the fiercest fighting of the whole war', 'a bitter slugging match in which the enemy had to be forced back yard by yard'.[43] Montgomery recorded that 'the enemy parachute troops fought with a fanaticism unexcelled at any time in the war […] the volume of fire from enemy weapons was the heaviest which had so far been met by British troops in the campaign'.[44] Montgomery had intended to follow the British and Canadian assault with the full weight of the American 9th Army to the south, but this was prevented by the release of water from the Schwammanuel Dam. This flooded the River Roer along the whole front of the 9th Army, and it was not until two weeks later that they were able to attack. By this time though, most German defenders had been drawn away, and the Americans were able to advance against weaker opposition. In the first days of March, British and American units reached the Rhine. Although they had suffered heavily, great numbers of the German defenders were able to escape across the river, blowing the bridges behind them.

Goebbels followed the Allied advance through the Rhineland with alarm but not despondency. He was reassured that the retreating German troops were on the whole fighting well and maintaining a defensive front, but was deeply troubled by the news that some German towns and villages had hung out white flags to the invaders. His home town of Rheydt, which lies between the Roer and Rhine, a few miles west of Düsseldorf, was occupied by the Americans on 3 March, and Goebbels brought a personal slant to this:

> The news that the town of Rheydt received the Americans with white flags makes me blush. I can hardly realise it, especially not the fact that one of these white flags flew from the house where I was born. At the moment, however, I do not even know who is living in the house and I can only suppose that this deed of madness was done by evacuees or people who had been bombed out. It makes a first-class sensation for the Americans of course, just as it is shameful and humiliating to me. If we ever return to Rheydt, however, I shall try to clear the matter up.[45]

Further south, the Americans also attacked towards the Rhine, but from a greater distance, from inside Alsace. Here they encountered a new phenomenon, considerable numbers of German soldiers giving themselves up as prisoners; for the first time whole headquarters of large formations were captured. At the tactical level many of the American commanders were bold and imaginative, and prepared to take risks. German resistance was much weaker and the Americans were able to move quickly, with few casualties. By 6 March they had reached the Rhine at several points, and taken the ruins of Cologne. Russell Weigley has described the famous moment when advanced units of the American 1st Army pushed through the town of Meckenheim, a few miles from the Rhine, on 7 March, and realised that one of the bridges across the river was still intact:

> The morning was well along before bulldozers cleared a path through the rubble of Stadt Meckenheim for Engelman's lead tank platoon, equipped with the new T26 Pershings, to break free. Brushing aside sporadic light opposition, Task Force Engelman reached woods just north of Remagen a little before noon. Just before 1:00 P.M., 2nd Lieutenant Emmet J. Burrows, commanding the lead infantry platoon, emerged from woods onto a cliff overlooking the Rhine. Before him he saw, plainly enough despite a low haze, the town of Remagen and, still standing, the Ludendorff railway bridge.[46]

With great initiative the Americans from Burrows up in the chain of command moved to seize the bridge. At the last minute, the demolition charges were ignited but did not work as planned, leaving the bridge damaged but useable. There was no German force of sufficient size to retake the bridge and the Americans were able slowly to fan out around it, and to establish a defensive perimeter on the east bank. Hodges, Commander of the 1st Army, learnt at about 6 p.m. that his men had got hold of the bridge, and promptly diverted substantial forces to exploit the crossing. Bradley and Eisenhower confirmed this, quickly authorising the diversion of four or five divisions to Remagen. German generals have been scathing about Eisenhower's inability to alter his ponderous plans and to exploit the bridgehead at Remagen more, but the Americans displayed considerable skill and tenacity in what they did. The Germans made a concerted effort to destroy the bridge, including prolonged artillery fire, aerial bombing, attack by frogmen with explosives, and even a V2 rocket fired from Holland, which landed some 300 metres from the bridge. The bridge collapsed four days after its capture, but by this time the Americans had built several temporary structures alongside it and were moving thousands of men across.

To Montgomery, the bridge at Remagen made little difference. Since October 1944 he had been planning an operation on the scale of D-Day to cross the Rhine. On the British front, north of the Ruhr basin, the Rhine was a broad river with a strong current. It was from four hundred to a thousand metres wide, depending on local conditions. The British and Canadian armies were by this time huge engineering organisations, with many units specialising in the construction of Bailey bridges, pontoon crossings, and deploying thousands of small boats and amphibious vehicles. Montgomery knew that if his forces could get across the Rhine, there were no substantial barriers on the flat plains of northern Germany to prevent further rapid advance. He planned to support a number of simultaneous crossings on a wide stretch of the river north of the Ruhr with a large airborne landing, the first since Arnhem. The paratroopers would be landed on the opposite side of the river, but this time close enough to be within range of artillery support and to get help from ground forces in a very short time. Thousands of aircraft were to be deployed in support of the crossings, which were intended totally to overwhelm any remaining German defences. This was the last great demonstration of combined British military might in the Second World War, and Churchill came to watch the operation unfold.

The operation was sprung on the night of 23/24 March, but although planned on the scale of D-Day, there was nothing like the opposition faced then. The German army in the west was no longer a great, coordinated fighting force. Rundstedt had been dismissed by Hitler after the debacle at Remagen, as if a change of commander could change anything at this late stage. Kesselring, the new commander, had no reserves, very few of his units were at all mobile, and disorganisation set in as they became separated from one another. The strongest elements of the German defences were the hundreds of anti-aircraft guns, and these took a heavy toll on the aircraft carrying the airborne forces. Within twenty-four hours Montgomery's forces established a large, well-protected bridgehead and were able to start construction of temporary bridges. Within a week Montgomery had 2,000 tanks and self-propelled guns on the east bank of the Rhine. The American 9th Army, on the right of Montgomery's assault, made particularly rapid progress, and drove across the north of the Ruhr valley; it was not part of any Allied plan to get snarled up in this huge industrial agglomeration. South of the Ruhr, Hodges' 1st Army had expanded the Remagen bridgehead, and Eisenhower was now able to plan a huge encirclement of the whole Ruhr valley.

South of Remagen, the Rhine crossings were more improvised, and increasingly unopposed. Patton's forces famously managed to cross the Rhine south of Mainz a few hours before Montgomery. In the next few days, his men crossed the Rhine gorge between Boppard and Koblenz, and further south, at St. Goar and Oberwesel; Patch's army got across at points north and south of Worms on 26 March. Further south still, the French army under de Lattre was urged by de Gaulle to cross the Rhine, and crossed at Speyer and Germersheim on 31 March. All along the river from the British crossings down, as armoured columns fanned out, typically the strongest defences they encountered were groups of anti-aircraft guns turned against them. Everywhere the Allied soldiers passed through villages hung with white flags. A CBS correspondent reported: 'you pass through one undamaged village after another, punctuated occasionally by a complete mess of a town which happened to be a railway junction, or which was unfortunate enough as to offer resistance to our advance'.[47] Within what was left of Germany, rumours abounded as to which places were in the hands of the invaders, and which not. On 1 April the American 9th and 1st armies met at Lippstadt, completing the encirclement of the Ruhr and more than 300,000 German troops under Field Marshal Model.

What was the mood amongst Germany's leaders, as its empire shrank, and its remaining territory cowered under air assault? If we are to believe Goebbels' diary, which records events almost hour by hour in March 1945, he still clung to hope. He placed absurd confidence in the potential of the new U-boats, partly because of his belief in the National Socialist conviction of their commander, Dönitz. He followed eagerly the limited progress made by local German counterattacks in Hungary, in East Prussia, and in the Rhineland. Most of the senior officers and leaders who survived the war claim at this time to have been trying to send out peace feelers, and to have been searching for ways out of the impending disaster. Several memoirs, like that of Speer or Guderian, recount private conversations where one or other top Nazi sought to probe the allegiance of another, and to see whether they would stay loyal to Hitler. Himmler had been entrusted by Hitler with the command of an Army Group in Alsace, and then another on the Eastern Front in April 1945, but was not in any way able to fulfil these responsibilities. He had fled to a clinic at Hohenlychen near Berlin, from where he was desperately trying to direct his remaining SS operations. Himmler also nursed the deluded idea that he would be accepted as the leader of a post-Hitler government, unaware that most Allied leaders were thinking more of shooting him out of hand if he was captured. Speer in his memoirs makes much of his realisation that the war was lost, and that the end could only be prolonged. He had also realised, rather late in the day, that Hitler intended to take down all of Germany with him to destruction. Speer records that he made special arrangements with Guderian to prevent the armed forces implementing Hitler's orders to demolish all bridges and buildings across Germany as they retreated. Guderian similarly claims credit for having averted much needless destruction.[48]

Hitler alone appears never to have wavered. We know little about his thoughts in the final months of the 'Third Reich', but he at least was clear that there was no hope to be expected from negotiations, and no profit to be had from even exploring such a possibility. His nihilistic and Darwinist views now came to the fore. Famously, when confronted by Speer after a situation conference, he declared:

> If the war is lost, the people will be lost also. It is not necessary to worry about what the German people will need for elemental survival. On the contrary it is best for us to destroy even these things. For the nation has proved to be the weaker, and the future belongs solely to the stronger eastern nation. In any case, only those who are inferior will remain after this struggle, for the good have already been killed.[49]

Goebbels, who saw Hitler frequently at this time, was full of admiration for his steadfast attitude and for the example he set. Both still clung to the trappings of power, and continued to make plans and to order operations. Goebbels still supervised the production of newsreels and newspapers, and fretted about the problems of getting them to the troops. Hitler designated fortresses, changed commands, and demanded punishment for those who did not do their duty. Hitler and Goebbels were agreed that the officers who had failed to destroy the bridge at Remagen should be tried. They were, and five were swiftly executed. At a more personal level, Goebbels pursued his private vendetta in Rheydt, where the Americans had earlier reported that his birthplace had flown a white flag. In his diary for 10 March 1945 Goebbels wrote:

> I am vexed most of all by the behaviour of people in my home town of Rheydt. The Americans have struck up a real triumphal chorus about it.

A certain Herr Vogelsang, known to me from the early days as a down-right National-Socialist philistine, has placed himself at the disposal of the American occupation authorities as Oberbürgermeister. In doing so he stated that he had only joined the party on compulsion from me and otherwise had had nothing to do with it. I am going to draw a bead on this gentleman. I am preparing an operation to liquidate him at the first opportunity.

The next day, Goebbels told Hitler 'in detail' about Rheydt and his plan to assassinate Vogelsang, adding 'The Führer is in full agreement.' On 28 March he recorded:

It is good news that Oppenhoff, who was installed as Burgomaster in Aachen by the Anglo-Americans, was shot during the night Tuesday/Wednesday by three German partisans. I think that Vogelsang, the Burgomaster of Rheydt, will suffer the same fate in the next few days.[50]

The anti-Semitic hatred of both Hitler and Goebbels also came to a frenzied peak in these final weeks. Victor Klemperer, now a homeless refugee like so many others in Europe, was still observing the media in Germany, and recorded many instances of anti-Semitic ranting in German newspapers, and in broadcast speeches. More tellingly, he noted how deeply this propaganda had affected many ordinary people. One night, late in March 1945, he was kept awake by air-raid alerts, and talked with a young woman. She was beginning to have many doubts about the course of the war, and about the Nazi regime. But, she said, 'It's only the Jews I hate, I think I've been a bit influenced in that.' Klemperer, who was of course concealing the fact that he was a Jew, 'merely smiled'.[51]

4

THE LIBERATION OF THE CAMPS

Buchenwald, Belsen, and Nordhausen. One cannot speak here of inhumanity or
even of pitilessness. What has taken place in these camps has never before been
recorded in all history. There are no words to describe this obscene savagery, this
abandonment of every moral precept, this collapse into the slime of bestiality.

From an article by William Rust in the Daily Worker, *21 April 1945.* [1]

By the end of March 1945, it was clear to the Allied leaders in the West
that the German army was a broken force. Increasingly their thoughts
turned to the end of the fighting, and to the problems of a post-war
Germany. With the crossing of the Rhine accomplished, and the most
coherent German forces encircled and isolated in the Ruhr, it was clear
that no major defensive or geographical obstacles remained to prevent the rapid advance of American and British forces into the heart
of Germany. Attention focused on the potential difficulties of entangle-
ment with the advancing Soviet troops, and above all on Berlin. It had
long been assumed that the German capital was the ultimate target of
the Allied advance, and there was a natural sense of competition amongst
the officers and troops on the ground about who would get there first.
Since the end of January the Soviet armies on the eastern bank of the
Oder, only fifty miles from Berlin, had largely stood still, consolidat-
ing their position. Now it seemed that there was a real possibility that
American or British forces might take the great symbolic prize.

Montgomery, as ever, had his own ideas, and late on 27 March he sent a message to Eisenhower that he intended now to strike for the River Elbe, and 'thence by autobahn to Berlin, I hope'.[2] Eisenhower had become deeply frustrated with Montgomery's tendency to act as if he were the Supreme Commander, and was at the end of his tether. On 28 March he received a message from George Marshall in Washington, suggesting that he concentrate his forces on an axis south of Berlin, to prevent the formation of a centre of German resistance in the mountainous country of Bavaria and Austria, in other words the fabled 'National Redoubt'. Eisenhower determined now to assert his authority: he bluntly informed Montgomery that the American 9th Army, which had been under Montgomery's command, was to be transferred back to Omar Bradley's 12th Army Group, and that this would be given the responsibility for the central thrust into Germany. Montgomery was to concentrate on a rapid advance to the Baltic coast, well to the north of Berlin. More significantly, Eisenhower cabled Stalin directly to inform him that after dealing with the German forces in the Ruhr, he would strike towards Erfurt, Leipzig, and Dresden, that is to the south of Berlin, to meet Soviet forces there and split Germany into two. Although the British Chiefs of Staff immediately protested against this decision, and Churchill telephoned him personally on 29 March to urge him to take Berlin, Eisenhower stood firm. He was supported by his own Chiefs of Staff, and the Combined Chiefs of Staff did not overrule him.

Eisenhower's decision has been interpreted in many different ways. At the pettiest level he has been accused of wanting to deny Montgomery the prestige of a triumphal entry into Berlin. More seriously he has been accused of political naivety, of not understanding the potential importance of Berlin. On a purely military level, he has been accused of undue caution, and of overestimating the remaining German potential for resistance. It is only fair to consider his defence. He argued that his proposed axis of advance offered more favourable terrain, cut by fewer rivers. Furthermore, he wrote:

Berlin, I was now certain, no longer represented a military objective of major importance. The Russian advance and the Allied bombing had largely destroyed its usefulness, and even the governmental departments were understood to be in process of evacuation. Military factors, when the enemy was on the brink of final destruction, were more important in my eyes than the political considerations involved in an Allied capture of the capital.[3]

Eisenhower also highlighted the potential difficulties of the Americans and Soviets becoming entangled in the ruins of a strongly defended city. To an extent, Eisenhower was still keeping his options open. Over the next two weeks, as his forces pressed forward, he hinted at various points that they might still take Berlin. Churchill kept stressing the importance of this to Roosevelt: on 5 April he told him 'we should join hands with the Russian armies as far to the east as possible, and if circumstances allow, enter Berlin.'[4] Churchill by this time was desperately concerned that the Soviets would not fulfil the obligations they had undertaken at Yalta, and that they would occupy all of Austria. He wanted to be in as strong a position as possible on the ground in Germany to counter this. Roosevelt was very ill, and did not intervene. He died on 12 April, a day of many momentous events. Eisenhower later wrote: 'Before the day ended, the scenes I saw and the news I heard etched the date in my memory.'

Eisenhower flew up to the front line troops, and spent the day with Bradley and with Patton. By this time American forces had reached the river Elbe, within sixty miles of Berlin, but Eisenhower instructed Patton during the course of the day that his forces were not to take Berlin, but were to stop on the line of the Elbe and Mulde rivers, to the west of the capital. Patton's protestations were to no avail.[5] After visiting a number of front-line units the generals were taken to two sites nearby. The first was a deep salt mine near Merkers, where a huge cache of art works, money, and gold bullion had been found. Eisenhower described how they saw 'huge piles of German paper currency', and 'an enormous number of paintings and other pieces of art'. In another tunnel, they found:

> a hoard of gold, tentatively estimated by our experts to be worth about $250,000,000, most of it in gold bars [...] Crammed into suitcases and trunks and other containers was a great amount of gold and silver plate and ornament obviously looted from private dwellings throughout Europe. All the articles had been flattened by hammer blows, obviously to save storage space, and then merely thrown into the receptacle, apparently pending an opportunity to melt them down into gold or silver bars.[6]

After this, Eisenhower, Bradley, and Patton were taken to a camp at a place called Ohrdruf; we will return to this shortly. At midnight, after long discussions, they heard on the BBC that Roosevelt had died.

Further down the chain of command, the news of the President's death came through at about the same time as the realisation that American troops would not take Berlin. Ken Hechler, with frontline American troops near Weimar, described how they heard the news:

> I remember the major called us all together and said, 'We have just received the sad news of the death of our Commander in Chief, Franklin D. Roosevelt.' Then he said, 'The current information' – and he picked up a piece of paper as though he didn't know what he was going to say – and he read it, and said, 'The current information is that a man named Harry Truman will succeed him; at least that's the latest report.'[7]

Although Hitler and Goebbels briefly rejoiced over the death of one of their main opponents, in practice Roosevelt's death made little difference to events in Germany, where American divisional commanders, who had been vying with one another in the race to get to Berlin, were amazed and frustrated by the decision to halt. They had understood since crossing the Rhine that Berlin was their target, and had made an extraordinary dash across central Germany. On 15 April, Eisenhower's decision to stop on the Elbe was finally communicated to the commanders already there.[8] Eisenhower confirmed this to Marshall on the same day: 'an immediate effort against Berlin', he wrote, 'would be foolish in view of the relative situation of the Russians and ourselves at this moment'.[9] Eisenhower met with Churchill in London on 18 April, and was again pressed to take Berlin, but he would not change his mind.[10]

Montgomery did not discuss the decision not to take Berlin in his immediate post-war memoirs, but his silence spoke volumes. Writing some years later, Montgomery did briefly refer to Eisenhower's decision, and to a message he received from him on 31 March 1945, confirming that Berlin was not an immediate target. Montgomery states: 'It was useless for me to pursue the matter further. We had had so much argument already on great issues; anyhow, it was now almost too late.'[11] Frustrated in his hopes of capturing Berlin, he turned his attention further north, and here he was strongly supported by Churchill and the British Chiefs of Staff. He was instructed to press on with all speed towards the ancient Hanseatic city of Lübeck on the Baltic coast. As he went, the units on his left flank would strike north towards the German North Sea coast, cutting off Holland, and securing the port cities of Bremen and Hamburg.

Above all, a successful advance to the Baltic would prevent the Soviets from occupying Denmark, and from gaining access to the North Sea. There were immediate military objectives here, notably the capture of U-boat bases, but the British were now concerned overwhelmingly with the post-war map of Europe. The leading units of Montgomery's forces advanced rapidly, impeded more by demolition than by German resistance: Montgomery records that over five hundred bridges had to be constructed by engineers to keep the troops moving.[12] A CBC correspondent captured the mood of the advance:

> You start out for the front. On a fixed battlefront you can drive from Army Headquarters to the front line in an hour. But now you leave Army and pass the Corps Headquarters and the traffic thins out. And then you're driving through miles and miles of villages and forest and farmland, where there's not an army vehicle to be seen. You race along a lonely forest road, alert, uncomfortable. The fighting units have gone through, but you may be ambushed by paratroopers or sniped at. You round a corner and see two or three German soldiers, your heart stops, and you see they have their hands in the air. They're asking to surrender, but you can't be bothered with prisoners, and on you go.

He commented on the German citizens he encountered: 'Some of them are grim, but thousands of them want to be friendly. They're obviously glad it's over, and they show no rancour, that's the simple fact of the case.'[13]

As the soldiers advanced beyond the Rhine in early April 1945, events were to divert the attention of politicians and generals from their strategic considerations.

HELL ON EARTH

On 4 April 1945, American soldiers of the 4th Armored Division, looking for a rumoured German communication centre near Gotha, came across the abandoned labour camp of Ohrdruf-Nord, a sub-camp of Buchenwald. What they saw there almost beggared description: more than three thousand emaciated and decomposing human bodies were lying uncovered in shallow graves, and piled up in sheds. Some bodies, half burnt, still lay on a makeshift funeral pyre made of railway tracks.

There was a smaller number of prisoners still in the camp, but they were desperately ill and emaciated. These were able to tell their liberators that some 9,000 other prisoners had been marched out of the camp only days previously. The shocking news was quickly passed up the American chain of command, and on 12 April Eisenhower, Patton, and Bradley were taken to the camp.

Eisenhower, who as we know already had very strong feelings about Nazism, was deeply shocked, and insisted on visiting 'every nook and cranny' of the camp. Patton, not known as a fragile or overly sensitive man, was unable to face some of the scenes. Ohrdruf was actually a relatively small labour camp, housing at most 10,000 inmates. The unburied corpses found by the Americans were of prisoners who had died since the beginning of 1945, and there had apparently been a belated attempt by their German guards to burn the bodies before they evacuated the camp. Before fleeing on 2 April, they had shot a number of other prisoners. Eisenhower, who later recorded that visiting Ohrdruf affected him more than any previous experience in the war, immediately reported back to Washington and London, recommending that 'newspaper editors and representative groups from the national legislatures' should be sent to record the evidence being uncovered in Germany.[14]

It was by this time all too evident that Ohrdruf was not an isolated aberration. The day before Eisenhower and his generals went to Ohrdruf, their soldiers had reached Buchenwald outside Weimar. This was one of the earliest concentration camps, established in 1937, and by 1945 it had grown to the size of a small town. Here the Americans found 20,000 prisoners still living, some in a condition of emaciation and degradation, in their striped uniforms, whose images still haunt us. As well as unambiguous evidence of mass killing through starvation and overwork, there was proof of organised torture and sadism. Medical experiments had been carried out on living people without regard for their well-being. Crematoria had been constructed to dispose of huge numbers of corpses. Women as well as men had worked as guards and overseers in Buchenwald. The prisoners themselves came from all over Europe, and included Germans alongside other nationals. Evidently the Jews amongst them had been segregated and singled out for the worst excesses of brutality and ill-treatment. Mel Mermelstein was one of these. He had been one of the thousands marched out of Auschwitz in January 1945, and was one of the few to reach Buchenwald alive. Here he was put in the 'Little Camp', an isolation compound for the sick and the dying. By the time the Americans arrived, he was reduced to eating grass.[15] Buchenwald had by this time become a collection point for thousands of prisoners from other camps; like the other camps liberated in April 1945, the provision of water, food, and sanitation had broken down, and dead bodies lay unburied all over the camp. Half-burnt corpses were found in the crematorium ovens.

Over the next few weeks, as they struggled to provide food and medical help for the living, the Americans forced local people to help to bury the dead, and to see the places of execution and torture. Delegations of soldiers, news reporters, cameramen, and politicians were immediately invited to see and record the terrible scenes there. On 16 April a team of officers from the Psychological Warfare Division arrived to make a comprehensive study of the camp and its role in the Nazi state. The Americans were helped in this task by the well organised prisoner resistance in Buchenwald, several of whose members had detailed knowledge of different departments of the camp. The resulting report played an important part in later trials.[16] Partly because of the wide publicity given to it, Buchenwald became the representative image of the concentration camp in the American imagination.

Buchenwald, like many of the camps, was sited near stone quarries, where prisoners had been compelled to undertake gruelling manual labour. At Nordhausen in the Harz Mountains, the Americans on 12 April discovered a concentration camp linked directly to the most advanced industry and war production, Dora Mittelbau. Here an army of prisoners had been brought from all parts of Nazi-occupied Europe in 1943 to excavate deep tunnels into the mountainside. The survivors, constantly supplemented with fresh prisoners to fill the places left by the dead and dying, were forced in conditions of extreme hardship and brutality to work on the construction and assembly of V2 rockets. The whole hellish complex was run by the SS, but Speer had visited it, and was – despite his subsequent denials – aware of the conditions at Nordhausen.[17] All there, German scientists, guards, and prisoners, had to walk past the gallows at the entrance, where the bodies of executed prisoners were displayed. The conditions were appallingly unhygienic and thousands of prisoners fell ill and died; so many indeed that the SS built a camp outside to house the sick. Here, in concrete hangars, these wretched prisoners suffered and died. Some were killed in the air attack of 3 April. When the Americans found the camp on 12 April there were more than three thousand dead there. In some of the hangars two or three living people were found amongst the dead.

Worse was to follow. The British, advancing largely unopposed across the flat heaths of northern Germany, had become aware that there was a large camp before them near Celle. In an unprecedented arrangement they agreed a neutral zone around the camp, and entered the camp, still guarded by German and Hungarian units, on 15 April. Nothing could have prepared them for what they found: scenes which, on newsreel film, have been seen by millions, and represent a low point in human history. Alongside 60,000 living inmates in indescribable condition, there were more than ten thousand unburied dead. Brigadier Glyn-Hughes later testified:

> The conditions in the camp were really indescribable; no description nor photograph could really bring home the horrors that were there outside the huts, and the frightful scenes inside were much worse. There were various sizes of piles of corpses lying all over the camp, some outside the wire and some in between the huts. The compounds themselves had bodies lying about in them. The gutters were full and within the huts there were uncountable numbers of bodies, some even in the same bunks as the living. Near the crematorium were signs of filled-in mass graves, and outside to the left of the bottom compound was an open pit half-full of corpses. Some of the huts had bunks but not many, and they were filled absolutely to overflowing with prisoners in every state of emaciation and disease. There was not room for them to lie down at full length in each hut. In the most crowded there were anything from 600 to 1000 people in accommodation which should only have taken 100.[18]

Bizarrely, although some of the SS guards had left Bergen–Belsen before the British arrived, the camp Commandant, Josef Kramer, together with some eighty of his staff, including thirty SS women, had stayed behind to hand the camp over to the British. They were placed under arrest, and set to work to bury the dead. Many of the guards were beaten by British soldiers and by prisoners. Some were killed. Kramer himself, a veteran of the concentration camp system, who had served as commandant at Natzweiler and Auschwitz, was initially surprised by the shock and anger of the British.[19]

As Buchenwald for the Americans, Bergen-Belsen became for the British the representative example of the 'concentration camp'. The newsreel film, shot over the next few days and weeks, was seen all over Britain by huge audiences by the end of the month, and has been endlessly reproduced since. The images of thin, frightened prisoners, living in totally neglected conditions alongside piles of the dead, and of German guards forced to carry the corpses to mass graves are still totally shocking. 'Belsen', as it became known in English, was not in fact a representative concentration camp, but a product of recent developments. The camp had been established later than most of the others, initially as a 'detention camp' for Jews whom Himmler imagined had some kind of exchange value. In March 1944, as the concentration camp universe began physically to shrink, Bergen-Belsen was renamed a 'recuperation camp'; in August 1944 a 'women's camp' was added. Increasingly Belsen served as the collection point for transports of ill prisoners from around the 'Third Reich'. They became ever more numerous, especially after January 1945. Many arrived in a desperately poor condition. Kramer and his administration made less and less effort to safeguard any health amongst the prisoners, and when typhus spread in the last weeks of the war, the death rate spiralled out of control. In fact, before the British arrived, almost the last act of the Kramer's staff was to try to bury the bodies. All those strong enough to carry the dead had been made to drag bodies to mass graves, while two bands played dance music.[20] After 15 April, while the British tried to provide water, food, and medical treatment, another 14,000 of these prisoners died.

Scarcely a day passed without the discovery of new horrors. In the last days of Himmler's concentration camps, hundreds of groups of prisoners were marched pointlessly from one place to another, or shut up on trains which were shunted from place to place. In many places the Allied soldiers found terrible traces of these last cruel movements of people. Near Gardelegen, American soldiers found on 15 April a large brick barn, in which over one thousand prisoners had been burned alive. Survivors told them that they had been evacuated from Nordhausen and other concentration camps by train, but offloaded from the train on 12 April. They had been marched from there towards Gardelegen, many being killed along the way. The next day SS guards had herded all the survivors into the barn, poured petrol over the straw inside and set fire to it. Those prisoners who managed to get out of the resulting inferno were machine-gunned outside. A survivor recorded that the SS were helped by members of the town police and local Hitler Youths.[21] General Frank Keating, Commander of the 102nd Infantry Division, ordered that the residents of Gardelegen be taken to the site to view the atrocity. He then ordered the townspeople to create a military style cemetery, making them dig a separate grave for each victim. They had to put a cross or Star of David on each grave and enclose the cemetery with a white fence.[22] Sometimes the living were found: two trainloads of prisoners, evacuated from the hell of Belsen only days before the British arrival, were found abandoned, one by the Americans near Magdeburg, and one near Trölitz by the Soviets.[23] Historians estimate that between as many as 350,000 people were killed in the 'death marches'.[24]

By the time the Americans reached Dachau, outside Munich, in the south of Germany at the end of April, this, the first of all the camps, was hugely overcrowded with prisoners from outlying camps who had arrived in the last months of the war. German method and efficiency had broken down to the extent that a fifty-car train full of dead prisoners stood outside the camp. Confronted with the now familiar scenes of starvation, cruelty, and death, some of the liberators shot a number of the German guards out of hand. Donald Miller reported:

> A U.S. Army squad guarding about 122 SS prisoners, who continued swearing threats at their former prisoners, opened fire with machine guns and killed all of them. At that point soldiers turned over the remaining guards to the inmates. One GI gave an inmate a bayonet and watched him behead a guard. Many of the guards were shot in the legs and could not move. A number of these disabled guards were ripped apart limb from limb.[25]

At Dachau, the Americans also found evidence of medical experiments on a large scale, and they discovered a number of gas chambers. It appears now that these were used for disinfecting clothing, and that the killing in Dachau was done by other means. Slower to emerge was the evidence of medical killing on a mass scale. In fact the Americans had started to uncover the 'euthanasia' programme at Hadamar even before they reached Ohrdruf. Here they found not a concentration camp but an asylum for the mentally ill which had become a centre for mass murder. The asylum's cemetery held thousand of bodies, killed, according to the surviving patients, by the medical staff.[26]

The impact of the discovery and liberation of the concentration camps has been extensively discussed. The changes it brought to modern consciousness have been charted, and not overstated. Humanity had not previously been confronted with such graphic and horrible evidence of systematic cruelty. The images of the camps in April 1945 – the piles of bodies like matchsticks, the bulldozers pushing mountains of corpses into mass graves, the eyes of the starving prisoners, the barrack huts, the barbed wire, and the crematoria – are engraved on the memory of all who see them. They certainly affected the Allied soldiers in Germany, above all those who saw them directly. Paul Fussell had described how the American army took on a new sense of purpose and mission, fuelled in part by anger, after the liberation of the camps. He notes how many German prisoners taken later in April and May 1945 were beaten and abused by American soldiers, not given to making fine distinctions between *Wehrmacht* and SS. A company commander said: 'we had just mopped them up before, but we stomped the shit out of them after the camps'.[27] Nor was retribution confined to the ordinary soldiers. When Field Marshal Milch surrendered his baton in early May 1945, a British soldier recalled how his commanding officer, Brigadier Mills-Roberts, 'disgusted at the sights we had uncovered at Belsen and Lübeck, [...] broke the baton over the field-marshal's head.'[28]

As well as immediate reactions like these, the discovery of the camps strengthened enormously the desire of the Allies to destroy Nazism altogether. The Americans and the British were deeply angered by the juxtaposition of the camps with well-fed local populations and stores of food. After Eisenhower visited Ohrdruf, he ordered that the mayor and citizens of nearby Gotha should be taken around the camp and confronted with the evidence of what Nazism meant for its opponents and racial others. This became a regular practice, and the pictures of German civilians, mainly women and elderly men, looking in horror at mass graves, or burying the dead, have also taken a place in our visual perception of the camps. The mayor of Gotha and his wife went home and hanged themselves.[29] Other Germans enraged the Allied soldiers by denying knowledge of the camps and refusing to acknowledge any guilt for what had gone on in them.

We may well ask why the horrible discoveries of April 1945 came as a surprise, or why they had such an impact, given that the Allies had months previously come across other concentration camps. As we know, the Soviets had found evidence of industrialised killing in Maidanek in August 1944, and at Auschwitz in January 1945. A Polish crew made a documentary about Maidanek, filmed only hours after the Germans left.[30] Several newspapers in Britain published reports and photographs of Maidanek after thirty Western reporters were taken there in September 1944.[31] The Soviets also occupied the site of Treblinka, north-east of Warsaw, at this time. Although great precautions had been taken by the SS to destroy the evidence of mass killing here, the Soviets quickly discovered from the few survivors, and from local people, what had gone on. Vasily Grossman was taken to Treblinka, and wrote an article which was extraordinarily accurate in its depiction of the camp. Grossman's article was published in the Soviet Union in November 1944, but Stalin's government did not wish to give publicity specifically to the Nazi extermination of the Jews. Grossman, whose mother had earlier been killed in a mass execution of Jews, was overwhelmed by the horror of Treblinka, and his subsequent collapse may also have had something to do with the Soviet unwillingness to recognise the Holocaust.[32]

In the west, the French army had found the empty but intact site of the concentration camp at Natzweiler-Struthof in Alsace in November 1944, and US Army investigation teams had been sent there to examine and report upon what they found. Canadian troops had come across the concentration camp at Vught in the south of Holland on 26 October 1944. There was a running fight with SS guards who were trying to evacuate some of the remaining prisoners. Between 500 and 600 prisoners had been killed earlier that day: their bodies lay unburied in the camp compound. From well before the war, the public in Britain, France, the USA and the Soviet Union had been informed about the 'concentration camps' in Nazi Germany, and during the war there had been a great deal of accumulated knowledge of Nazi brutalities. The Polish government in exile in London was very well informed from underground sources in Poland, and as early as 1941 provided the Allies with extensive documentation about the concentration camps. One such report in May 1941 stated: 'The camps whose names will mark the most horrible pages in the annals of German bestiality are those of Oświęcim (*Auschwitz*), *Oranienburg, Mauthausen*, and *Dachau*.'[33] The Allied governments, above all the British, knew far more from accumulated intelligence. The British were reluctant to reveal how much German material they were successfully decoding at Bletchley Park, or indeed that they could break key codes at all. The British government did not reveal until the 1990s details of the accumulated decrypts, notably those of the *Einsatzgruppen* and Order Police in 1941–1942, which made it clear that these groups were shooting hundreds of thousands of Jews and others in the Soviet Union.[34]

There was, understandably, much anger in April 1945 amongst those who had been documenting Nazi atrocities for years. The indefatigable journalist Victor Gollancz was bitter about those who had for so long ignored the evidence, and now sought to blame the Germans collectively for what was being uncovered:

> An influential section of the Press, and many writers and public men, are using these revelations – which are no revelations at all to those who have lived in an agonised consciousness of them, day after day, for twelve long years – as proof at last of the utter wickedness of all Germans, and of the 'collective guilt' of the whole German people.[35]

Some were honest enough to admit that they had been wrong. The editor of the *Boston Globe* said with reference to the earlier Soviet publicity about Maidanek: 'Now we know that the Russians told the truth.'[36]

There were two factors in April 1945 which had unprecedented impact: the huge scale of what was uncovered, and its horrible actuality. The discovery of some of the larger and more notorious sites has been charted here, but there were literally hundreds of others. The huge centres of the concentration camp universe were all surrounded by extensive networks of sub-camps, invariably sites of horror and suffering. Alongside these were the hundreds of labour camps, great and small, and of POW camps. Some of these, like Sandbostel which the British liberated on the day the Americans entered Dachau, were huge, swollen like the concentration camps with thousands of recent evacuees, often in desperate condition. There were more than 20,000 British and American prisoners at Sandbostel, many terribly starved, and thousands more recently arrived concentration camp prisoners. The dead lay unburied around the camp as at Belsen. The other end of the scale may be seen in a letter written by a British officer, ironically from very near to Belsen itself:

> Near the farm where I was sitting was a sort of barbed wire cage, surrounding a hut. I broke down part of the fence, and was amazed to find over a dozen

men and women of various nationalities, some French, ragged and in squalid conditions. They were slave workers who had been there for two or three years, and they 'belonged' to the farmer, who locked them in at the end of each day's work. They ate what was passed through the wire. I got all of this out of them, astonished at their casual and matter-of-fact description of their lot: they were totally dispirited and submissive, but I felt quite otherwise. I hauled the farmer and his family and made them tear all the wire down, no tools allowed. The ex-slaves sat and watched, smoking our cigarettes after eating a hot meal from our rations, and visibly came alive again. We had passed within two or three miles of Belsen, not seen it but heard about it, and the liberation of this miniature concentration camp gave me great satisfaction...[37]

The immediate impact of the discovery of the camps was greatly heightened by the American and British decision, taken almost immediately at the highest levels, to document what had been found, to prevent any allegations that this was mere 'atrocity propaganda'. Churchill spoke to the House of Commons on 19 April:

I have this morning received an informal message from General Eisenhower saying that the new discoveries, particularly at Weimar, far surpass anything previously exposed. He invites me to send a body of Members of Parliament at once to his Headquarters in order that they may themselves have ocular and first-hand proof of these atrocities... I have come to the conclusion that eight Members of this House and two Members of the House of Lords should form a Parliamentary Delegation, and should travel out at once to the Supreme Headquarters... Photographs will be shown of the Members in these gruesome scenes... The object of this visit is to find out the truth... [38]

Through April and May 1945 a succession of visitors, from troops stationed locally to journalists, politicians, and churchmen, were taken to the camps; official reports were drawn up and published by Congressional and Parliamentary delegations. Similar efforts were made in Poland and in areas of Germany occupied by the Red Army. A British delegation, including representatives of the Archbishop of Canterbury and from Oxford University, was taken to Auschwitz.

It was above all the medium of film which brought images of the camps to a much wider audience, rapidly and with overwhelming force. British army film units photographed scenes in Belsen in the days after the liberation there, and American film crews were present at the liberation of Dachau and other camps. The footage they shot was widely shown in Britain, America, and across much of Europe in the next few weeks. No one who saw these films was likely to forget them. As we shall see, they were to play an important part in subsequent denazification, and in 'war crimes' trials.

THE LAST BATTLES

In the first days of February 1945, Soviet troops had crossed the river Oder near Berlin. The most advanced formations were an hour's drive from the German capital. In the vanguard were troops commanded by General Chuikov, one of the defenders of Stalingrad in 1942. Just as American and British commanders were amazed to be told they were not to press on to Berlin, Chuikov was halted by orders from above. In late January, his forces had been advancing at twenty-five to thirty kilometres every day, meeting little resistance. The ground was frozen and movement was relatively easy. It was clear to him that the Germans were withdrawing into fortified towns and major transport junctions, and trying to hold them as a delaying tactic. His inclination was to leave these behind, isolated and contained. But, just as the Americans had earlier determined that they must take Brest and Metz before advancing too much further, Chuikov was ordered to take the fortresses of Poznan and Schneidemüll. He had to divide his forces, leaving several divisions to invest the fortresses but pushing on with the remainder towards Berlin. On 6 February he and other senior commanders were summoned to a conference with Zhukov. The meeting was interrupted by a telephone call from Stalin, who ordered Zhukov 'to consolidate on the Oder, and to turn all possible forces north, to Pomerania, to join with Rokossovski and smash the enemy's "Vistula" group'.[39] Chuikov devoted many pages in his memoirs to this decision, and argued strongly that by concentrating in the centre, and pushing on, the Red Army could have captured Berlin quickly. Instead, he wrote, there was 'excessive caution': 'the fate of Berlin, and with it that of Nazi Germany as a whole, could have been sealed then, in February'.[40]

As it was, the Soviet forces which had crossed the Oder and established bridgeheads so close to Berlin had to concentrate on tactical improvements to their position while ammunition and supplies were brought up. An initial few days turned into a few weeks, while elsewhere on the Eastern Front Stalin attempted to safeguard and improve the Soviet position. Zhukhov's remarkable advance across hundreds of miles of frozen land had left behind large groups of German soldiers, in fortresses like Poznan, or 200 miles to the east, in the ancient city of Königsberg. A pitiful remnant still held out in Budapest, and a much larger force was isolated in Courland. The weather changed at the same time, and a thaw set in, making movement more difficult. Stalin, like Eisenhower, overestimated the offensive capacity left to the Germans: before attacking Berlin he turned both south and north of the city to push back the remaining German forces. Astonishingly, they still found strength to resist, and defended their ancestral lands with great tenacity. Chuikov, drawn towards the 'lair of the Fascists', found himself commuting between the front line on the Oder, and Poznan; it took weeks to reduce the huge seventeenth-century fortifications, strengthened by twentieth-century concrete. Finally, on 23 February, the remaining 12,000 German defenders surrendered. Chuikov was able to turn his attention back to Berlin.[41]

South of Berlin, Koniev was ordered to attack further into Silesia, and at the same time to avoid unnecessary damage to the industrial facilities there. His forces encircled Breslau, but their offensive ground to a halt in the second week of February. The Breslau 'fortress' was commanded by one of the staunchest of Hitler's *Gauleiter*, Karl Hanke. Unlike a number of local Party chiefs who deserted their posts as the Allies approached, Hanke mobilised the city's population for defence, and contested every building with the Soviets. His force held out. In mid-February the Germans even found forces for local counterattacks, and these had some success in East Prussia. By 21 February all the Soviet offensives into Germany had been halted. More systematically, the Red Army prepared for the next.

Further to the south, Hitler had spent his last serious offensive force in a pointless effort in Hungary, initially to relieve Budapest. Sepp Dietrich's Sixth SS Panzer Army had been moved from the Ardennes to Hungary, and there, late in January, it was committed. Budapest itself fell to the Soviets on 11 February, after a siege which, in Earl Ziemke's words, paralleled Stalingrad. Hitler still had wild dreams of a successful offensive and insisted on another being made in Hungary in early March. This last effort, styled *Frühlingserwachen* or 'Spring Awakening', had nothing like the success enjoyed in the Ardennes. Nor did it have any strategic objective. The Soviets allowed it to develop, conceding some territory, and then counterattacked. The exhausted Germans and their few Hungarian allies were thrown into retreat. For the first time, many surrendered or deserted. Orders to counter-attack, or to stand and defend where they stood, were ignored. The Red Army swept to the Austrian frontier by the end of March, and invaded what had been called, since March 1938, the *Ostmark*. There was no will amongst the retreating Germans for another Stalingrad or Budapest, and after some fighting, Vienna was renounced to the Soviets on 12 April.

Before striking at Berlin, the Red Army also turned on the Germans still along the Baltic coast. In the last week of February isolated garrisons were forced to surrender, and the main front was pressed back as far as Stettin, where the new Polish frontier was soon to be established. Only in Königsberg, and along strips of the flat coastal lands, were pockets left. The evacuation of German citizens by sea from the Baltic states and East Prussia had gathered pace, but was now threatened. As many as 1.5 million people, mainly civilian, had been taken by German navy and merchant vessels from these areas and landed further to the west, but they came increasingly under attack from aircraft and submarines. As the German enclaves they travelled to and from became smaller, they were threatened also by artillery fire from the land. Many of the ships were desperately overcrowded, and there were terrible tragedies. The Soviet and British attackers did not know, or take the trouble to establish whether they were carrying soldiers, civilians, or concentration camp prisoners. Innumerable small boats were sunk, but the most grievous loss occurred when some of the largest liners of the German merchant navy were sunk. A Soviet submarine torpedoed the *Wilhelm Gustloff* on 30 January 1945. A few days later it sank the *Steuben*. Between them these two vessels had been carrying more than 10,000 people, almost all of whom drowned.[42]

The evacuation continued from pockets along the Baltic; it was clear that the Germans were in headlong retreat. By the end of March Stalin felt free to concentrate again on Berlin. His forces were well-positioned to add Austria and Czechoslovakia to the list of Eastern European countries they now occupied. Railway lines had been laid up to the front line along the Oder, and reinforcements brought up for the final offensive.

IN BERLIN

Since the alarm of late January, when the Soviets had advanced so close, the inhabitants of Berlin had experienced ten weeks of relative calm. Relative, because although there was virtually no apparent activity on the front line along the Oder, there were frequent air raids, some very heavy. The city was already largely in ruins. There was no evacuation of government offices though, and no official evacuation of civilians. Hitler rarely emerged above ground, often staying in his bunker below the Reich Chancellery. Speer has described him in these last days:

> Now, he was shrivelling up like an old man. His limbs trembled; he walked stooped, with dragging footsteps. Even his voice became quavering and lost its old masterfulness. Its force had given way to a faltering, toneless manner of speaking. When he became excited, as he frequently did in a senile way, his voice would start breaking. [...] His complexion was sallow, his face swollen; his uniform, which in the past he had kept scrupulously neat, was often neglected in this last period of his life and stained by the food he had eaten with a shaking hand.[43]

Goebbels also stayed in Berlin, taking a certain pleasure in seeing defences prepared there and in maintaining the output of propaganda. In his more lucid moments, Goebbels could see that the end was near, and was preoccupied with the impression that he might leave on history. Every day in his diary he commented in detail on the military situation, noting exactly where different Allied forces were attacking. He gave prominence to reports of local German successes, and used one of them to stage one of his last propaganda efforts. In early March, a counterattack in Silesia retook from the Soviets the small town of Lauban. In his diary, Goebbels recorded:

> At midday I drive out to visit Görlitz. The weather is clear and frosty; the whole countryside is bathed in wonderful sunshine. On leaving the ruins of Berlin one enters a region apparently quite untouched by the war. One feels really happy to see open country and breathe fresh air again. Everywhere, not only in Berlin but also along the road, barricades against the advance of Soviet tanks are being built.

Goebbels had an enjoyable day out, taking inspiration everywhere from the people he met: 'We have to stop for a short time outside Görlitz. A group of women come up to the car and give me a rapturous welcome.' Once there, Goebbels met with Colonel-General Schörner, by this time one of the few generals still trusted by Hitler. Schörner made a great impression on Goebbels, and took him to Lauban to meet the soldiers and Hitler Youths who had recaptured the town. Goebbels noted how Schörner was motivating his soldiers, by dealing with 'professional stragglers': 'His procedure with such types is fairly brutal; he hangs them on the nearest tree with a placard announcing: "I am a deserter and have declined to defend German women and children."' Goebbels then returned to Görlitz, seeing as he went the evidence of 'indescribable' atrocities, 'everywhere along the road'. Back in Görlitz he spent time urgently discussing the situation with Party men and officers, noting 'the fighting spirit here is like that of the good old days'. Goebbels then addressed 'soldiers and men of the *Volkssturm* in the overflowing Town Hall', and had a big meal in a local hotel. 'Once again I observe that firm faith in victory and in the Führer is prevalent among these men. [...] These are fine moments which really do one good.'[44]

Some of these 'fine moments' were recorded on film. A film crew accompanied Goebbels and scenes from the visit were shown in one of the final Nazi war newsreels. Goebbels was shown in Lauban talking with a sixteen-year-old Hitler Youth who had been awarded the Iron Cross. In the film of him addressing the crowd in Görlitz, the camera lingered on the face of a nun, wearing a habit, as Goebbels spoke of the 'slaughtered children and dishonoured women' left behind by the Soviets.[45]

Stalin received Eisenhower's message on 25 March that he was attacking south of Berlin, towards Leipzig and Dresden, with suspicion. He knew that the Americans and the British were negotiating in Switzerland with German representatives to try to arrange a surrender of German forces in Italy. He was alarmed by the rapid eastward advance beyond the Rhine, and by rumours that the German forces on the Western Front were surrendering in large numbers. He assumed that Eisenhower's message was deceitful, and that the Americans would try to take Berlin. He faced the distinct possibility that large areas of the agreed occupation zone of the Soviets would very soon be held by American troops. Behind these immediate military considerations he thought it very likely that the Americans and the British would treat the conquered Germans too 'gently'. He immediately called a meeting of the Soviet Defence Committee, and summoned the commanders in the field outside Berlin, Zhukov and Koniev, to attend. At the meeting, Stalin gave Zhukov and Koniev forty-eight hours to prepare their plans for an assault on Berlin, to start by 16 April, and afterwards he sent a message to Eisenhower.

In this, Stalin agreed to Eisenhower's plan to meet in the Leipzig-Dresden area, and said that his own attack would develop in the second half of May. He also agreed with Eisenhower that Berlin was not an important objective and said that the Soviets would allot only second-ary forces to this. In the next two weeks, as the Americans and British swept through central and northern Germany, the Red Army carried out a massive redeployment of its forces, which during February and March had been largely diverted well to the north and south of Berlin. Although Stalin had made it absolutely clear to his commanders that Berlin was the main objective, he planned also to advance on a much broader front, well beyond Berlin. In the centre, the largest concentra-tion of force was given to Zhukov's army group, which was tasked with the direct assault on Berlin from the bridgeheads on the Oder. To the south, Koniev was given the opportunity to circle around Berlin, but also directed to press towards the Americans on the Elbe. In the north, Rokossovski was directed to attack directly across the flat plains towards the Baltic seaports and the advancing British.

The Soviets gathered huge forces for this, their last great offensive in Europe. The three army groups amassed 2.5 million soldiers, with 6,250 tanks, 41,600 guns and mortars, and 3,255 rocket projectors in preparation. Over 41,000 aircraft would support the attack.[46] Against this onslaught the Germans had only a pitiful remnant of the huge forces they had earlier deployed against the Soviet Union, and these were not well used. Hitler and Schörner were still convinced in early April that the real Soviet offensive would be directed further south, and the best of their remaining tank formations were deployed here. Berlin itself, for all the Nazi bombast of preceding weeks, had only limited defensives. The German forces opposite Zhukov on the Oder had well prepared posi-tions on the Seelow Heights, an arc of hilly land overlooking the Soviet bridgeheads, and some positions in a secondary line behind these, but they had only limited reserves of ammunition and fuel. They successfully beat off a rather inept preliminary attack on the Seelow Heights by the

Soviets on 14 April. The next day, Hitler issued what turned out to be his final Directive to the troops on the Eastern Front, combining typically his hatred of the Jews and the Bolsheviks, and drawing upon the evidence of recent Soviet atrocities:

> For the last time our deadly enemies the Jewish Bolsheviks have launched their massive forces to the attack. Their aim is to reduce Germany to ruins and to exterminate our people. Many of you soldiers in the East already know the fate which threatens, above all, German women, girls, and children. While the old men and children will be murdered, the women and girls will be reduced to barrack room whores. The remainder will be marched off to Siberia.

After threatening any who failed to do their duty with dire punishments, Hitler declared defiantly: 'Berlin remains German, Vienna will be German again, and Europe will never be Russian.'[47]

The full Soviet offensive opened on 16 April, and Zhukov's forces, accompanied by a huge barrage, swarmed across the river, and out of the bridgehead. So concentrated was the Soviet assault that the mass of men and vehicles became tangled up, and for two days the German defences on the Seelow Heights held. At Hitler's headquarters in Berlin, 18 April was, amazingly, a 'day of optimism'.[48] Encouraged by his supine collaborators, Keitel and Jodl, Hitler was confident that the defences could hold firm, but in reality the outcome was predictable. On that day, Zhukov's forces finally smashed through and pushed west on the road to Berlin. The next day, Koniev's men broke through and advanced rapidly to the south of Berlin. On 21 April they overran the German army headquarters at Zossen. By now, only a few SS and Hitler Youth units were offering any serious resistance. Most of the German forces, despite their grandiose titles as 'Armies' or 'Divisions', consisted now of disorganised and leaderless groups of stragglers, intent above all on escaping from the Soviets. Some 40,000 were pushed back towards Berlin itself, where they combined with *Volkssturm* units, groups of anti-aircraft gunners, and armed civilians in the smouldering ruins of the city. The first Soviet shells started to land there on 21 April.

The previous day, Hitler had celebrated his birthday, emerging from the bunker to award decorations to a few SS men and Hitler Youths. After the ceremony, many of the senior Nazis, including Dönitz, Goering, and Himmler, took the opportunity to escape from the city, while there were still corridors open. On 22 April, Hitler confronted the facts. At the daily situation conference he lost his temper, and declared that the war was lost. Trevor-Roper's account, written in 1946, captures something of the drama:

> Hitler flew into a rage. He shrieked that he had been deserted; he railed at the Army; he denounced all traitors; he spoke of universal treason, failure, corruption, and lies; and then, exhausted, he declared that the end had come. At last, and for the first time, he despaired of his mission. All was over; the Third Reich was a failure, and its author had nothing left to do but to die.[49]

There were moments in the succeeding days when Hitler briefly flickered back into life, enquiring about 'counter attacks', like that supposedly to come from General Wenck's Twelfth Army, to the west of Berlin, but inwardly he seems to have given up. He had determined to stay and die in Berlin. Keitel and Jodl, those 'collaborators in futility'[50] who had for so long encouraged Hitler's absurd military pretensions, fled on 23 April. Even at this late stage, Hitler's influence over some followers was strong. Goebbels had determined also to stay in Berlin, and had moved into the bunker together with his wife Magda and their six children. Eva Braun, Hitler's mistress, had also moved in. Hitler's secretary Martin Bormann also stayed, although he cherished hopes of escaping later.

Speer returned to Berlin to see Hitler for the last time on 23 April, and claims to have advised him to stay there and end his life. After a final conversation with Magda Goebbels, Speer said goodbye to Hitler and left the bunker. His aircraft took off from an improvised runway between the Brandenburg Gate and the Victory Column: 'Then we were in the air, and undisturbed. In and around Berlin we saw many large fires, the flashes of artillery, flares that looked like fireflies.'[51] Speer, like Himmler, made his way north, towards Hamburg. On 25 April, Ritter von Greim, the new 'commander' of the *Luftwaffe*, and the female test pilot Hanna Reitsch actually flew into Berlin in a light aircraft and landed close to the bunker. They offered to fly Hitler out of the capital but he declined. Astonishingly they managed to fly out themselves, but they were among the last to escape from the bunker. On the same day, Zhukov and Koniev's forces met at Potsdam, to the west of Berlin, effectively encircling the city. Seventy miles to the south, Soviet and American forces met at Torgau on the Elbe, cutting the 'Reich' in two. In an act which symbolises the pointless resistance of the German armed forces in the last days of the war, engineers blew up the bridge across the river there hours before the Allied troops met. Were they trying to prevent the Soviets advancing to the West, or the Americans to the East? It matters not; they failed to demolish the bridge completely, and Soviet troops were able to get across the twisted wreckage to meet the Americans on the west bank of the river.

5

OCCUPATION AND PARTITION: APRIL–JULY 1945

What had been clear to the Soviet people from the first day of the war has now become obvious to the whole world: The Hitlerite brigands badly over-reached themselves when they prepared their attack on the Soviet Union.

From a book on the Red Army published by the Soviet Embassy in
Britain in 1944.[1]

In the early hours of 29 April 1945, as the fighting on the outskirts of Berlin intensified, and shells landed in the city centre, Hitler married Eva Braun in a bizarre ceremony conducted deep below the Reich Chancellery. Joseph Goebbels and Martin Bormann witnessed the union, and afterwards champagne was served. Hitler, who did not drink alcohol, retired to dictate his personal and political testaments to his secretary, Traudl Junge. Three copies of these documents were made and signed, and at about midday three officers were despatched to take the documents to Field Marshal Schörner in Bohemia, now appointed Commander in Chief of the German army, to Munich – the Party headquarters – and most importantly, to Admiral Dönitz in Flensburg on the Baltic coast. Hitler had appointed Dönitz to succeed him as 'Reich President and Supreme Commander of the Armed Forces'. Only hours before the wedding, Hitler had heard that Himmler had tried to open negotiations with the Allies through Count Bernadotte of Sweden. Earlier, news that Goering had tried to assume office as Hitler's successor had come through to the bunker, but appears not to have affected Hitler so grievously. Himmler's he considered the ultimate act of treachery, and in his political testament, Hitler expelled both Himmler and Goering from the Party and dismissed them from all their positions of responsibility.

Although Hitler held a number of brief situation conferences after this, he was now preoccupied with arrangements for his death and the destruction of his body. In the small hours of 30 April he said farewell to the staff who had attended him in the final days. Traudl Junge described the leave-taking:

> He comes very slowly out of his room, stooping more than ever, stands in the open doorway, and shakes hands with everyone. I feel his right hand warm in mine, he looks at me but he isn't seeing me. He seems to be far away. He says something to me, but I don't hear it.'[2]

At midday Hitler ate a final lunch, before retiring to his room with Eva Braun. She took poison, and Hitler shot himself. The most senior Nazis still in the bunker, Goebbels and Bormann, then entered the room and found the bodies. Shortly afterwards, Artur Axmann, head of the Hitler Youth, arrived and also saw the bodies. Three of Hitler's SS staff carried the bodies upstairs and into the Chancellery garden, followed by Goebbels, Bormann, and Axmann. The SS men had been previously ordered to find petrol; they had siphoned off some 180 litres from vehicles in the Chancellery garage, and they now used this to burn the bodies. Shells were travelling overhead and falling nearby, and none of the witnesses to the funeral pyre wanted to expose themselves unnecessarily to further danger. They therefore, after an initial salute, retired to the shelter of the bunker, emerging at intervals to pour more petrol on the flames. Over the next twenty-four hours, Hitler's suicide was followed by others. Most notably, Goebbels and his wife Magda killed themselves, after poisoning their six children in the bunker. Bormann and Axmann were amongst those who attempted to escape from the bunker and, by various routes, to get out of Berlin. According to Axmann, who did escape, Bormann was killed near the bunker.

Before killing himself, Goebbels had managed to send a telegram to Dönitz, informing him of Hitler's death, and of his appointment as 'Reich President'. At 21.30 on 1 May, Hamburg Radio interrupted its programme with news of an important announcement. Over the next hour, it broadcast music by the Nazis' most cherished composers, Wagner and Bruckner, before Dönitz himself came on air to announce, misleadingly, that Hitler had died 'a hero's death' fighting 'the Bolshevik storm flood' in Berlin, and that he had assumed the succession.[3] This broadcast was monitored outside Germany, and all over the world, the news of Hitler's death was spread further. Although the Soviets were later to provoke uncertainty about Hitler's death, at the time, the accuracy of Dönitz's statement was widely accepted, and it produced a wide range of reactions. For the Allies, Hitler's death came as a huge relief, not least because it ended once and for all the debate on what to do with him if he was captured alive. There had been no enthusiasm amongst the Allies for any kind of judicial process, which Hitler might conceivably have manipulated for political purposes, or used to portray himself as a martyr. Equally, they were aware of the potential difficulties which might have been caused by any kind of summary execution. Their concern now focused entirely on the verification of his death, and the Soviets, who entered the bunker on 2 May, immediately set about trying to find Hitler's body. Within days, they established that charred dental remains found in the Chancellery garden were those of Hitler.[4]

Amongst the surviving German population, the news of Hitler's death, which filtered through to people in different ways, had surprisingly little impact. Some were shocked and saddened; for fanatical loyalists this was the end of the world they had known. One of the soldiers still defending Berlin, Ulf Ollech, later wrote:

> Hitler had once said: 'I am National Socialism, if I no longer exist, there will be no more National Socialism', in other words, everything was focused upon him. We young men were very upset. We'd believed him when he said that. We'd grown up with it. We felt he had let us down. It was like losing an all-powerful father. What was going to happen to us now? We wondered. It seemed hopeless to carry on.[5]

Across Germany there was a wave of suicides. For those who had suffered under Hitler, the news came as some kind of relief. For most though, it was curiously irrelevant. The 'Third Reich' was obviously coming to an end. By the time Dönitz made his broadcast, much of Germany was already occupied, and people were trying to come to terms with a totally changed situation. In those parts of Germany not yet occupied, it was obvious that the authority of the Nazi Party was crumbling, and that military defeat was imminent.

Above all, Germans everywhere were totally preoccupied with their immediate survival. Everywhere communications were breaking down, rumours had taken the place of reliable news, and normal public services had either ceased or were on the verge of collapse. Millions of Germans were on the move, fleeing from the Soviets, trying to escape from bombardment, or to find temporary accommodation wherever they could. Most were concerned more with the immediate necessities of food, drink, and shelter than with bombastic declarations about Hitler in Berlin. Ursula von Kardorff, a journalist sheltering like many former city dwellers in a village now occupied by the Americans, heard Dönitz's broadcast, and told a number of other villagers about Hitler's death the next day. They all reacted in the same way, saying: 'So. At last. Unfortunately too late.'[6] Nonetheless, the importance of his death should not be underestimated. The whole Nazi movement, its social programme, its war of conquest and aggression, and its racial war against the Jews and other minorities, were overwhelmingly identified with the person of Adolf Hitler, and there was no one to take his place. Dönitz, although a convinced Nazi and a competent naval officer, was in no sense a politician, and there was not the slightest possibility that he would resurrect the Nazi Party. Hitler's death was a fundamental precondition for the denazification that was swiftly to follow.

THE 'NATIONAL REDOUBT'

While the drama of Hitler's suicide was played out in Berlin, the Allied armies continued their relentless occupation of Germany. Although they came up against isolated pockets of resistance, and were in places even thrown back by fierce counterattacks, for the most part, the real fighting was over. In the last weeks of the war, most German soldiers gave up trying to hold their positions, and concentrated instead on their own survival. Many who found themselves in the path of the Red Army fled westwards, hoping to give themselves up to the Americans or the British. On the American front, Eisenhower was concerned above all with the imagined 'National Redoubt' in the Alps. The huge pocket in the Ruhr offered surprisingly little resistance, and most of the 300,000 German soldiers trapped there had surrendered by 19 April. Their commander, Field-Marshal Model, was one of many senior German officers who committed suicide rather than face captivity and trial. On the Elbe, American units stood still, and devoted their attentions largely to trying to process the ever increasing number of refugees streaming across the river. In some cases they were able to enjoy the brief experience of celebrating with Red Army units which advanced from the east.

Further south, Patton's 3rd Army, and Patch's 7th Army were still on the move. In their path stood several places which had played a central part in Nazi mythology, and some of these were defended with determination. Between 16 and 20 April, the 7th Army fought street by street and through Nuremberg, the 'City of the Reich Party Rallies', facing suicidal resistance from SS, *Volkssturm*, Hitler Youth, and civilians armed with *Panzerfäuste*. The city's many anti-aircraft guns were again a formidable obstacle. Outside the city, the now abandoned grounds of the rally site were captured, and an American newsreel crew filmed the demolition of the huge stone swastika above the Zeppelin Tribune, from which Hitler had reviewed his Party faithful. At Bayreuth, where the tradition of Wagner had been appropriated by the Nazis, there was fierce fighting around the Festival House.

By the time that American units approached Munich, the cradle of the Nazi movement, site of the Party Headquarters and the 'House of German Art', the mood was beginning to shift, and here some of the citizens rose up against the Nazi authorities. Elsewhere in the city, there were pockets of Nazi resistance. The first American unit to reach the city centre was a group of 'psychological warriors', from the 'Information Control' section of Eisenhower's headquarters, tasked with the reform of the city's newspapers. On 29 April troops from Patch's 3rd Army crossed the Austrian frontier at Füssen and pressed on, largely unopposed, towards Innsbruck. There was great competition amongst different units to capture Hitler's mountain retreat at Berchtesgaden, and this was accomplished on 4 May by French troops in Patch's Army. Salzburg surrendered on the same day, as did Linz on the Danube. This was where Hitler had gone to school, and he had subsequently adopted Linz as a 'home town'. In the testament he dictated on 30 April, he had left his collection of paintings to Linz.[7] The Americans found a more substantial and enduring testimony to Hitler outside the city, when on 5 May they reached Mauthausen.

Like the other camps they had liberated, Mauthausen was the centre of a whole network of sub-camps. The largest of these, Gusen, Ebensee, and Melk, were by the end of the war large camps in their own right, and like the others, horribly overcrowded. Thousands of dead bodies were found alongside the living, there was further evidence of torture, and of medical experimentation on humans. In Mauthausen the Americans found a chamber in which poison gas had been used to kill thousands of prisoners. They also soon discovered that a gas van had been used to transport prisoners between Mauthausen and Gusen. During the voyage prisoners from one camp were gassed, and afterwards burnt in the crematorium of the other. Near Mauthausen was the castle of Hartheim, which had been a centre of the Nazi 'euthanasia' programme. It also had a gas chamber, and many prisoners from Mauthausen were killed there.[8] Although the American armies did make further advances in early May, towards the Italian frontier, and into Czechoslovakia, their penetration into Austria was their final advance into the former 'Third Reich'. The granite walls of Mauthausen, and the horrible discoveries there were a fitting culmination to their campaign in Europe.

To the right of the American armies, the French army of de Lattre had managed to cross the Rhine in March, and in the last days of the war, it was urged on by de Gaulle, now head of a Provisional Government in France. De Gaulle realised the enormous prestige to be gained from the reassertion of French military strength, and from a claim to a significant role in a post-Nazi Germany. Although there had previously been agreement on the boundaries of the zone allotted by the Americans and British to the French, de Gaulle was, like Churchill and Stalin, convinced that actual possession would confer a position of strength in the post-war situation. He stressed to de Lattre the importance and prestige he attached to the capture of German territory, and urged him to take Karlsruhe and Stuttgart.[9] French soldiers faced increasingly weak resistance as they moved through the Black Forest and into Tübingen and Reutlingen. Disregarding the orders of their American Army Group commander, on 22 April they entered Stuttgart. The Americans had wanted to encircle the city to trap German forces there. Eighty kilometres further east, the French competed with the Americans for the capture of Ulm, taken by Napoleon in 1805.

In the extreme south, the French advanced through Freiburg to the shores of Lake Constance, and from there to the Austrian frontier. By 6

May they were within a few kilometres of the Italian frontier near the Arlsberg Pass. Although the Americans, who had equipped the French army, were often vexed by the French, particularly in these last stages of the war, when they repeatedly ignored the demarcation lines set between French and American forces, de Gaulle's instincts were absolutely correct. Churchill had not at Yalta argued for a French Zone for reasons of sentiment or kindness. He recognised that there would be a need for French manpower in a post-war occupation, and the increasing participation by the French armies in the invasion of Germany proved that their military power was genuine.

Although the French narrowly failed to reach the Italian frontier, the Americans did. A group of soldiers from Patch's 7th Army reached the Brenner Pass on 4 May, and met there fellow Americans advancing from northern Italy. Since mid-February, the Americans had been conducting a guarded negotiation with SS General Wolff in Switzerland, about the surrender of German forces in the Italian theatre. The Soviets were aware of these negotiations, and although they were told roughly what was going in them, they were understandably disquieted by the prospect of a separate surrender by the Germans. The surrender in northern Italy was finally signed on 2 May, and this was the beginning of the end.

Eisenhower, having told Montgomery that he was not to drive on Berlin, had been pressing him to push his forces towards the Baltic, and during April, the old concerns about Montgomery's slowness had resurfaced. North of Berlin, the Soviet offensive launched at the same time as Zhukov's attack on the city had faced little resistance, and across the flat lands of northern Germany, troops, civilians, and former prisoners were fleeing towards the advancing British. Montgomery in fact had plenty on his hands. In the centre of his advance was the huge port city of Hamburg. On the right, 400 kilometres from his initial crossing of the Rhine, he intended to reach the Baltic at Lübeck. On the left, the Canadian army under his command had a large area of northern Germany to occupy, including several ports, as well as the densely populated area of Holland still occupied by the Germans. In addition to dealing with millions of surrendering soldiers, refugees, and liberated prisoners, the British were concerned to occupy German naval bases, to destroy or capture any warships there, and also to secure intact examples of the most advanced German submarine technology.

The advance picked up speed as the resistance before it collapsed, and British units arrived outside Hamburg at the end of April. Two days after Dönitz announced Hitler's death, the city was thankfully surrendered without a fight. Hamburg's *Gauleiter*, Karl Kaufmann, had no stomach for an extended and pointless resistance in the city, and with Speer's help, convinced Dönitz to permit the surrender. The radio station was handed over intact to the British, with most of its staff. Dönitz had by now retreated, with a motley group of Nazi Party officials, SS, *Wehrmacht*, and Navy units to Flensburg on the Danish frontier. His intention was not to prolong a fanatical resistance against the British and Americans, but to buy time for the escape of German soldiers and civilians from the East. Like so many at all levels in the German armed forces, Dönitz assumed that the British would understand this, as they, with the Americans, would soon be in conflict with the Soviet Union. Dönitz was still supervising a huge ongoing evacuation from Courland and East Prussia, despite continuing losses in ships, and amongst their wretched crews and passengers. Until 14 May, thousands of refugees daily from these places were unloaded at points along the Baltic behind the furthest point of the British advance at Wismar. Here indeed, some fifty kilometres beyond the agreed boundary of the future British Zone, Soviet forces were surprised when they arrived on 2 May to find British paratroopers patrolling the streets of the ancient port. They had arrived only a few hours earlier, after an unopposed drive of forty miles.

Berlin was not a second Stalingrad. It was in fact defended by only 40,000 German soldiers and foreign SS auxiliaries, and these were formally surrendered by their commander, Weidling, on 2 May. In the next few days, as Soviet soldiers looted, raped, and celebrated in the ruins of the capital, a huge column of Germans trudged out of the city towards the West. The Soviet flag, in a famous photographic moment, was raised above the Reichstag. Bemused groups of soldiers, reporters, and investigators roamed through the rubble of the Nazi administration, through the wrecked Propaganda Ministry on Wilhelmstrasse, and the ruins of the Gestapo headquarters at Prinz-Albrecht-Strasse, where six living prisoners were found. The other prisoners there had been massacred by the Gestapo on the night of 23/24 April.[10] Cornelius Ryan has recounted how Major Boris Polevoi explored the silent and deserted corridors and chambers of Hitler's bunker. He found the bodies of two

Generals, Burgdorf and Krebs, and an SS Captain, Franz Schedle, who had shot themselves. Then he found a room containing the bodies of six children, aged between four and twelve, and the charred remains of two adults. Polevoi immediately recognised one of them as the body of Josef Goebbels. All the children had been poisoned, and it appeared that the eldest had been bruised in a struggle.[11] Vasily Grossman wandered around the Reich Chancellery, and recorded his final impressions of the war:

> Hitler's office. The reception hall. A huge foyer in which a young Kazakh, with dark skin and broad cheekbones, is learning to ride a bicycle, falling off it now and then. Hitler's armchair and table. A huge metal globe, crushed and crumpled, plaster, planks of wood, carpets. Everything is mixed up. It's chaos.[12]

Significantly, while Soviet soldiers rejoiced in the ruins of Berlin, their political superiors were already engaged in more serious tasks. Although all the occupiers were to rely heavily on the services of individual German émigrés, many of them Jewish, in their future administrations, the Soviets had specifically prepared a whole group of German communists. Two groups of these, fortified by Marxist-Leninist training at 'anti-fascist schools' in the Soviet Union, were flown into Germany in the last days of the war, ironically in American aircraft, and told to organise new administrations. Ten members of the 'Ulbricht Group', whose leader would later emerge as effective ruler of the GDR until 1971, left Moscow on 30 April 1945. Wolfgang Leonhardt described their arrival in Berlin on 2 May: 'It was a hellish picture. Ruins, hungry people in tattered clothes wandering around; helpless German soldiers, who no longer seemed to grasp what was going on around them. Singing, celebrating, and often also drunken Red Army soldiers.' Even before the fighting had ended, the 'Ulbricht Group', and a similar group under Anton Ackermann in the operational area of Koniev's Army Group, had begun the construction of new Communist administrations run by 'anti-fascists'.[13]

SURRENDER

The largest surviving concentration of German troops was not in a 'National Redoubt', but under Schörner's command in Saxony and Bohemia. As the situation deteriorated all around them, these forces withdrew into the mountainous terrain, and it was from here that the last great exodus of German civilians took place. This was another of the human disasters which unfolded in early 1945, and have gone largely unnoticed since outside Germany. Bohemia had included a German population from well before 1939, when it was annexed by the Nazis after the Munich Agreement. This population had grown during the war, with the 'Germanisation' of the Czech economy, and of cultural and educational life. By 1945 many more Germans had arrived, either to escape from Allied bombing, or as refugees from further east and south. In the first days of May 1945, and in the subsequent weeks and months, they fled or were driven from their homes by a Czech population which had been oppressed for years. Long columns, sometimes protected by armed units, made a weary trek back towards the German frontier. Many were killed, beaten, or humiliated. They had to leave their possessions behind. The American units they hoped to reach, had like those facing Berlin, been finally ordered to stop, much to the anger and disappointment of Patton, who had hoped to end the war by taking Prague. Schörner himself, nicknamed the 'Hanging General' for his summary treatment of deserters, escaped in a light aircraft to the west, where he was arrested by the Americans.

After the months of dogged resistance, the end came quickly. Montgomery was informed on 27 April that peace feelers had been proffered in Sweden, and after the surrender of Hamburg it was clear that the remaining German forces opposite his own were looking for a way out. On 3 May a party of four German officers was allowed through to Montgomery's trailer headquarters, now on Lüneburg Heath. Montgomery received them with two peremptory questions, directed not to them, but about them. 'Who are these people?' he asked, and 'What do they want?'[14] Friedeburg, the leader of the delegation, tried, as did all German negotiators in the next few days, to gain time to allow their men and as many civilians as possible to give themselves up to the British and Americans. Montgomery, like Eisenhower, was mindful of the potential for harming relations with the Soviets in any surrender which was manipulated by the Germans, and insisted that he could only accept the surrender of forces opposing him, and not those still fleeing from the Soviets. Friedeburg and his colleagues retired to consult with Dönitz and Keitel by telephone. At 18.30 on 4 May 1945, the German delegation reassembled to sign a prepared 'Instrument of Surrender'. All German forces in Holland, north-west Germany, and in Denmark were to cease hostilities the next morning.[15]

Keitel and Jodl, having escaped the bunker in Berlin, conducted the wider German surrender. Keitel had made it to Flensburg, where he operated as the crestfallen and doomed commander of the German forces there, authorising Friedeburg to sign the surrender to Montgomery. Friedeburg was now despatched to play a similar role with the Americans. He was flown by the British to Eisenhower's HQ at Rheims in France on 5 May. On the same day, the German armies which had fled before the Americans into Austria surrendered to General Devers. At Rheims, Friedeburg again tried to temporise, asking in effect for a separate surrender to the Americans. Eisenhower made it absolutely clear that there was no possibility of this, and had to threaten to seal the American front against all incoming refugees before Dönitz gave his agreement on 7 May to the unconditional surrender which had been demanded all along. General Suslaparov, representing the Soviet Union, had flown in to sign, and France was represented by General Sevez. Alfred Jodl was delivered to act as representative of all the German armed forces. For reasons of diplomatic prestige, the ceremony was re-enacted on Soviet controlled territory, at Karlshorst in eastern Berlin, on 9 May. Keitel and Friedeburg, again flown in by the British from Flensburg, signed on behalf of the German armed forces; a group of officers, including Eisenhower's deputy, Air Chief Marshal Tedder, Zhukov the conqueror of Berlin, Spaatz, and de Lattre represented the Allies, and signed the document.

The American, British, and French officers and pressmen had flown in from Rheims, and were fascinated by their first impressions of the shattered capital of the Reich, and of the Soviets. Bizarrely, they were taken from the airfield at Tempelhof to the surrender ceremony at Zhukov's headquarters in a convoy of commandeered German vehicles. In front of more than one hundred Soviet cameramen, and just three from the West, Keitel, Friedeburg and Stumpf were brought in. Harry Butcher, Eisenhower's naval aide, was particularly struck by Keitel's demeanour:

It was one of arrogance and defiance. [...] Keitel surveyed the room as he might have looked over the terrain of a battlefield. Here was the living Prussianism of which I had heard so much. His attitude contrasted sharply with that of the German civilians I had seen during the day, all of whom appeared completely whipped and cowed.[16]

When he realised that the French were also signing the surrender, Keitel said 'What? The French as well?'[17]

These surrenders were followed by a remarkably swift transition from a condition of extreme violence to one of relative peace. The once powerful German army had totally disintegrated. Its political guidance, its military leadership, communications, supply, and above all the will to fight, had vanished. Literally millions of soldiers of all kinds gave themselves up in early May, their numbers swelled by many SS men and others who were identified as war criminals. There were sporadic outbursts of fighting, typically when Hitler Youths naively attacked occupying forces or their vehicles. In both Courland, where the sea-borne evacuation continued, and in Slovakia, where Schörner's army group sought to disengage from the Russians, fighting continued for a few days after the formal surrender. But over most of Germany, scarred and embattled, the agony was ended. There was a palpable sense of relief amongst German civilians, Allied soldiers, and most German soldiers. The guns fell silent, and the fleets of aircraft which had flown over Germany largely disappeared.

Strikingly, no organised group of German soldiers fought on in the way which had been feared. In Holland, Norway, Denmark, the Channel Islands, and on isolated Greek islands in the Mediterranean, the Germans gave themselves up. The garrisons which had been encircled since August 1944 in Dunkirk, La Rochelle, Lorient, and Saint Nazaire laid down their arms. The British were concerned that individual German U-boats still at sea might ignore the instruction to surrender, and indeed two Allied merchant ships were sunk in the Firth of Forth on 7 May by U-boats. Over the next few weeks, others gave themselves up: by the end of the month forty-nine U-boats had surrendered at sea.[18] There were many individual instances of German resistance after the surrenders in early May, but they were just that. Nowhere did a large body of men with heavy weapons attempt to prolong the struggle.

STUNDE NULL

The moment of transition when Allied soldiers first arrived in a given locality came at different times all over Germany. In German consciousness this became known as *Stunde Null*, or 'Zero Hour', the moment when history stopped and the clock was restarted. Sometimes the moment was marked by violence; at other points it was more peaceful. This was a strongly gendered encounter, when the experience of Germans depended very greatly on whether they were male or female. The transition from Nazi rule to Allied military occupation, and the first transactions between occupiers and Germans, were marked above all by suicide, rape, and a complete shift in authority. This was still an extraordinarily violent situation. Hitler's suicide was both preceded and followed by thousands of others across Germany, particularly in the east, where whole groups of people killed themselves rather than face the Soviets. In Leipzig the Americans found the mayor and his wife dead in his office, their daughter – a nurse – dead on the sofa in the same room. Max Hastings recounts how the German commander in Pilsen, after surrendering the town to the Americans, concluded the ceremony by shooting himself.[19] Many senior officers killed themselves, including two of the four who had arrived at Montgomery's trailer on 3 May. Many Nazi Party officials took poison before they were captured, or, like Himmler, after they were captured and recognised.

There were of course many different reasons why Germans killed themselves at this point, and much of the debate about this is highly speculative. One testimony comes from Rudolf Höss. He had ended up, like so many, with his wife and family, with the Dönitz government in Flensburg. Höss was one of a group of SS men who had much to fear. He had been working with the Concentration Camp Inspectorate in Berlin, the body which actually administered the whole ghastly system. With him now were Himmler's most senior aides in this administration, Oswald Pohl and Richard Glücks, and other notorious individuals like Glücks' deputy Gerhard Maurer and Carl Gebhardt, Himmler's personal physician. Höss described his reaction to Hitler's death:

> With the Führer gone, our world had gone. Was there any point in going on living? We would be pursued and persecuted wherever we went. We wanted to take poison. I had obtained some for my wife, lest she and the children

fall alive into the hands of the Russians in the event of their making an unexpected advance.

Nevertheless, because of the children, we did not do this. For their sake we wanted to take on our own shoulders all that was coming. But we should have done it. I have always regretted it since.

Höss was subsequently dumbfounded when, after it became clear to Himmler that Dönitz would not tolerate him in his 'government', Himmler told the SS men to change their uniforms and 'hide in the army'. Höss disguised himself in a Navy uniform, as a 'boatswain's mate', and submerged himself amongst the others at a Naval Intelligence School on the island of Sylt.[20]

The front line soldiers who moved through Germany in April and May 1945 had participated in and witnessed violence on a huge and grotesque scale, as had many of the citizens. The horrible knowledge of Nazi atrocities poisoned the atmosphere. It is hardly surprising that many Allied soldiers behaved in an extraordinarily violent way when they met German civilians. In the first moment of what is usually thought of as either liberation or occupation, soldiers frequently felt completely loosened from normal restraints of law or civilised conduct. Often they felt themselves beyond the reach of any sanction; individually, or more often in groups, they raped women all over Germany. There has long been a horrible knowledge that almost all women who came under Soviet occupation in Germany in 1945 were raped, unless they hid, or were very lucky. Great numbers of women killed themselves rather than face this prospect. Some realised after repeated sexual assaults that their best hope was to offer themselves to a single Soviet officer who might then protect them from the attentions of other soldiers. One woman in Berlin summed this up, writing 'I have to find a single wolf to keep away the pack.'[21]

There was also widespread rape in other parts of Germany. In areas occupied by the French, folk memory still affirms that the situation was as bad as in Soviet-occupied areas, that from very young to very old, most women were raped. Everywhere, a terrible risk was posed by former slave labourers, now often free, but searching for food, drink, and in some cases revenge. There clearly was not rape on the same scale in towns and villages first occupied by the British or Americans, but there was more than is commonly affirmed. In certain cases, it appears very closely linked with revenge. A German woman interviewed years later by Alison Owings recalled that in Schwäbish Hall, in southern Germany, when the Americans arrived, they ransacked the mayor's office and raped his daughter.[22] Strikingly, some reactions to rape in the future British Zone were like those elsewhere: the Germans deserved anything they got, and might consider themselves lucky that they had escaped at all. This testimony from a British witness is all the more remarkable as he was a priest: 'Fortunately', he wrote, the Germans were getting 'their just deserts… In most cases they [the slave labourers] are taking their revenge. Some are going about in organised bands. [...] There is a good deal of rape going on, and those who suffer have probably well deserved it.'[23]

Before the occupation, the British and Americans had agreed a policy of 'non-fraternisation': their forces would not be permitted to speak to Germans, of any age, unless it was necessary. 'Non-fraternisation' is typically dismissed lightly, with a remark about how quickly it was disregarded by most soldiers. Where it was in fact applied, it certainly had a chastening effect. Sybil Bannister was in the unusual position of being a British person coming under this new dispensation in Hamburg in May 1945, and she recounted the chilling effect of the non-fraternisation policy:

> We were ordered to stay indoors whilst the occupation of the town was taking place. Anyone seen outdoors would be shot. For several days we were shut in and saw nobody. [...] Soldiers were only allowed to speak to civilians on necessary business and they led an entirely separate existence. Uniform was a dividing line. Those in uniform were the conquerors. Those not in uniform were the conquered, the underlings, the scum of the earth. Being a civilian, whether I liked it or not, I was automatically herded amongst the Germans, the underlings.[24]

'Non-fraternisation' was pursued not from spite, but because of memories of 1918. Montgomery's behaviour gives an insight into this. He was mindful above all of the outcome of the First World War, and the legend that had arisen then of an undefeated German army. He also wanted to impress on the Germans now under his control that they must take responsibility for the terrible things done in their name. On 10 June 1945 he issued a message 'to the population of the British area in

Germany': this told them that 'you have been defeated, which you must know by now', and that 'you, your nation, were guilty of beginning the war. [...] every nation is responsible for its rulers, and while they were successful, you cheered and laughed. That is why our soldiers do not smile at you.'[25] Montgomery was also conscious of the potential problems which could arise from undisciplined behaviour by his troops, and of the example they had to set. He was particularly troubled by his men's habit of driving around in stolen German vehicles. As early as 6 May he issued orders that 'looting by individuals, or bodies of individuals, was of course forbidden at any time', and he made it clear that 'any contravention of this order would be tried by court martial, whatever the rank of the individual concerned'.[26]

Looting was nonetheless a major problem. By no means all Allied officers were as high-minded as Montgomery, and nothing speaks more eloquently of the licence of the early days after the surrender than the way senior American and British officers referred to their own acquisitions. Harry Butcher was able to get out on a tour of southern Germany and Austria in early June. He saw Munich, the Rally grounds at Nuremberg, and went up to the famed 'Eagles' Nest' at Berchtesgaden. A soldier there told him that the previous unit 'had collected so many souvenirs that now the Eagle's Nest was carefully guarded to prevent any further pilfering'. Butcher then went down to Hitler's former chalet, where he 'collected a few pieces of marble from Hitler's fireplace', one especially for a friend.[27] Admiral Andrew Cunningham was in Berlin for the Potsdam meeting in July, and when he flew back, he took with him 'a few mementoes', including 'two books from one of the palaces at Potsdam', a piece (he hoped) of Hitler's marble-topped desk from the Reich Chancellery, and 'a handful of Iron Crosses and medals'.[28]

Individual, uncoordinated looting of the kind which bothered Montgomery was quickly replaced by more organised activity. All the Allies had prepared teams of specialists to accompany the troops into Germany, with instructions to seize particular people and things. All wanted to capture as many German scientists as possible, particularly those associated with high technology, like rockets, jet aviation, or nuclear physics. They were all after documents and materials related to these areas. All planned to seize German archives, particularly those relating to the Nazi Party, the German government and the armed forces.

Particular teams were charged with recovering stolen works of art and cultural monuments. Alongside these more official activities, there was much wanton destruction, and theft.

In many places there was a temporary breakdown of all law and custom. Edith Hahn was in the city of Brandenburg, near Berlin, and she described what happened when Soviet soldiers found a bank: 'The Russians had broken into the vaults and taken out all the reichsmarks, and now they threw the money into the street so that it blew like flying leaves in the hot wind from the fires all around. When the Germans ran after the money, the Russians roared with laughter.'[29] Remarkably, in such a chaotic situation, the breakdown in law and order was often very short lived. In most places the Allies pragmatically ordered the local police to continue their normal duties, even to carry firearms, wearing armbands showing that they were operating in the name of the military government. Where Allied soldiers were shot at after the surrender, the response was typically ruthless. Soldiers of the British 7th Armoured Division were relaxing in their camp in the foothills of the Harz Mountains on the night of 8 May; for the first time they had permission to light fires. During the evening they were disturbed by gunfire, explosions, and shouts. The men immediately combed through the forest around them and rounded up a number of Hitler Youths from a nearby training centre. One of the British soldiers, Alan Ritchie, described what happened: 'They were shot under the terms of the Geneva Convention as they were not in uniform – they had Nazi armbands, but that was not sufficient. They were shouting and screaming "Heil Hitler" and "Gott strafe England". They had also been found setting fire to some parts of the forest to try and burn us out. And on this particular occasion, they were also armed, so they had to be disposed of.'[30] Only has to imagine the salutary effect these incidents had on any others inclined to prolong the war.

There were not many of these in any case. Peter von Zahn was one of hundreds of thousands of German soldiers evacuated from the Baltic coast and landed in the British Zone after the surrender. His account speaks volumes:

Before the Germans were marched off by British Royal Marines, they threw their rifles on the ground. The Marines picked them up with great effort and care, and, with bundles of German rifles under their arms, raced after their prisoners. They did not use their butt ends on them but tried to make the Germans carry their weapons themselves. This was vigorously refused.[31]

These men were done with soldiering. Remarkably, there were virtually no problems with the disarmament of the German army. Most of its heavy weapons had been destroyed or damaged in the last weeks of the war, and many of those which had survived were destroyed by German soldiers before they finally surrendered. A striking example is provided by Germany's fighter chief, Adolf Galland. In the last weeks of the war, out of favour with both Goering and Hitler, he was given command of an elite unit of fighter aces equipped with the ME-262 jet. This was the single most advanced aerial formation in the world in April 1945. By 3 May, Galland's sixty jets had been forced to retreat to Salzburg. He described their end: 'As the rattle of the first tank was heard on the airfield, there was no other possibility left; our jet fighters went up in flames.'[32] Everywhere the Allies tried to capture examples of German military technology as trophies, or for evaluation and research. Examples are to be found all over the world today in museums and military collections. At Nordhausen the Americans removed hundreds of tons of partially assembled V2 rockets.

Admiral Cunningham, while in Germany for the Potsdam meeting, also went to Kiel, where 'the harbour seemed full of floating cranes, lighters, tugs and floating docks, sufficient to have provided Portsmouth, Plymouth and Chatham.' At the nearby torpedo works at Eckernforde, Cunningham's party 'saw a captured film of Dr. Walther's experiments with a 27 knot submarine of a special type with streamlined hull and very fast under water [...] We then saw Dr. Walther himself, who demonstrated his fuel called 'Engelin', which I understand consisted of oxygen derived from the decomposition of hydrogen peroxide by a platinum process.' Cunningham was 'supremely thankful that the war had ended when it did'.[33]

The few surviving surface ships of the German Navy were parcelled out amongst the Allies, and their fate was somehow representative. The heavy cruiser *Prinz Eugen*, which had accompanied the *Bismarck* on its abortive break-out in 1941 and the *Scharnhorst* and *Gneisenau* in their successful dash through the English Channel in 1942, was surrendered in Copenhagen. It was allocated to the Americans, who used it as a target in nuclear bomb tests in 1946. The British got the light cruiser *Leipzig*;

they filled it with gas munitions and sank it at sea. The Soviets inherited a similar ship, *Nürnberg*, which they renamed and used in their Navy. They also raised the scuttled wreck of a planned aircraft carrier from the harbour in Königsberg, but never completed their attempted rebuild of the ship. A number of *Luftwaffe* aircraft were used for civilian purposes after 1945, but none of the advanced designs of 1945 were realised in Germany. Production of weapons, military aircraft, tanks, and warships ceased almost entirely. No large or significant group of German weapons was used in warfare after the surrender. Nor, despite fears, were they used for underground resistance. In early July 1945, General Lucius Clay, who had been appointed Deputy Governor of Germany, and would over the next four years play a significant role in post-war Germany, reported: 'There is no evidence of an attempt to organise a Nazi underground'.[34]

Several million German soldiers surrendered to the Allies in the last weeks of the war and the first of the peace. Only rarely were they immediately confined. The Allies had no camps prepared on anything like the necessary scale. Many prisoners were required to set out on long marches towards camps further west or further east. In the British area, the surrendering Germans were confined to coastal peninsulas and simply required to wait there. The Americans were similarly overwhelmed with the numbers which surrendered to them. In the first few months of 1945 they took charge of some 3 million German prisoners, many of whom were eventually held in improvised camps in the Rhineland. In April and May these camps consisted of nothing more than fields enclosed by barbed wire, with a few buildings serving for the camp administration. Food was desperately short, and sanitation almost non-existent. Later, barracks, kitchens, and latrines were built, but these camps were primitive in the extreme. The thousands of men languishing there experienced, in addition to great physical hardship, total uncertainty. Their pre-existing world had vanished forever, and now they heard only rumours, that they would all be sent to France or to the Soviet Union for forced labour, or that certain groups of them – the young, or the old – might be released. It is incredible that more of them did not die. Rüdiger Overmanns has surveyed the available evidence, and discounts some of the more lurid estimates; he reckons that between 5,000 and 10,000 German prisoners died in the camps of the Rhineland, out of one million interned there.[35] Many more fell ill, but the provision of food and sanitation did improve, and by June 1945 the first were allowed to return home.

Everywhere the Allies were looking for war criminals, but any screening of such a huge number of prisoners was bound to be superficial. Most SS men could be identified by a tattoo under their left arm, but this included hundreds of thousands of *Waffen-SS* men who had served as frontline soldiers or as auxiliaries. Others escaped even this cursory inspection. Rudolf Höss, posing as a seaman, was confined with thousands of others on the Baltic coast, but in the summer he was released as he claimed to be a farmer. In rare individual cases, a 'major Nazi criminal' was recognised and separated for further investigation. Many thousands of suspected criminals were confined separately, awaiting further review. In several places, the occupiers used the concentration camps they had so recently freed from the Germans. It is well know that the Soviets used Buchenwald for many years as a prison, after they took it over from the Americans in July 1945. It is not such common knowledge that the British used Neuengamme, which they had liberated shortly before occupying Hamburg, to house prisoners they suspected of being dedicated Nazis or potential war criminals. This reminiscence, from Brigadier David Baines suggests that their treatment there could be very harsh:

> I was given an interesting job [...] at the Hamburg headquarters, being able to speak a little German. I had to go and collect SS officers from the German divisions which were still in being up in Schleswig-Holstein and near Buxtehude, and take them to a British 'concentration camp' on the Elbe at Neuengamme. They thought they would be shot – perhaps they were.[36]

Again and again one comes across this indifference to German suffering, particularly in April, May, and June of 1945. There was plenty of awareness of the suffering of the Germans, of the plight of their refugees, of the rape of women, and the ill-treatment of prisoners. But few had any sympathy for them, so great was the revulsion felt at what was still being discovered all over Germany.

The transition from Nazi authority to military government was also very rapid, but took different forms in different places. Once Hitler had gone, central government in Germany disappeared. The pathetic history of Dönitz' 'government' has been told from several perspectives, but in reality it never exercised any great power, and none at all in some parts of the former 'Reich'. Quartered on a ship off Flensburg, it did still meet, and issue orders; Speer relates how some members of the government addressed memoranda to one another. He himself was prone to similar flights of fantasy. The British allowed Dönitz to carry on like this for a few days, primarily to help with the huge task of administering the transition to military government and to help look after German soldiers, but were angered when Field-Marshal Busch appeared to exceed his authority on 11 May. He was reprimanded by Montgomery, and after this the Dönitz 'government' was more carefully observed. The Soviets were also anxious to see this body wound up, lest it emerge under British tutelage as some kind of replacement central authority in Germany. They need not have worried: the British had no intention of allowing this and on 23 May all members of the 'government' were arrested.

Although the Allies had planned to rule Germany through a 'Control Council', this was not ready in May 1945. In practice martial law was declared in all areas of the country as they were occupied. In the absence of central authority or direction, in each city or town, there was an *ad hoc* transition of power, with temporary 'councils' and 'committees' assuming responsibility, or being assigned it, often for a short initial period. In some cases Allied officers literally walked into the town hall, and after brief consultations appointed someone as 'mayor', giving them responsibility for the maintenance of law and order and essential services. Those identified as Nazis, rightly or wrongly, were dismissed or arrested if they were present, and replaced by others who could claim a more respectable background. Each new military administration assumed complete power in its locality and often these first civilian appointments were quickly revoked when news of past Nazi affiliations was received. In even the larger German cities though, there were relatively few occupying soldiers, and in many towns and villages there were none.

In the vacuum, 'anti-fascist committees', composed largely of former trade unionists, communists, and social democrats, with a leavening of Catholic and Protestant clergy, were typically formed. Often these German 'antifas', as they were styled, undertook their own denazification, dismissing men and women from the police and local administration, and removing swastikas and other obvious traces of the Nazi regime. Most of the 'antifas' were dismissed by the different Allies within weeks of the surrender, and disappeared leaving little or no historical trace, but they should be credited for the important work they did in maintaining sustaining law and order, and in safeguarding public health at a critical point in German history. Gareth Pritchard, who has researched their role in the Soviet Zone, recounts an event in Leipzig:

> On one occasion a crowd of several thousand was bent on plundering the food stores. Six members of the committee faced them, in danger at any moment of being trampled underfoot. There were moments of tension and then someone from the crowd shouted 'These are the right people'. The mood of the crowd changed and they eventually dispersed.[37]

In rural communities and small villages, the transition to Allied authority was more informal, as Germans tried to guess what might be the most expeditious behaviour in the new circumstances. Victor Klemperer had by the time of the surrender reached the small village of Unterbernbach in Bavaria, and it was here that he heard of Hitler's death, and saw for himself the Americans at first hand. On 28 April, he recorded, 'unbelievable, but completely true!' that the mayor had removed the swastika above the district office. On 2 May he walked to nearby Kühbach, and recorded a peaceful first encounter, with an 'American emergency or repair column' on the church square:

> a truck with a winch, one with tyres, etc., smaller vehicles, jacked up high on one was a long, thin-necked machine-gun with cartridge belt hanging down. A grinding machine or a lathe stood against the wall of a house. Black, more precisely, brown Negro soldiers in indefinably grey-green earth coloured jackets and trousers, all with steel helmets stuck on their heads, bustled and swarmed around – village children stood close by and among them. Later I also saw individual blond soldiers in dark leather jackets, revolver strapped on, rifle slung over the shoulder. All the shops were shut, admittedly it was not quite three o' clock. I turned into a side street, a young blonde, certainly no peasant woman, presumably from Munich, answered my enquiries. [...] On the first day of the occupation the troops had taken everything out of the shops, but otherwise had been altogether decently behaved. 'The blacks too?' She almost beamed with delight. 'They're even friendlier than the others, there's nothing to be afraid of.'[38]

Cologne was one of the largest cities occupied outside Berlin, and here the Americans quickly chose Konrad Adenauer, former mayor of the city, to head a new administration. Earlier, while awaiting the arrival of the Americans, he had received a telephone call from his sister, who, 'quite excited', told him: 'We are free, we have Americans here – quite nice people, by the way.' A few weeks later, American officers arrived at Adenauer's country house, and drove him in an open jeep the few miles into Cologne. There the Commandant, Lieutenant Colonel Hyles, asked him to become *Oberbürgermeister*. Adenauer, who set about his task with great energy, recalled that 'The Americans with whom I dealt were all intelligent and reasonable men. We soon understood one another.'[39]

The many similar recollections of initially harmonious shifts of authority should not mask the abruptness and severity of other initial transactions between occupiers and Germans. We have seen that all over Germany, people living near concentration camps or scenes of atrocities were forced to visit them, and often to bury the dead. Sometimes this process was visited on the Germans least responsible. Elfie Walther was a schoolgirl living in Delmenhorst in northern Germany. On 28 April she was peremptorily told by the British to report for work at seven o' clock the next morning, 'with things for several days'. She and other school-girls were taken to the camp at Sandbostel, which had recently housed many thousands of British and Soviet prisoners of war, and political pris-oners. Elfie and her companions were set to work to clean up the camp, and she recorded her shocked impressions in a diary. After being told about some of the horrific things which had gone on in the camp, she wrote: 'If it is as the orderlies have told us, then the pictures of Bergen-Belsen are certainly true too.' After cleaning barracks, the German girls were told to clean the surviving prisoners:

> I lack the right words to describe all the misery. They are hardly people. Skeletons lie there in their filthy beds, smeared with excrement from head to foot, and stare at us with huge eyes... How ashamed I am in these minutes to be German! We caused this! And my mother does not believe that Germans could do something like this!

Elfie had to carry corpses outside to be buried, and then to witness a suicide attempt, when a woman peeling potatoes 'started to scream dreadfully and suddenly cut her artery with a potato knife'. Apparently the woman had a son who was in the SS, and feared that he would be shot. On 10 May Elfie and her group were sent home, to be relieved by girls from Bremen. Several of her school friends subsequently died

from typhus, contracted in the camp. She was unable to tell her par-
ents for several days all she had seen and heard. When she did tell them,
they were 'speechless. A world collapsed for them too'.[40] One can hardly
imagine a more brutal 'denazification'.

Another kind of denazification was swiftly conducted by the
Americans in Ahrweiler in May 1945. Here an American military tribunal charged four minor Nazi officials and villagers with the murder of
an American airman in August 1944. Three were sentenced to death and
hanged on 2 June; the fourth was sentenced to life imprisonment. At the
execution, according to a British journalist, the 'row of official witnesses
turned pale and swayed when the trap crashed open, and the American
hangman wept'.[41]

THE ALLIED CONTROL COUNCIL

In the first weeks of military occupation, authority in Germany devolved
completely on local military commanders. The nature of the occupation depended very much on they way they governed their troops, the
masses of 'displaced persons', and the German population in the areas
they temporarily controlled. Although the Allies had agreed a plan for a
'Control Council', and had in various ways prepared for it, they could
not immediately establish this. The Soviets were determined first to get
the Americans out of the substantial area they occupied in Saxony and
Thuringia which had been designated part of a Soviet zone; conversely,
the British and Americans were determined to occupy a sector of Berlin,
as agreed. The French fumed impotently on the sidelines, wanting to be
treated as an occupier on equal terms, but refused this. Although Churchill
particularly wanted to embrace French participation in the occupation,
Stalin was utterly contemptuous about the French, and insisted that anything conceded to them must come from areas previously designated to
British and American control. When the Allied leaders met at Potsdam,
outside Berlin, in July 1945, the French were not invited.

In the weeks immediately after the surrender, the Allies jockeyed for
position at a number of levels. In Germany itself, the respective army
commanders paid one another visits, and formal military ceremonies
were staged, with parades of soldiers and displays of weapons. Celebratory
meals were laid on, and toasts were drunk. All sides made fulsome

declarations of thanks and bestowed medals on one another. This was not mere window dressing or empty rhetoric. There was genuine good feeling between fellow soldiers and officers, who had indeed been engaged on a great common enterprise. Outside Germany, the Allied leaders negotiated separately and tried to establish their positions before the planned meeting in Potsdam.

Harry Truman felt at a disadvantage because he did not share the working relationship already established between the 'Big Three' before Roosevelt's death. He was weighed down by a mass of military and political decisions, not least those related to the war with Japan, and the details of a settlement in Germany were beyond him. Churchill was absolutely determined to drive a hard bargain with Stalin, but equally conscious of Britain's diminishing power and influence. It is difficult to know whether Stalin had any definite vision for post-war Germany. As far as can be judged, the Soviets were incredibly vague about this. Truman was quite ready to withdraw American soldiers from the 'Soviet Zone', and the Soviets proved equally ready to allow the British and Americans into Berlin. Indeed, they staged there on 5 June the inaugural meeting of the Allied Control Council. Montgomery and Eisenhower flew separately into Berlin with accompanying retinues, and met with Marshal Zhukov. At a formal ceremony the Allies signed a 'Declaration regarding the Defeat of Germany', and assumed 'supreme authority' over the country.[42] Lucius Clay also attended the meeting in Berlin. He was struck by how ill prepared the Soviets were, reporting that 'neither I, nor members of my party found any evidence of Russian organization for Control Council government'.[43]

Five days later, Zhukov made a visit to Eisenhower's HQ, now in Frankfurt am Main. Montgomery was there too, and all were treated to an awesome demonstration of military strength, a fly-past by over 1,700 American and British aircraft. Behind the scenes the Allied governments were moving towards agreement to withdraw from or advance into the agreed zones, and at the end of June another meeting was held in Berlin to arrange this. In the early days of July 1945, American and British soldiers pulled back, and the Red Army marched into Saxony and Thuringia, and along the Baltic coast to Lübeck. According to communist historians, this was the real moment of liberation for these parts of Germany. Otto Winzer, one of the members of the 'Ulbricht Group', described how the Red Army entered Eisleben on 3 July, where 'the market place was a sea of red flags.'[44] Separately, there was a sharp exchange between Eisenhower and the French, who were reluctant to withdraw from Karlsruhe and Stuttgart to the areas conceded to them by the Americans and British. Reluctantly the French pulled back, and American units took over the administration of both cities.[45]

On 4 July, advance parties of American and British forces arrived in Berlin, and established provisional headquarters there. The Americans took over the south-west of the city; the British sector covered the north-west. Road and rail routes from the American and British Zones to Berlin had been agreed with the Soviets, and over the next few weeks the presence of both in the city grew rapidly. On 15 July, Stalin, Churchill, and Truman arrived in Berlin for the Potsdam Conference. They confirmed at the meeting that the French could have a sector in Berlin, taken from the American and British areas. On 30 July the first executive meeting of the Allied Control Council was held.

The Control Council was made up of four representatives, one each from the Soviet Union, America, Britain, and France. A 'Co-Ordinating Committee' of the deputies of these four, and a 'Control Staff' divided into twelve divisions completed its administration. Although the Control Council acted as a central governing body, it affirmed the separate authority of each country in its own zone: this gave official recognition to what was already a reality, that Germany was divided, with new external and internal frontiers, and that the first signs of a different direction were already apparent in separate zones. On 30 August 1945 the Control Council issued its first Proclamation, addressed 'To the people of Germany', formally announcing its assumption of 'supreme authority' there. It gave Allied military law in Germany absolute precedence over any pre-existing laws. Control Council Order No. 1 forbade 'former members of the German armed forces, and other German civilians' from wearing 'military uniform', or any 'military badges of rank, medals or insignia'.

Significantly, the Control Council's Law No. 1 repealed twenty-six Nazi Laws. All had been passed since 1933, and most embodied discriminatory provisions against the Jews. The laws repealed included those commonly known as the 'Nuremberg Laws' of 1935 which had deprived Jews of German citizenship, and prevented marriage or sexual intercourse between 'Aryans' and 'non-Aryans'; the law of August 1938 demanding that Jews take uniform 'Family Names and Christian Names', and the law of September 1941 enforcing the wearing of the yellow star in public for Jews. The Control Council also repealed a number of laws concerning the Gestapo and the Hitler Youth.[46] At a stroke the legal basis of the 'Third Reich' was dismantled. Carl von Clausewitz, the great military philosopher of the nineteenth century, wrote that a war could not 'be considered to have ended' until three conditions were fulfilled. The fighting forces of the enemy had to be destroyed, its country occupied, and its will broken. Not only must the enemy government be 'driven to ask for peace', but its population must also be 'made to submit'.[47] All these conditions were satisfied by the defeat of Hitler's 'Third Reich' in 1945. The Allies turned now to the 're-education' of Germany, and to the punishment of Nazi criminals.

6

DENAZIFICATION:
MAY–SEPTEMBER 1945

The nature of the German *nation* is hideously warped and diseased. Unless that is manfully recognised, there is no chance of peace in the world. Even that chance will not exist unless both we and the United States have not only a clear policy, but the resolve to fit it with the means of accomplishment at whatever cost of cash and convenience.

> *From a pamphlet published by the British Foreign Office diplomat Sir Robert*
> *Vansittart in 1943.*[1]

The 'denazification' of Germany was a long and complex process. It evolved over a several years, had several distinctly different dimensions, and involved many different agencies and individuals, both Allied and German. By 1945 Nazism had penetrated deeply into German society, its institutions, its culture, and the fabric of everyday life. Even the German language had been warped by Nazi usage. The Allied intention to destroy Nazism, stated consistently during the war, in policy declarations, in key planning directives, and in the early legislation of the Control Council was clear, but necessarily very general. The 'Principles' adopted at Potsdam in August 1945 are representative. The meeting of the Allied leaders has often been seen as a failure, because they could not agree on a long-term future for Germany; this, it is said, is where the Cold War started. Stalin, Truman, and Attlee – the new British Prime Minister – did in fact agree that Germany would be governed, at least for an interim period, by the Control Council, and they were able to agree on a programme of denazification.

The Allies restated in the 'Potsdam Declaration' their commitment 'to destroy the National Socialist Party and its affiliated and supervised organizations, to dissolve all Nazi institutions, to insure that they are not revived in any form, and to prevent all Nazi and militarist activity or propaganda'. They also committed themselves to the dissolution of the German armed forces, the repeal of Nazi laws, the arrest and internment of war criminals and 'influential Nazi supporters', the removal of Nazis from 'public and semi–public office', and to the restructuring of German education, 'to make possible the successful development of democratic ideas.'[2]

How was this programme to be enforced? In early 1945 there were 8 million members of the NSDAP, or Nazi Party. They came from all walks of life. The Party had become a huge organisation in its own right, employing many people, with a plethora of smaller administrative bodies. These organisations operated in all areas of German cultural and social life, as well as in the field of politics. The Hitler Youth organisation affected millions of young people. Women, although excluded from professional life and politics, had their own Nazi organisations. The Reich Chamber of Culture involved hundreds of thousands of artists in different fields, and professional bodies like the *NS-Lehrerbund* (the National Socialist Teachers' League), or the *NS-Ärztebund* (the National Socialist Doctors' League) exerted influence in the workplace. The German educational system had been put under huge pressure to accept Nazi practices like the use of the Hitler salute, and school curricula had been distorted to carry the crudest propaganda. Everyday life had been saturated with Nazi symbolism and imagery. Millions of people were clothed in uniforms displaying endless examples of this. The swastika was everywhere, decorating public buildings, in people's lapels, even on Christmas trees. The Nazi eagle was ubiquitous, from huge stone statues which dominated parade grounds and Party buildings to tiny images on postage stamps and decorative letterheads. In only twelve years, as Victor Klemperer so lucidly documented, the Nazis had changed the German language, introducing new terms, and giving new meaning to old ones.

The Allied occupation forces, entering Germany in April and May 1945, could hardly know in any detail how, and in what ways Nazism had seeped into German society. The Allies had to proceed largely from what they knew of Nazi Germany before 1939, and from what they had been able to add to this during the war. There had been a sustained debate in different countries about how to get rid of Nazi ideology, and what later became known as denazification stemmed from these debates. The Allied programme had several distinct strands: the arrest and punishment of Nazi criminals; the abolition of the Party and its institutions; and the repeal of Nazi laws. To these were added the intention to get rid of Nazism from public discourse, the mass media, and from education, to purge the public sphere of all Nazi insignia, and most contentiously, to exclude Nazis from all areas of responsibility and influence in public life.

In practice it proved more straightforward to get rid of Nazi symbolism from the public sphere, and this task was largely accomplished in the initial post-war period. Other aspects of the denazification programme ran into major difficulties. During this time, many 'war criminals' were apprehended and preparations were set in hand to bring them to trial. Although many of these trials were concluded by the end of 1946, the machinery set in motion ground on for some years, before the responsibility for pursuing war criminals was turned over to German authorities. Many war criminals escaped from Germany, and others were not even identified until later. A disturbing number who were implicated in grave crimes were put through various legal processes, but escaped with only light punishments. The denazification of public life proved an impossible task. Put bluntly, if the Allies had actually dismissed all ex-Nazis from all positions of responsibility and influence in Germany after 1945, they would have had all essential services there desperately depleted, and an enormous body of resentful people either unemployed or working as labourers. They would have had to employ armies of investigators and lawyers to purge the different professions, the economy, and other areas of public employment. There would inevitably have been many miscarriages of justice, and examples of petty unfairness. Confronted with the need to restore public services, and lacking sufficient numbers of police and lawyers, the Allies in post-war Germany had to make pragmatic judgements about which individuals to exclude from different areas of public life; all worked in an environment in which denunciation flourished and misinformation was rife. They had to balance their anti-Nazism with the practical demands of reconstruction, and with the need to build a constructive relationship with the German people.

It is hardly surprising that many war criminals escaped, and it is easy with the benefit of hindsight to find fault with the Allies in this area, collectively and individually. All practised double standards with the different treatment they accorded to ex-Nazis whom they wanted for their weapons programmes. To a lesser extent they operated similar double standards in critical social fields like the police, the operation of the judiciary, and in public health. It is equally unsurprising that numerous people continued to work in the professions, and in prestigious institutions, who appear now as seriously compromised. Both these areas of denazification – the punishment of war criminals, and the purge of elites – were obviously compromised by the developing tension between the Soviets and the other occupiers. On both sides of this east-west divide the pressure grew after 1945 to use war crimes trials less as instruments of punishment and more as tools of publicity. After 1948 both sides became increasingly unwilling to antagonise German opinion in their zones, and correspondingly keen to enlist German support in the Cold War.

The Allied programme to eradicate Nazi symbolism from the public sphere in Germany, was, in contrast, very successful. Strikingly, this was an area where there was close agreement between all the occupiers. Their analysis of the causes of Nazism differed greatly; but they shared a genuine loathing for Nazism, its institutions and symbols. On this issue there were no significant differences in the Control Council, and between the four separate military governments taking shape in Germany. All four wartime Allies linked this aspect of denazification with the programme of 'demilitarisation': they sought to eradicate military insignia, symbols, and linguistic usages at the same time as they outlawed all manifestations of Nazism in German life.

ABOLITION OF THE NAZI PARTY

After repealing Nazi laws, the Allies dismantled the Party organisation. Control Council 'Proclamation No. 2' of 20 September 1945 stated: 'The National Socialist German Workers' Party (N.S.D.A.P.) is completely and finally abolished and declared to be illegal.' It also abolished all German armed forces. Control Council Law No. 2, 'Providing for the Termination and Liquidation of the Nazi Organisations', went into greater detail: 'The National Socialist German Labour Party, its formations, affiliated associations, and supervised agencies, including paramilitary organisations and all other Nazi institutions established as instruments of party domination are hereby abolished and declared illegal.' This Law listed sixty-two Nazi Party organisations which were expressly abolished, including well-known bodies like the SS, the SA, the Hitler Youth, the Gestapo, and National Socialist Women's Movement, as well as more obscure ones like the 'the Reich Committee for the Protection of German Blood'. This was a comprehensive institutional ban, and none of these agencies have since been revived. There is no evidence that any body of Party workers in Germany tried to keep alive a sense of the Nazi Party as an organisation after May 1945. Law No. 2 also provided for the confiscation by the Allies of 'all real estates, equipments, funds, accounts, records and other property' of all Nazi organisations.[3] Ironically, buildings which had been used by the Nazi Party, or its agencies, if they survived the destruction at the end of the war, often provided the occupiers with the best available offices for their own administrations. Similarly, Nazi Party stationery was often the only paper available to Germans in the immediate post-war period, and new German administrative bodies, even 'antifas', sometimes had to use the reverse side of old forms decorated with Nazi insignia.

As the Allies entered Germany, they all tried to capture as much as they could of the Nazi Party's archives. There were collections of documents all over Germany that related to the administration of the Party, its security services, and its different agencies, as well as more mundane material like membership lists, which might be of huge help in any denazification programme. In the enormous destruction visited upon Germany in the latter stages of the war, whole collections of these records were destroyed. Bombs and shells fell indiscriminately, and archives were sometimes hit. Our historical knowledge of Nazi Germany has suffered as a result. As the Allies advanced into Germany in 1944 and 1945, many more documents, particularly those of an incriminating nature, were deliberately destroyed or hidden. Many of the most sensitive records, like those of the concentration camps and of the Gestapo, were deliberately destroyed before the Allies arrived. A remarkable quantity survived, so many in fact that some have hardly been processed since. Hundreds of tons of paperwork relating to the Nazi Party and its activities were seized in April and May 1945, or found after the surrender. Although specialist teams of investigators were sent into Germany, they could only direct their attention to the most pressing documents. Much of the captured material, particularly when it related to obscure branches of the Party, simply had to wait.

Certain key finds were made which should be mentioned here, because they played an important part in future developments. The Americans found, at a paper mill in Bavaria, the entire card index of Nazi Party membership; it had been sent there to be pulped, but the order had not been carried out. This card index was to provide, with a few exceptions, a remarkably sound base for establishing if, when, and for how long anyone had held membership of the Nazi Party. The British based the Intelligence Section of their 'Information Control Service' in Berlin in the offices of the former Reich Chamber of Culture, on Schlüterstrasse, and discovered in August 1945 that its personnel archive was, remarkably, still in place on the top floor of the building. It held details of some 250,000 people who had held membership of the Chamber.[4] There is no detailed overview yet available of exactly what material the Soviets captured in 1945, but there was undoubtedly a great deal of it.

We know most about the documents captured and collected by the Americans, who established collecting points for the tons of archival material they captured. The Party material was gathered at what subsequently became known as the Berlin Document Center, and in later years was augmented by material which the British decided they no longer wanted. Even in the 1950s the Berlin Document Center was collecting thousands of additional Nazi documents. The membership records of the Nazi Party alone referred to more than twelve million individuals.[5] Today the entire collection has been returned to the German Federal Archive, and is still being processed.

ARREST AND INTERNMENT

The immediate arrest of suspected Nazi criminals after May 1945 can be seen in one sense as a continuation of the war. The Allies, as they invaded Germany, had teams of military police, and various security agencies tasked with the arrest of lists of suspected criminals. Operating alongside, or even ahead of the fighting units in the final days of the war, these teams were heavily armed and steeped in the violent atmosphere of front-line combat. They thought nothing of an armed shoot-out, and were not inclined to treat those arrested with any great sensitivity. The Soviet secret police, the NKVD, operated autonomously alongside the Red Army, and many of its units moved with it into Germany in 1945. In the American-occupied areas the Counter-Intelligence Corps (CIC) was one of several security agencies looking for Nazi criminals. The British Field Security Police, and, in areas occupied by the French, the *Sureté*, were equally active. These teams had lists of named 'major war criminals' to search for. As the Allied knowledge of Nazism increased in the final months of the war, other groups of suspects were identified: senior government officials and administrators; high ranking Party officials; senior army officers; the SS leadership; Gestapo and SD officers; doctors who had participated in medical experiments; and businessmen who had exploited slave labour. After the Moscow Declaration of 1943, a 'United Nations War Crimes Commission' had been established, and one of the responsibilities of this body was the identification of suspects and the preparation of lists. The Soviets refused to take part in this Commission, creating from the start a divergence in the Allied approach to the whole problem of war crimes. Nonetheless, the Commission in 1944 established in Paris a Central Registry of War Criminals and Security Suspects (CROWCASS), and this provided a constantly updated list of suspects. By 1947, when the CROWCASS list was published, it contained no fewer than 60,000 suspects.

All four occupiers also had specific cases, typically of alleged crimes against their own nationals, which they particularly wished to prosecute, as the Americans did in Ahrweiler in June 1945. The Soviets had an enormous catalogue of atrocities, committed in their territory since 1941, which they were determined to investigate. The French similarly wished to pursue specific crimes committed by the Nazis in occupied France, or against French nationals in Germany. As well as trying those accused of murdering captured airmen in Germany, the Americans were committed to pursuing the perpetrators of the massacre of their soldiers at Malmédy in the Ardennes in December 1945, even though as a war crime it paled into insignificance alongside many such events on the Eastern Front. Although the majority of British POWs had been relatively well treated in German captivity, a number, including fifty RAF officers from Sagan in March 1944, had been executed after escaping from various prison camps, and the British intended to punish the perpetrators of these crimes. The British similarly wished to pursue the case of three female intelligence agents who had been caught by the Germans and executed at Ravensbrück on Himmler's specific order.[6]

The agenda of the different Allies was also shaped by their experience in Germany itself. In several cases, the Allies felt duty bound to prosecute the staff of concentration camps they had liberated. Thus for the British it became very important to stage rapidly a trial of the captured male and female staff of Bergen-Belsen. Outside Germany, six officials of the Maidanek concentration camp had already been arraigned before a Polish Special Criminal Court in Lublin. After a trial lasting five days all were found guilty and sentenced to death. They were hanged on 3 December 1944.[7]

Although the mythology of the 'national redoubt' turned out largely to be just that, there was one respect in which it was borne out. As Germany was invaded, many compromised Nazis fled to the mountainous areas of the Tyrol and of south Bavaria. Those who did not kill themselves feared Soviet captivity more than any other, and a large number therefore ended up in areas under American control. Here, in the weeks after the surrender, as American patrols searched the countryside, many were captured, including Goering, Kaltenbrunner, Ley, Frick, Rosenberg, Keitel, Frank, and Julius Streicher. At a lower level the Americans were zealous in tracking down guards from the large camps they had liberated. At Mauthausen they were given active help by surviving prisoners, including an American OSS agent, Jack Taylor, in tracking down the fugitive commander of the camp, Franz Ziereis. He was captured near the camp after a brief exchange of fire by CIC agents on the night of 23/24 May, and died shortly afterwards in hospital. The Americans were told that Ziereis' deputy Georg Bachmayer had committed suicide after killing his family; a CIC team led by Gerard Oppenheimer exhumed his body some twelve kilometres from Mauthausen and verified its identity. Another seventeen key suspects who had worked there, or in its sub-camps, were quickly arrested.[8] By March 1946 the number had grown to sixty-one, all men, who went on trial at Dachau before an American Military Court in March 1946.[9] Those who were arrested and put on trial might consider themselves relatively lucky. As former prisoner Jack Taylor was driven away from Mauthausen on the day of liberation, he saw German Kapos from the camp being murdered 'with fenceposts' by released prisoners.[10]

The British similarly captured a number of senior Nazis and major criminals who had fled to northern Germany. It was British police who arrested Himmler, disguised and in civilian clothes, in Meinstedt on 21 May 1945. Taken to a nearby internment camp, Himmler committed suicide when he realised that he had been correctly identified. When they took members of the Dönitz government into captivity on 23 May 1945, as well as Dönitz himself, the British captured Albert Speer and Alfred Jodl. Later they captured Artur Seyss-Inquart, previously the Nazi leader in Austria, and latterly Reich Commissar in the occupied Netherlands. On 14 June they arrested Hitler's Foreign Minister Joachim von Ribbentrop, hiding in Hamburg. Speer was transferred to the high-security prison at Monsdorf in Luxembourg. He later wrote, 'the whole hierarchy was there: ministers, Field Marshals, Reichsleiters, state secretaries, and generals.'[11] Only in July 1945 was the British War Crimes Executive formed to conduct further investigations in Germany. One of its first concerns was the Krupp industrial empire, run from Essen, now in the British Zone. Airey Neave, a young officer, arrived in Essen in August 1945 with instructions from Henry Phillimore, the head of the Executive, to investigate 'anything that linked the firm with the Nazi Party; the production of any weapon which would be a breach of international law; and the scope and treatment of slave labour employed by the firm'.[12] Neave's investigation immediately threw up the kinds of problem which have bedevilled all attempts to bring Nazis to trial. The proprietor of the company was an old man, obviously incapable either of running a company or of standing trial. It proved incredibly difficult over the next few years to establish who was responsible, in particular for the huge and appallingly cruel exploitation of slave labourers by the Krupp concern. Many relevant documents had been burnt or hidden, and the British investigators often faced a wall of silence. They nonetheless dismissed no fewer than 600 executives in the first week of their investigation.[13]

It is difficult to know exactly how many suspected war criminals were arrested in the initial post-war period; the Allies did not compile an accurate list. Even Lucius Clay reported that he had 'no reliable information' about the Soviet Zone. He nonetheless estimated in July 1945 that some 75,000 Germans had been detained 'on basis of black list and arrest directives'.[14] We have precise figures for the French Zone, where by August 1945, 10,815 Germans had been arrested and held in internment camps. The sum of 410,000 Reichsmarks had been sequestered by the Military Government.[15] The French have often been criticised for letting ex-Nazis escape through their zones in Germany and in Austria, from there to Italy, and on to other destinations, notably Syria and Argentina. In fact they were energetic in the first few months of their occupation in applying the principles of denazification announced at Potsdam. In October 1945, de Gaulle visited the French Zone in Germany, now administered from the undamaged spa town of Baden-Baden, and spurred on its commander, General Laffon, to 'a rigorous purge'. Laffon himself demanded that his regional commanders act with 'energy and swiftness'.[16] In some areas, like public health, the French took sanctions against more than half the working officials in the first few months of their occupation in Germany.[17] We should not underestimate the impact of these sanctions. As well as being dismissed from employment at a time of great economic insecurity, those 'denazified' might be turned out of their homes, fined, and deprived indefinitely of civic entitlements like the right to vote or to play an active part in politics.

In contrast, relatively few senior Nazis fell into Soviet hands. After the surrender they held Grand Admiral Erich Raeder, former commander of the German Navy, and Hans Fritzsche, one of Goebbels' deputies at the Propaganda Ministry. They had, though, captured huge numbers of soldiers and officers of all ranks and were not prepared to let these go as quickly as the western Allies. By early 1946 the NKVD was running eleven special camps in the Soviet Zone for ex-Nazis, and for 'sectarian' enemies on the German left. Conditions in these facilities, which included the former concentration camps at Buchenwald and Sachsenhausen, were appalling, and as many as 42,000 Germans died in them 'as a result of sickness' before 1950.[18] Hundreds of thousands of German POWs, including many ex-Nazis, were taken back to the Soviet Union, where they faced lengthy interrogations about their involvement in war crimes. Siegfried Knappe had been a staff officer in Schörner's Army Group at the end of the war. After his capture by the Soviets, Knappe was flown to a camp for officers at Krasnogorsk, near Moscow, where he was kept for the next two years, before being moved on to another camp. At Krasnogorsk the Soviets held many senior German officers, including Schörner, who had been delivered to them by the Americans, and a number of German civilians, including aristocrats and intellectuals. All were put under sustained psychological pressure to confess to participation in war crimes, and to incriminate others.[19] Over the next few years, as many as 10,000 Germans were executed for alleged 'war crimes' in the Soviet Union.

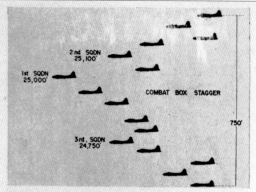

Side view of combat box. *The symmetrical formation of many heavy bombers is not arranged for aesthetic reasons. There is an extremely practical purpose...*

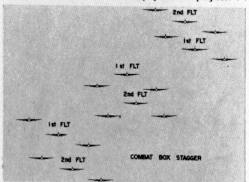

Tail view. *That purpose is to utilize the great defensive power of our Forts and Libs by providing maximum mutual protective fire of the bomber's guns...*

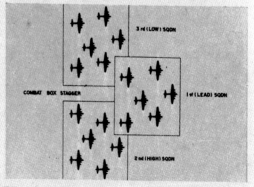

Plan view. *The positions indicated in these diagrams represent the ideal battle formation. In combat it is seldom possible to attain this degree of perfection.*

Above: 1 The Americans hoped that carefully grouped 'combat boxes' of their B-17 bombers would be able to defend themselves in daylight from fighter attack.

Right: 4 From subsequent photos the Americans claimed that two-thirds of the plant at Regensburg was destroyed.

2 In practice it was very difficult for the American bombers to maintain the prescribed formations; the vapour trails left them visible for miles.

3 The daylight attack on the Messerschmitt plant at Regensburg on 17 August 1943 was the first American attempt to hit a target deep inside Germany.

5 Speer, Ley, and Goebbels, three of Hitler's closest supporters.

6 Bulgarian soldiers on anti–partisan duties; in 1944 eastern European countries which supported Hitler melted away under the Soviet onslaught.

7 German propaganda made much of their technological strength, but in practice the Wehrmacht relied increasingly on horses.

Above left: 8 During the war, the Mercedes–Benz 'star' was closely associated with German militarism, as in this advertisement.

Above right: 9 General Guderian presents a medal to a Dutch armaments worker.

Above: 10 Smiling young Germans help with the distribution of bread after a British raid.

Left: 11 The morning after a British raid on a German city.

Left: 12 Despite the British and American bombing, German armaments production continued to rise until the end of 1944.

Below: 13 Armaments Minister Speer and senior German industrialists enjoy a sociable evening.

Below left: 14 A propaganda image shows a fashionable lady at a German newspaper kiosk, surrounded by newspapers for foreign workers.

Below right: 15 The Allied invasion of Italy in 1943 did not bring an early end to the war.

16 Hitler, before the bomb plot of 20 July 1944, which left him physically weakened.

17 Many photographs like this, showing Nazi atrocities in the Soviet Union, were published in Britain and America during the war.

18 Seventeen-year-old German boys doing labour service in 1943; these were the future officers of the '1945 class'. How many of these boys survived the war?

19 In 1943, the Germans began a long retreat through Ukraine.

20 German grenadiers on the Eastern Front, with Tiger tanks.

21 German rocket artillery on the Eastern Front. Although these multi-barrelled weapons were advanced, the smoke trails they left made their location all too plain.

Opposite below: 24 This aerial view shows clearly the artificial breakwaters used to create a harbour around the D-Day landing beaches at Arromanches.

21 ARMY GROUP

PERSONAL MESSAGE
FROM THE C-in-C

To be read out to all Troops

1. The time has come to deal the enemy a terrific blow in Western Europe.

The blow will be struck by the combined sea, land, and air forces of the Allies—together constituting one great Allied team, under the supreme command of General Eisenhower.

2. On the eve of this great adventure I send my best wishes to every soldier in the Allied team.

To us is given the honour of striking a blow for freedom which will live in history; and in the better days that lie ahead men will speak with pride of our doings. We have a great and a righteous cause.

Let us pray that "The Lord Mighty in Battle" will go forth with our armies, and that His special providence will aid us in the struggle.

3. I want every soldier to know that I have complete confidence in the successful outcome of the operations that we are now about to begin.

With stout hearts, and with enthusiasm for the contest, let us go forward to victory.

4. And, as we enter the battle, let us recall the words of a famous soldier spoken many years ago :—

"He either fears his fate too much,
Or his deserts are small,
Who dare not put it to the touch,
To win or lose it all."

5. Good luck to each one of you. And good hunting on the mainland of Europe.

B. L. Montgomery
General
C.-in-C 21 Army Group.

1944.

Above left: 22 Winter on the Eastern Front.

Above right: 23 This message from Montgomery to his troops before D-Day is typical of his personal approach.

Left: 25 The town of Villers–Bocage in Normandy, on 25 May 1944.

Below: 26 Villers-Bocage on 18 July 1944 after Allied bombing.

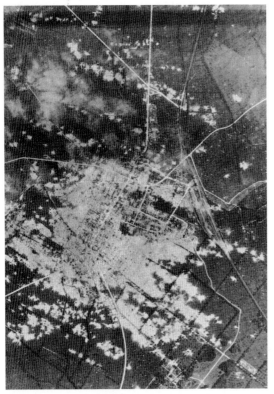

Opposite above: 27 The entrance to the concentration camp at Natzweiler in Alsace, abandoned by the SS in November 1944. The camp is preserved today as a memorial site. The German for concentration camp was *Konzentrationslager*, this was abbreviated to '*KZ*'.

Opposite middle: 28 After the failed attack on Arnhem in September 1944, it was not until April 1945 that British troops liberated the town.

Opposite below: 29 A British tank equipped with chains for mine clearing moves through burning streets in Arnhem, April 1945.

Opposite above: 30 German prisoners are marched past a British tank in April 1945.

Opposite middle: 31 Tracked amphibious vehicles in the mist near the Rhine; note the groups of German prisoners.

Opposite below: 32 British troops relaxing during the final stages of the campaign in Germany.

Right: 33 A propaganda leaflet announces that the Allies are coming to restore law and to punish war criminals; where, it asks, are the German 'wonder weapons' now?

Below: 34 In March 1945, as his troops advanced into Germany, Montgomery issued this order with advice: 'Be just; be firm; be correct; give orders and don't argue.'

mit ihren Stahlkolossen, Jabos und Flammenwerfern.

SIE KOMMEN

denn jetzt kann nichts und niemand sie mehr halten.

SIE · KOMMEN

denn jetzt liegen auch Nord- und Mitteldeutschland offen vor den Anglo-Amerikanern und Russen. Der grösste Betrug der Weltgeschichte ist bald vorbei:

WO BLIEBEN die deutschen Wunderwaffen?
WO BLIEBEN die operativen Reserven?
WO BLIEBEN die Parteigenossen und „Hoheitsträger", die immer zum fanatischen Widerstand aufgerufen haben? Die alliierten Armeen nehmen Deutschland im Sturm.

SIE KOMMEN

um den deutschen Militarismus endgültig auszurotten.

SIE KOMMEN

um die Kriegsverbrecher ihrer Strafe zuzuführen.

SIE KOMMEN

---

disregard by their leaders of any form of decency or of honourable dealings: the same Germans whose brothers, sons and fathers were carrying out a system of mass murder and torture of defenceless civilians. You will have to remember that these same Germans are planning to make fools of you again and to escape the loathing which their actions deserve.

5. Our consciences are clear; "non-fraternisation" to us implies no revenge; we have no theory of master races. But a guilty nation must not only be convicted: it must realise its guilt. Only then can the first steps be taken to re-educate it, and bring it back into the society of decent humanity.

6. German discipline, though not our sort, is thorough. The people will judge you with no amateur eyes: and any slackness will be the cue for the resistance movements to intensify their efforts.

7. Be just; be firm; be correct; give orders, and don't argue. Last time we won the war and let the peace slip out of our hands. This time we must not ease off—we must win both the war and the peace.

B. L. Montgomery
Field-Marshal,
C-in-C 21 Army Group.

March, 1945.

PSS 1810 3.45

LETTER

BY THE

COMMANDER-IN-CHIEF

ON

NON-FRATERNISATION

TO ALL OFFICERS AND MEN OF 21 ARMY GROUP

1. Twenty-seven years ago the Allies occupied Germany: but Germany has been at war ever since. Our Army took no revenge in 1918; it was more than considerate, and before a few weeks had passed many soldiers were adopted into German households. The enemy worked hard at being amiable. They believed that the occupation was due to treachery, and that their army had never been beaten. They remained unrepentant and attached to their worship of brute force.

2. The fight was continued by the German General Staff, who concealed war criminals and equipments, built up armaments, and trained a new striking force. To evade the Armistice terms they had to find sympathisers, and "organising sympathy" became a German industry. So accommodating were the occupying forces that the Germans came to believe we would never fight them again in any cause. From that moment to this their continued aggression has brought misery or death to millions, always under the familiar smoke screen of appeals for fair play and friendship, followed by the barrage of stark, brutal threats.

This time the Nazis have added to the experience of the last occupation; they have learned from the resistance movements of France, Belgium, Holland, and Norway. These are the type of instructions they are likely to give to their underground workers:

"Give the impression of submitting. Say you never liked the Nazis; they were the people responsible for the war. Argue that Germany has never had a fair chance. Get the soldiers arguing; they are not trained for it, and you are.

"Use old folks, girls, and children, and 'play up' every case of devastation or poverty. Ask the troops to your homes; sabotage or steal equipment, petrol or rations. Get troops to sell these things, if you can. Spread stories about Americans and Russians in the British zone, and about the British to other Allies."

3. Because of these facts, I want every soldier to be clear about "non-fraternisation". Peace does not exist merely because of a surrender. The Nazi influence penetrates everywhere, even into children's schools and churches. Our occupation of Germany is an act of war of which the first object is to destroy the Nazi system. There are Allied organisations whose work it is to single out, separate and destroy the dangerous elements in German life. It is too soon for you to distinguish between "good" and "bad" Germans: you have a positive part to play in winning the peace by a definite code of behaviour. In streets, houses, cafes, cinemas, etc., you must keep clear of Germans, man, woman and child, unless you meet them in the course of duty. You must not walk out with them, or shake hands, or visit their homes, or make them gifts, or take gifts from them. You must not play games with them or share any social event with them. In short, you must not fraternise with Germans at all.

4. To refrain from fraternisation is not easy. It requires self-discipline. But in Germany you will have to remember that laughing and eating and dancing with Germans would be bitterly resented by your own families, by millions of people who have suffered under the Gestapo and under the Luftwaffe's bombs, and by every Ally that Britain possesses. You will have to remember that these are the same Germans who, a short while ago, were drunk with victory, who were boasting what they as the Master Race would do to you as their slaves, who were applauding the utter

---

TO ALL MEMBERS OF 21 ARMY GROUP

1. I have been considering the present orders about non-fraternisation.

We cannot let-up on this policy.

2. But these orders need no longer apply to small children.

3. Members of the British Forces in Germany will be allowed to speak to, and play with, little children. This will come into effect at once. In all other respects the orders issued by me in the card dated March 1945 will remain in force.

B. L. Montgomery

Field Marshal,
C-in-C, 21 Army Group.

12 June 1945

Above: 35 In the order, Montgomery urged his men not to repeat the mistakes of 1919.

Left: 36 Montgomery allowed his men to speak to, and to play with little German children only after the first six weeks of occupation.

TO ALL MEMBERS OF THE BRITISH FORCES IN GERMANY

Great progress has been made in the de-Nazification of the British Zone and in removing Nazis from all responsibility in German life. Further, the Germans have shown themselves willing to obey my orders and to co-operate in the reconstruction of their country on non-Nazi lines.

I have already modified my orders about non-fraternisation and allowed you to speak and play with little children. I now consider it desirable and timely to permit a further modification of these rules. You may now engage in conversation with adult Germans in the streets and in public places.

You will not for the present enter the homes and houses of the Germans nor permit them to enter any of the premises you are using except for duty or work.

I know the non-fraternisation policy has been a strain upon many of you who have to live and work in close contact with Germans, and I appreciate the loyal way in which you have honoured it.

B. L. Montgomery

Field Marshal,
Commander-in-Chief,
British Zone.

14 July 45.

Above: 37 By July 1945 British troops were allowed to speak to German adults in 'streets and public places'.

Right: 38 Eisenhower's final message to the troops of the Allied Expeditionary Force in July 1945.

SUPREME HEADQUARTERS
ALLIED EXPEDITIONARY FORCE

TO ALL MEMBERS OF THE ALLIED EXPEDITIONARY FORCE:

The task which we set ourselves is finished, and the time has come for me to relinquish Combined Command.

In the name of the United States and the British Commonwealth, from whom my authority is derived, I should like to convey to you the gratitude and admiration of our two nations for the manner in which you have responded to every demand that has been made upon you. At times, conditions have been hard and the tasks to be performed arduous. No praise is too high for the manner in which you have surmounted every obstacle.

I should like, also, to add my own personal word of thanks to each one of you for the part you have played, and the contribution you have made to our joint victory.

Now that you are about to pass to other spheres of activity, I say Good-bye to you and wish you Good Luck and God-Speed.

Dwight Eisenhower

JOURNAL OFFICIEL DU CONSEIL DE CONTRÔLE EN ALLEMAGNE	ВЕДОМОСТИ КОНТРОЛЬНОГО СОВЕТА В ГЕРМАНИИ
NUMÉRO 1	НОМЕР 1
29 octobre 1945	29 октября 1945 года
BERLIN SECRÉTARIAT ALLIÉ 32, Elssholzstraße	Берлин Союзный Секретариат Эльсхольцштрассе 32
OFFICIAL GAZETTE OF THE CONTROL COUNCIL FOR GERMANY	AMTSBLATT DES KONTROLLRATS IN DEUTSCHLAND
NUMBER 1	NUMMER 1
29 October 1945	29. Oktober 1945
BERLIN ALLIED SECRETARIAT 32, Elssholzstraße	Herausgegeben vom Alliierten Sekretariat Berlin, Elssholzstraße 32 Einzelpreis RM 2,—

Left: 39 The first issue of the *Official Gazette of the Control Council for Germany,* published in four languages.

Below: 40 Field-Marshal Montgomery inspects troops of the Gloucestershire Regiment in occupied Germany, 1946.

Above: 41 Montgomery in 1946, now Military Governor of the British Zone of Germany.

Right: 42 Preface to an emergency edition of a textbook in the British Zone of Germany.

PREFACE

1. This textbook is one of a series which is being published by order of the British Commander-in-Chief for emergency use in German schools in the area occupied by his Forces.

2. It has been selected after a thorough examination of many of the books in use in Germany before the Nazi accession to power. It is a textbook of German authorship and has been reprinted without textual alteration.

3. Its issue does not imply that it is entirely suitable from an educational point of view or otherwise. It is merely the best book which could be found in the circumstances and must serve until Germany produces better textbooks of its own.

VORWORT

1. Das vorliegende Buch gehört zu einer Reihe von Schulbüchern, die auf Anordnung des britischen Oberbefehlshabers veröffentlicht werden. Es dient zum Behelfsgebrauch in den deutschen Schulen, die sich in dem von seinen Truppen besetzten Gebiet befinden.

2. Dieses Buch wurde gewählt nach gründlicher Untersuchung vieler Schulbücher, die in Deutschland vor der Machtübernahme durch den Nationalsozialismus in Gebrauch waren. Es ist von Deutschen geschrieben und wird hiermit ohne jedwede Textänderung neugedruckt.

3. Die Tatsache des Neudrucks bedeutet nicht, daß dieses Buch vom erzieherischen oder anderen Gesichtspunkt aus völlig einwandfrei ist. Aber unter den gegebenen Umständen ist es das geeignetste Buch, und es ist zu benutzen, bis Deutschland selbst bessere Schulbücher hervorbringt.

Left: 43 At Nuremberg, the
Soviets accused the Germans of
the Katyn Forest massacre; during
the war German propaganda
accused the Soviet secret police,
using forensic evidence gathered
from the mass graves in this
exhumation in 1943.

Below: 44 Goering in the dock
before the International Military
Tribunal at Nuremberg.

THE INTERNATIONAL MILITARY TRIBUNAL

As we have seen, a number of Allied leaders during the war had expressed their view that senior Nazis should be summarily executed if they were captured. Churchill and others in Britain had sought to establish the legality of such executions by reference to the archaic notion of the outlaw; others had clutched at similar notions of the 'drumhead court-martial', and searched for historical precedents.[20] A number of factors crystallised the decision-making of the Allies in regard to the treatment of major war criminals in early 1945, and pushed them, more or less reluctantly, towards acceptance of legal process.

Firstly, it was one thing to talk of summary executions, and another to contemplate their actuality. As the Allied leaders anticipated the final defeat of Germany in 1945, they had also to contemplate the effect summary executions of Nazi leaders would have on public opinion worldwide. Whatever their personal feelings, they recognised that they had to be seen to observe a higher standard of morality. Secondly, Hitler's suicide removed the enormous potential difficulty of trying him. The Allies could, with far greater equanimity, contemplate the trial of any of his subordinates. Thirdly, Roosevelt's successor, Harry Truman, was an ex-judge, and energetically pursued Roosevelt's earlier commitment to trying the leaders of the Nazi regime. Truman instructed Roosevelt's personal advisor on war crimes, Judge Samuel Rosenman, to press the issue with the British, the Soviets, and the French at the founding conference of the United Nations in San Francisco in early May 1945. According to Truman, 'Eden stated that the British War Cabinet had recently changed its position, because many of the top Nazis had already committed suicide or had been killed and no doubt many more would follow before any trial could be held'.[21] Rosenman secured broad agreement in San Francisco to the trial of major war criminals before an international tribunal.

Truman had on 2 May appointed Associate Judge Robert Jackson, a former Attorney-General, as his Chief Counsel for the preparation of the trial, and from this time forward it was driven by the Americans. Jackson submitted a progress report on 6 June 1945 which contained in essence the procedures later adopted at Nuremberg. Jackson declared: 'Fair hearings for the accused are, of course, required to make sure that we punish only the right men for the right reasons.' He disposed of the idea that a head of state, or his close associates, were immune from legal liability (ironically, given earlier British resistance to the idea of a trial) by explicit reference to English constitutional precedent, 'the principle of responsible government declared some three centuries ago to King James by Lord Chief Justice Coke'. He asked:

> Whom shall we accuse and put to their defense? We will accuse a large number of individuals who were in authority in the government, in the military establishment, including the General Staff, and in the financial, industrial and economic life of Germany who by all civilized standards are provable to be common criminals.

Jackson also made clear that these proceedings would be concerned with more than mere retribution, and would serve a far larger historical task:

> Unless we write the record of this movement with clarity and precision, we cannot blame the future if it in days of peace it finds incredible the accusatory generalities uttered during the war. We must establish incredible facts by credible evidence...
>
> Those acts which offended the conscience of our peoples were criminal by standards generally accepted in all civilized countries, and I believe we may proceed to punish those responsible in full accord with both our own traditions of fairness and with standards of just conduct which have been internationally accepted.
>
> I think also that through these trials we should be able to establish that a process of retribution by law awaits those who in the future similarly attack civilization. [22]

This was the blueprint for Nuremberg.

Delegations from the Soviet Union, Britain, France, and the USA met in London in June to discuss the plans for an international military tribunal further, and at Potsdam on 2 August 1945, a formal declaration was issued: 'War criminals and those who have participated in planning or carrying out Nazi enterprises involving or resulting in atrocities or war crimes shall be arrested and brought to judgment.' [23] Previous Allied declarations had referred to arrest and punishment, but not to a trial. Significantly, the new British Premier, Clement Attlee, who participated in the later stages of the Potsdam conference, shared Truman's commitment to a trial. On 8 August the London Agreement was signed, providing for an International Military Tribunal and a Charter 'laying down the procedures and character of the trial'.[24] The London Agreement also resolved another problem. It specified for the first time the charges that would be brought against the accused, of 'crimes against peace, war crimes, and crimes against humanity'.

By creating these new charges, the International Military Tribunal (IMT) sought to link the accused to the wider patterns of Nazi aggression and barbarism. To establish this connection the Americans had adopted the proposal originally made by Murray Bernays, a lawyer working with Robert Jackson, to accuse the defendants of conspiracy, or a 'common plan'. This has attracted great criticism from other lawyers, then and since, but in 1945 it appeared attractive for several reasons. By accusing the defendants of complicity in Hitler's plans, it removed the defence that they were only following orders. It also allowed the prosecution to argue that crimes committed against Germans before 1939 were linked to crimes committed against other countries and their nationals during the war. Although individual defendants at Nuremberg were accused of specific crimes, they also stood there as representatives of a system and a political movement, which had persecuted its domestic opponents, waged aggressive war in a conscious effort to dominate the world, and murdered millions of Jews in pursuit of a doctrine of racial supremacy.

Murray Bernays had also in September 1944 put forward the linked idea of trying what came to be known as 'criminal organisations'. If, he argued, organisations like the SS and the Gestapo could be declared as criminal in intent, and part of the larger Nazi conspiracy, mere membership of one of these organisations would establish individual guilt and responsibility. In this way, subsequent proceedings against all members of the 'criminal organisations' could be greatly expedited. After the adoption of this idea, seven groups were isolated and charged: the SS, SA, SD, Gestapo, the Reich Cabinet, the General Staff, and the Leadership Corps of the Nazi Party.[25] Both the 'common plan' and the notion of 'criminal organisations' were subsequently to prove highly contentious, and to cause considerable confusion at the IMT, not least because the idea of conspiracy, although familiar to British and American lawyers, was alien to French and Soviet prosecutors, and to the German defence lawyers at Nuremberg. It was impossible to prove even that some of the 'criminal organisations' existed, let alone that all of their members had known about and been complicit in their criminality.

At Potsdam, the Allied leaders had not reached a consensus on the specific individuals to be brought before a tribunal, but later in August 1945 the British and Americans agreed on a list of twenty-four named individuals. After more discussion, on 29 August a list of those to stand trial before the IMT was formally announced.[26] In some ways the twenty-two names on this list represented a curious selection, but they were chosen both as individuals and as representatives of the Nazi system. There was universal agreement that Hermann Goering, involved in all major policy decisions of the Nazi regime, should stand trial. Keitel, Jodl, Dönitz, and Raeder stood as representatives of the armed forces; Hess and Bormann (who was tried *in absentia*) represented the Nazi Party itself, Alfred Rosenberg its philosophy. Wilhelm Frick, Hitler's Interior Minister, and Robert Ley, leader of the German Labour Front, were amongst the accused. Baldur von Schirach was accused effectively of corrupting the youth of Germany as well as being *Gauleiter* of Vienna. Speer, Fritz Sauckel, former Plenipotentiary for Labour Supply, and Hans Frank, the former Governor of occupied Poland, were accused effectively of the exploitation of occupied countries' human and natural resources; Seyss-Inquart was held responsible for the *Anschluss* with Austria in 1938 (construed as an act of aggressive war), and for the brutal occupation of Holland after 1940. Hjalmar Schacht, President of the *Reichsbank* between 1933 and 1939, and his successor Walther Funk, were alleged to have financed the Nazi regime's preparation for aggressive war. As Himmler had killed himself, and Heydrich, that earlier architect of the Holocaust, had been assassinated in 1942, Ernst Kaltenbrunner was chosen as the chief representative of the SS, the SD and the Gestapo. Similarly, as Goebbels was no longer alive, Hans Fritzsche, who had been captured by the Soviets in Berlin, stood as a representative of the Nazi propaganda machine. The elderly diplomat Konstantin von Neurath, who had been Hitler's Foreign Minister until 1939, and his successor in that post, Joachim von Ribbentrop, were accused of conspiring to wage aggressive war. Franz von Papen, the conservative Catholic politician who had helped engineer Hitler's appointment as Chancellor in January 1933, was effectively tried for this.

Perhaps the oddest choice was Julius Streicher, widely known as editor of the anti-Semitic magazine *Der Stürmer*, and earlier *Gauleiter* of

Franconia. Streicher, although active as a propagandist in the 1930s, had been forced out of public life in Germany since 1940, and played no direct part in the so-called 'Final Solution'. He stood accused, behind the formal charges, of poisoning the mind of a nation. Considerable efforts were made to include a leading German industrialist among the accused before the IMT. The largest German armaments company, Krupp, had not only profited greatly from providing weapons for the Nazi war machine, but had also exploited slave labour on a huge scale. The nominal head of the company, the elderly Gustav Krupp von Bohlen und Halbach, was on the list of defendants published on 29 August, but was subsequently judged incapable of standing trial. The Americans, who had particularly wished to include a representative industrialist, and the British, who had been learning at first hand of the most barbaric examples of Krupp's treatment of slave labourers in Essen, were most disappointed by this.

One aspect of the earlier wish summarily to execute the Nazi leaders was still apparent as preparations for the IMT evolved: it was widely assumed that those indicted were guilty. The documents of the time express this, and make it clear that a presumption of innocence until proven guilty was not to be taken for granted. One Control Council Directive at this time specifically distinguished between 'War Criminals' and 'Suspected War Criminals'.[27]

The twenty-one 'major war criminals' held for trial before the IMT represented only the tip of an iceberg. The Allies were also bound by the terms of the London Agreement to deliver to one another, and to other countries, alleged criminals wanted outside their own areas of jurisdiction. One of the first acts of the Control Council was to prevent any German national from leaving Germany without express permission,[28] and after this its Law No. 10 provided for a much wider application of the charges presented by the IMT, instructing the separate commanders of each zone in Germany to arrest and deliver for trial anyone suspected of crimes against peace, war crimes, or crimes against humanity. It authorised military governments in each zone to establish military tribunals to conduct their own trials against the accused. In 1945, under these provisions, and under the Military Law of the separate occupiers, many thousands were arrested in all four zones of Germany and held while evidence was gathered against them. A great number were delivered for trial to another zone, or to France, Poland, Czechoslovakia, and other countries occupied by Germany between 1939 and 1945. The punishments prescribed by

Law No. 10 should dispel any doubts about the severity of Allied denazi-fication. They consisted of 'one or more' of the following:

a) Death
b) Imprisonment for life or for a term of years, with or without hard labour.
c) Fine, and imprisonment with or without hard labour, in lieu thereof.
d) Forfeiture of property.
e) Restitution of property wrongfully acquired.
f) Deprivation of some or all civil rights.[29]

ABOLITION OF NAZI SYMBOLS AND INSIGNIA

As ever larger numbers of suspected Nazi criminals languished in various prisons and detention centres, the Allies moved to consolidate the ongo-ing destruction of visible Nazi symbols in the public sphere. The Control Council actually moved after the separate military governments had already instituted this in their own zones. An American Army Directive in July 1945 had already called for 'the renaming of streets, parks, build-ings, and institutions', as well as 'the removal of all monuments, statues, emblems, and symbols of Nazism and German militarism from pub-lic places'.[30] The Control Council acted first to prevent any revival of German militarism, and in passing to consolidate earlier prohibitions on Nazi symbols. In November 1945 it formally disbanded all German armed forces, and formalised the abolition of Nazi symbols in Law No. 8, 'Elimination and Prohibition of Military Training', Article IV:

> The use by any German of military or Nazi uniforms, insignia, flags, banners or tokens or of military or civil decorations, and the employment of distinc-tive Nazi or military salutes or greetings are prohibited; all other symbolic means of expressing the Nazi spirit are prohibited.[31]

It was not until May 1946 that the Control Council extended these ideas to other areas of civilian life. Directive No. 30, 'Liquidation of German Military and Nazi Memorials and Museums', declared:

> the planning, design, erection, installation, posting or other display of any monument, memorial, poster, statue, edifice, street or highway name marker,

emblem, tablet, or insignia which tends to preserve and keep alive the German military tradition, to revive militarism or to commemorate the Nazi Party, or which is of such a nature as to glorify incidents of war, and the functioning of military museums and exhibitions, and the erection, installation or posting or other display on a building or other structure of any of the same, will be prohibited and declared illegal; also the reopening of military museums and exhibitions.[32]

In fact, well before this time, much of the most obvious Nazi symbolism had long gone from public life in Germany. Allied soldiers took particular delight everywhere in smashing Nazi monuments and statues, the larger the better. Many Germans were angered by the catastrophe which engulfed them and similarly destroyed portraits and busts of Nazi bigwigs which adorned offices and public buildings. Swastikas were smashed; eagles knocked down. Potentially incriminating material of any kind was hurriedly thrown away, burnt, or hidden. Nazi literature of all kinds disappeared, and the notice-boards in which Streicher's anti-Semitic magazine *Der Stürmer* had been displayed to the public were dismantled. Victor Klemperer found one in Bavaria: he wanted to break it up for firewood, but lacked an axe for the job.[33] Ursula von Kardorff, in a celebratory act, threw a handful of swastika lapel badges which had been given to her into a nearby river, something she had wanted to do for years.[34]

Streets and squares which had been named *Adolf-Hitler-Strasse* or *Hermann-Goering-Platz* quietly reverted, often to former names. Institutions which had been given the names of Nazi heroes similarly resumed their former titles, if they were not closed down. Nowhere was it politic to display evidence of previous Nazi allegiance, and for the most part this huge work of denazification was carried out, willingly and unwillingly, by the Germans themselves. A telling reminiscence comes from the earliest days of British occupation in Celle, in north Germany, and concerns a mother and her children:

Today the children and I thought about what greeting they should use now. As they didn't know, they have not been using any greeting at all. I told them they could go on saying 'Heil Hitler' because Hitler had been the *Führer* to the end. But if they felt uncomfortable about it, they could say 'good day' or 'good morning'...[35]

One wonders how long it was before the children abandoned the salute.

Even in the one area where the Control Council's prohibition was obviously not enforceable, there was an effort to comply with the spirit of the law. Millions of people, not only ex-soldiers, in Germany after May 1945 still wore German uniform, or fragments of uniform, often because they lacked other clothing. But everywhere the service garments of the *Wehrmacht*, *Luftwaffe*, or Nazi Party agencies were worn without badges of rank or other insignia.

THE PURGE OF NAZI TEXTBOOKS

Well before the start of the war in 1939, there had been discussion outside Germany of what the Nazis were doing to education in that country. The systematic perversion of traditional educational values and the intrusion of Party organisations into the school system had been charted by a number of outside observers: a succession of horrified visitors from abroad had been allowed to look at German schools and youth organisations after 1933, and their reports back in their home countries had been supplemented by the critical news brought from Germany by émigrés, many of them intellectuals and academics. In Britain, left-wing and internationalist groups like the 'Friends of Europe' published many pamphlets on education under the Nazis. During the war, books like Gregor Ziemer's *Education for Death*, published in America and Britain, had a wide readership, and the need to 'denazify' education in Germany naturally assumed a prominent position in all wartime discussions on the future of Germany. An early purge of Nazi materials and teachers was high on the agenda of the occupiers, and of the Allied Control Council.

The denazification of schools was instituted by the invasion of Germany, and emerged from wartime violence. As the Allies entered Germany, those schools which were still functioning were closed for an indeterminate time. In many cases their buildings were destroyed or damaged; their pupils and staff dispersed, often very widely. Much the same applied to German universities. All education in Germany had come to an absolute standstill by May 1945, and the first measures of denazification were undertaken in the interim period which followed before any schools or universities were reopened.

Almost everywhere these first measures were taken by Germans themselves. As the dust literally settled, and an uneasy quiet hung over the rubble in German towns and cities, surviving teachers and others set about the task of throwing out Nazi textbooks, teaching materials, and insignia. Portraits of Hitler and Goering were taken down, piles of books were removed from storerooms and libraries, and incriminating documents were quietly disposed of or hidden away. Different motives were involved: for teachers who had endured Nazi tyranny and its crude anti-intellectualism, this was a time of relief. For the many who had perpetuated Nazism in schools and universities with varying degrees of enthusiasm, this was a time for change, and it was expedient to help get rid of the debris of the past. As military occupation took shape, the Allies made their intentions plain: all Nazi material was to be removed from schools, and there was to be a purge of staff before any reopened. The Control Council included education in its total prohibition of Nazi material in the public sphere. Its Order No. 4 called for the 'confiscation of literature and material of a Nazi and Militarist nature', including 'everything intended for children of all ages'.[36]

The purge of Nazi teaching materials was straightforward and successful in one sense. Almost all of the crudest Nazi propaganda, which typically came in the form of small pamphlets and supplementary materials issued by the *NS-Lehrerbund*, disappeared quickly, and the Allies rarely had to deal with schools which carried on using them, or with individual teachers who tried to infiltrate them back into the classroom. Much more problematic was the problem of what to do with textbooks and readers which contained some Nazi ideas worked in more or less crudely as a sub-text. The notion of mathematics problems which invited calculations on how best to transport bombs to Warsaw or how to save money by not feeding or caring for the mentally ill have gained wide currency, and by 1945 there was hardly an area of the school curriculum which had not been infused with Nazi race theory, with the crudest German nationalism, and with militarist ideas.

More than any other subject, the teaching of history had been corrupted. The whole educational system in Germany had before 1933 been strongly gendered, with different provision for boys and girls, but under the Nazis this had been greatly reinforced: boys had been subject to pre-military training, and girls to preparation for motherhood. The occupiers found, when their education teams got to work in Germany, that almost all of the books and teaching materials used in schools were in some way tainted. An American evaluation carried out from 1945 to 1948 found that no textbooks from the Nazi period were acceptable.[37] If they proscribed them all, a vacuum was left which could not be quickly filled, particularly given the chaotic state of the German economy. It would be years before the millions of new textbooks needed could be written, published, and distributed.

Nonetheless, all the Allies made a concerted effort, beginning a campaign which lasted years. Through the summer of 1945 desperate efforts were made to provide some substitute textbooks for schools which could reopen in September at the start of the new academic year. This was an area in which the French were particularly active. They were able to bring in a number of textbooks produced in Switzerland, and made great play of their achievement in getting many schools up and running again in September 1945. The British took another route, reprinting in austere emergency editions a number of German textbooks from the Weimar period. These carried a stern warning as a frontispiece, in German and in English, which in its tone and content speaks volumes about relationships between occupiers and occupied in post-war Germany:

1. This textbook is one of a series which is being published by order of the British Commander-in-Chief for emergency use in German schools in the area occupied by his forces.

2. It has been selected after a thorough examination of many of the books in use in Germany before the Nazi accession to power. It is a textbook of German authorship and has been reprinted without textual alteration.

3. Its issue does not imply that it is entirely suitable from an educational point of view or otherwise. It is merely the best book which could be found in the circumstances and must serve until Germany produces better textbooks of its own.[38]

In southern Germany, the Americans had to improvise. We are accustomed now to imagine the western parts of Germany as far more prosperous than the east, and therefore to associate the American Zone with images of prosperity from the 1950s, but material conditions there between 1945 and 1948 were as harsh as anywhere in Germany, and in many respects worse. There was a great shortage of paper, and it was years before replacement textbooks in any number were produced there. The Soviet Zone was better provided for, but the situation was still desperate. It contained Leipzig, the centre of the German publishing industry, and the Soviets quickly allocated large stocks of paper for educational reconstruction. They were also quickest to replace one set of ideologically oriented textbooks with another. In the educational, as in the cultural field, they set a pace which surprised the Americans and the British, and left them struggling to catch up. Ironically, the émigré musician André Asriel had been preparing a new communist songbook in Britain during the war, and by 1947, hundreds of thousands of copies of this had been produced for the 'Free German Youth' movement in the Soviet Zone.

The purge of Nazi teaching staff was similarly complicated. There was a high proportion of Nazi Party members amongst teachers, as indeed in other professions, and if this was rigorously used a criterion for exclusion, schools would have been left desperately understaffed. Many teachers were in any case missing, killed, injured, or in captivity as POWs. The Allies could not possibly deploy enough investigators in a few weeks to comb through all of Germany's schools and universities to establish who was fit to continue working and who should be dismissed. They had to rely to a great extent on the cooperation of teachers and academics, and it is no surprise that in their haste to get schools reopened, they allowed many ex-Nazis to start work again.

In teaching, as in other fields, all the Allies used early Party membership as a determinant in their denazification programme. They soon became familiar with the excuse that it had been necessary to join the Nazi Party in order to secure a career in Hitler's Germany, and that therefore this was done under duress. It is clear now that there were periods when the numbers of those joining the Nazi Party went up very dramatically, as for example in 1933, and again very late in the war. Many of those joining, particularly after 1933, no doubt had opportunistic and practical reasons for doing so, and career advancement was frequently one of these. The Allies took as a rule that earlier membership indicated a greater degree of Nazi conviction, and also tried to establish what roles individuals had played in other Nazi organisations. Involvement in the SS, the SA, or in the Hitler Youth was of course, if discovered, considered very critically. Many thousands of teachers were summarily dismissed from schools and universities, at every level of the hierarchies in both.

The proportion varied throughout Germany. Norman Naimark reports that the Soviets found that in Thuringia, 90% of *Volksschule* (or primary school) teachers had been Party members; throughout the zone, the average figure was 72%.[39] 16,000 teachers were dismissed in the British Zone.[40]

In the French Zone, by October 1945, 30% of schoolteachers in the Palatinate had been dismissed; in Württemberg, an astonishing 75%.[41] These figures probably encompass the larger spectrum in Germany, and reflect also the wide discrepancies from place to place. A French report in early 1946 included an annotated table showing how the 'Potsdam Principles' had been enforced in their zone. It claimed that out of a total of 149,000 public employees, 31,185 had been 'hunted out of all public or semi-public employment.' 8,430 officials in 'public education', proportionately more than any other sector, were 'hunted out'.[42] The French also exercised other sanctions. They suspended a great number of teachers and other officials, and moved others from one post to another.

The gaps left were hastily filled, where possible with anti-Nazis who had been excluded before 1945, or by retired teachers. In the Soviet Zone a crash course in teacher training was instituted in August, and workers with limited formal qualifications were urged to join up and play their part in a great social crusade. The course lasted three weeks, and 15,000 thus trained were put to work in the schools, which reopened on 1 October.[43] None of the western Allies was prepared to curtail teacher training like this, and their measures took years to implement. For years after 1945, the teaching profession in Germany was dominated by women, old people, and often ill-qualified new recruits. A French historian, writing in 1949, described the situation in the French Zone: 'The only ones left were a minority of resisters who had refused to join the party, or some aged and incapable functionaries'.[44] Inevitably, many teachers who had supported Nazism before 1945 continued teaching, but as in other areas of public life, the overwhelming majority had to repress and deny this. The collective amnesia which became such a pronounced feature of post-war Germany was as strong, and as necessary, in education as anywhere.

The continuation of Nazi staff was particularly marked in the universities. In their denazification programme here, the Allies faced particular difficulties. It was immensely difficult to establish in detail how far each individual professor, or researcher, was compromised by their behaviour before 1945, and academics proved to be particularly astute in denying, concealing, and re-presenting what they had done in these years. There were voices calling attention to the role that German academics and intellectuals had played in supporting Nazism, and in developing its ideas, but the Allies were reluctant to accept how far this had gone. They also needed lecturers, administrators, scientists, and technicians in their individual zones, and could not afford simply to dismiss everyone they had suspicions about. This was an area were there was great mobility, and academics dismissed from one university were often able to find a teaching post at another, perhaps in a different zone, in 1945 and 1946. Since the pioneering work of Max Weinreich on academic collaboration with the Nazis, an increasing number of detailed studies have revealed the most depressing cases of individual ex-Nazis who went on to prestigious careers in both East and West German universities after 1945.[45]

Often the denazification of universities was carried out in a relatively friendly way. Allied University Control officers were typically academics themselves, and sometimes had previous personal contacts with opposite numbers in the German university system. A good example was in Kiel, where a British control officer was helpfully shown around by Friedrich Blume, the musicologist, in September 1945. Blume, who held a senior position in the university and spoke good English, evidently struck up a friendly relationship with his British visitor, and reassured him that the University was ready to reopen with a limited, but reconstructed programme in September 1945, albeit on hulks moored in the harbour. Blume had a considerable international reputation from before 1939, and it does not appear to have been a concern to the British at this early stage that he might have been himself compromised by his involvement with the Nazi Party and its various activities in the musical field. Kiel University reworked some of its previously prepared material for the new academic year, and duly entered the post-war era. One document it published gave the addresses of academic staff, but still used the war-time street names: Blume's address in Adolf-Hitler-Allee was still listed.[46] At the official opening in November 1945 both British and German speeches declared that the University was 'to be devoted to the sciences, whose practitioners were aware of their social responsibility'.[47]

In the universities, as elsewhere, the Allies had to rely to a considerable extent on the Germans themselves either to confess, or to incriminate one another, and this was something few were prepared to do. Most, like Blume, were quick to accept the new dispensation, and to restructure their courses and their research programmes to conform to Allied requirements. There was some voluntary German cooperation. In Stuttgart the Americans put the renowned liberal writer Theodor Heuss (later President of the Federal Republic) in charge of education and culture for Baden-Württemberg. Heuss worked hard to convince the Americans that he had dismissed 'politically objectionable' staff, including the Director, from the State High School for Music, that prospective students would be screened with a questionnaire, and that the Music School would now embody internationalist principles in its curricula.[48] Elsewhere, internationally famous academics were likewise dismissed. The philosopher Martin Heidegger was dismissed from Freiburg University in the French Zone in the summer of 1945, because of the support he had given to the Nazi regime in its initial phase, and because of his early Party membership.[49]

September 1945 marked the end of the first period of Allied occupation of Germany in several ways. Institutionally, the first improvised administrations in post-war Germany had by this time been replaced by more permanent organisations, from the Control Council down. In many cases the soldiers who first entered Germany had gone, to be replaced by civilians, albeit in uniform and with temporary rank. All these military administrations were by now employing great numbers of Germans, as translators, clerks, drivers, and often in roles of responsibility.

Above all it was clear that early fears of continued Nazi resistance had been misplaced. There had been many individual acts of resistance, typically from young men, and in places these were claimed by '*Werwolf*' groups. These were no more than irritations to a military occupation enforced as strongly as that in Germany in 1945. All the occupiers used the death penalty against Germans convicted of shooting at their soldiers, or of carrying firearms. In July 1946 a young man in Hanover was sentenced to death after displaying a picture of Hitler in his window, and advocating that the Nazi Party be re-established. The sentence was only commuted after considerable public debate of the case in Britain itself.[50] The official historian of the British occupation conceded that

> in the early months there was tendency to inflict the death penalty for
> the unlawful carrying or concealment of firearms on disquietingly flimsy

evidence or where the circumstances afforded little justification. The number of weapons in the country was so vast, the risk of their falling into the wrong hands so great, and the resultant danger so real that this lapse from judicial objectivity can perhaps be understood, if not defended.[51]

In fact the Allies, in all four zones, were far more concerned with widespread lawlessness, whether from 'displaced persons', disaffected Germans, or indeed their own soldiers, than by armed resistance. Although they all noted the overwhelming note of submission, of passive and shocked acceptance of defeat in the German population, they had been pleasantly surprised by the level of cooperation that they had encountered, and by the energy with which many Germans had turned to the problems of reconstruction. Nowhere was this spirit of cooperation more evident than in the denazification of German mass media and the arts.

7

RE-SHAPING THE MASS MEDIA

The German authorities will comply with all directions which the Allied
Representatives may give regarding the use, control and censorship of all
media for influencing expression and opinion, including broadcasting, press
and publications, advertising, films, and public performances, entertainments,
and exhibitions of all kinds.

From a 'Proclamation' to the German people issued by the Allied Control Council,
September 1945.[1]

Since 1933, the self-conscious use of propaganda and the unashamed
manipulation of the mass media had been conspicuous features of Nazism.
Indeed, outside Germany they had been its best known features: the harsh
ranting of Hitler and Goebbels had been heard by millions over the radio;
newsreel images of Nazi demagogues, torchlit rallies, marching storm
troopers, and ranks of serried Nazi men with grim expressions had become
a recognised aesthetic, as had menacing formations of German bombers, or
joyful faces of women and children giving the Nazi salute to their leader.
Until the final weeks of the war, Goebbels' huge propaganda machine continued to produce films, and into the final days, newspapers. In the last
hours before individual towns and villages fell under Allied control, radio
broadcasts were often the last contact Germans had with the Nazi regime.

The Allies were absolutely determined to destroy the Nazi propaganda
machine in Germany, and to take the fullest control of all information

177

media there. They were not strangers to the use of propaganda themselves: the Soviets had been developing this, using new technologies, from 1917. They had their own distinguished cinematic tradition. The British had long experience of using propaganda, and used their national broadcasting service and a well-developed film industry for a worldwide projection of their national interests. The Americans dominated in the increasingly influential modes of popular culture, the Hollywood film, the Broadway musical, in jazz, swing, and boogie, but their huge cinema industry, extensive broadcasting networks, and sophisticated newspaper culture had also evolved a distinctive approach to wartime propaganda. The Soviets, the British, and the Americans had given a great deal of thought to the problems of replacing Nazi propaganda with their own information services in post-war Germany, and had prepared specialist teams for this. Typically they used a mixture of their own professionals, well versed in psychological warfare techniques, and émigré Germans, often of Jewish descent. Travelling with the frontline troops as the Allies advanced into Germany, these units were tasked with the immediate closure of all German media, and their subsequent replacement with licensed Allied services. Particular teams were assigned to radio, to cinema, to newspaper publishing, and to theatre and music. The French had less immediate experience, given that their own broadcasting, film, and newspapers had been controlled by the Nazis between 1940 and 1944, but they soon showed themselves to be quick learners.

The Americans and British had the most detailed plans for the control of information in a defeated Germany, and these plans were finalised in Military Government Law No. 191; Amended (1). Under this law, all public entertainments in Germany were to be prohibited. Meetings were not allowed except for religious services. Further detail was provided by Information Control Instruction No. 1, which was publicised in all areas occupied by the Americans and British. It declared:

> The sale, lending, and distribution of newspapers, books, brochures, journals, posters, and other publications, and of music, records, and other sound recordings is forbidden, insofar as through these
>
> a) National Socialist or similar 'völkisch' ideas (including racial science and racial hatred) are propagated;
>
> b) Fascistic or anti-democratic ideas are propagated;
>
> c) It is sought to create disunity between the United Nations, or to stir up hostility to them;

d) Militaristic (including pan-German and German-imperialistic) ideas are propagated;

e) Any rebellion or disturbance is incited, or the functioning of Military Government is in any way disrupted.

This instruction further forbade the printing of any material, or the production, distribution, sale, or showing of any films without the express permission of the Military Government.[2] These regulations were also adopted by the French in areas they occupied, and a similar blanket prohibition on all information media was applied by the Soviets, although they did not formalise the situation in their zone until September 1945.[3]

The British and the Americans envisaged three phases in the immediate aftermath of German defeat: first, the 'Prohibition of German Entertainment Services'; second, the 'Use of Allied Entertainments'; and third, the 'Re-establishment of German Entertainment Services Directed by Germans, under Allied Supervision'. During the second phase a reconnaissance would be made of all existing German entertainment facilities. No timetable was outlined, allowing for a flexible approach to the censorship and reconstruction of German media. This was a draconian programme, and the 'Manual' issued by SHAEF in May 1945 provided detailed instructions on how it was to be conducted. In the first phase, for example, a 'special watch' was to be made in case films were screened in churches. In the second phase, Information Control teams were to prevent 'all motion picture facilities' from being 'used, damaged, or dispersed by Germans'; and to report on the condition and seating capacity of all cinemas, theatres, and concert halls. They were to 'make a survey of local personnel engaged in all entertainment activities, obtaining any information available regarding their degree of Nazi collaboration and make every effort to discover personnel who may be presumed to be free of the Nazi taint'. In the third phase, licences would be given to 'producers in certain categories of entertainment'.[4] Obviously if any of these licensees contravened Military Government regulations, their licences would be withdrawn, and they would face other sanctions. This was a programme for the total control of a modern country's information media.

As with all aspects of their occupation, the Allies approached 'information control' with trepidation and uncertainty, an anxiety reflected in the idea that Nazi films might be surreptitiously screened in churches. They also accepted that they would depend on the cooperation of Germans, and that they would therefore have to try to sift out ex-Nazis from those active in the information services. The Americans, whose 'Information Control Division' was the best prepared, had a staff of 1,700 officers and men, with their own transport and communication facilities, at work in Germany by early July 1945.[5]

The commander of the British Information Control Service, Major-General William Bishop, did not arrive in Germany until July 1945, and his staff was initially pre-occupied with sorting out accommodation, food, and office facilities. The improvised nature of the British effort is clear from one of Bishop's early reports. He wrote: 'My IC team in Berlin has now risen to six officers. None of them knows anything at all about newspapers, theatres, film, radio, etc., but they are doing their best.'[6] Bishop rapidly established additional Information Control Units in Düsseldorf, Hamburg, and Hanover. The Soviets were less prepared in terms of policy. They had no handbooks or manuals ready in May 1945, but they had a significant advantage over the other Allies. As in the political field, they were prepared immediately to entrust trained émigré German communists with key posts in the reconstruction of the German media. They gave a surprising degree of freedom to these individuals, and were thus able to re-establish some information media in their zone with extraordinary rapidity.

RADIO

Radio was the most important mass medium of the mid-twentieth century. It was almost universally accessible in Germany, and by the later stages of the war was used by almost the whole population as the most immediate source of news. In the enveloping chaos of the end of the war and the confusion of the opening weeks of military occupation, radio took on an emergency role, but in times of greater normality after the surrender it provided a whole range of spoken word programmes, often aimed at specific groups like women or children, or at occupational categories like farmers; there was a great deal of broadcast music. Just as the Nazis had used the radio as a central tool in the building of the *Volksgemeinschaft* (or 'people's community'), the Allies in post-war Germany wanted to use the radio for more than merely the dissemination of news. They intended to use it to help construct a new society and a new model of citizenship, and would therefore seek to impose in Germany an entirely new radio culture.

The worst fear of the Allies was that clandestine radio stations, or transmitters still in Nazi hands, would broadcast to resistance groups and stir up opposition. Even though this fear later proved groundless, it was heightened by the numerous broadcasts encouraging the formation of *Werwolf* resistance groups which were sent out from German stations in the final weeks of the war.[7] The first and absolute priority of the Allies in the information control field as they took control of German territory was to close down German broadcasting. So effective were they that there was no Nazi broadcasting in Germany under military occupation.

As they advanced into Germany, the Allies took particular care not only to prevent Nazi broadcasting, but if possible to capture German radio facilities intact. When the British arranged the surrender of Hamburg in the final days of the war, they insisted as one condition that the still functioning radio station there, which had broadcast the news of Hitler's death on 1 May, be handed to them intact, with its staff. As soon as they entered the city they took possession of the building and within hours inaugurated a new era in German broadcasting with a recording of the British national anthem, followed by the words: 'This is Hamburg, a station of the Allied Military Government.'[8] Although the former Nazi directors of the station, and some of its best known announcers, were immediately dismissed, most of the lower grades of staff were kept on, pending more detailed investigations, so that the British could quickly develop a spoken word and music programme. In the first few weeks, they relied heavily on relays of programmes from the BBC or the British Forces Network, but with remarkable speed they developed new German-language programmes. The station was renamed the North-West German Radio (NWDR), and despite its peripheral geographical location, it quickly gained the largest audience of any station in post-war Germany. In August 1945 the British rebuilt a large transmitter in Cologne with its own studios.[9] From Hamburg and Cologne the NWDR reached a huge population in the Rhineland, the Ruhr, and in the cities of north Germany. From the first the NWDR was instructed not to engage in obvious propaganda, but 'to provide for the British Zone of Germany [...] a Home Service on the lines of the B.B.C. Home Service'.[10] It took from the model of the BBC a characteristically earnest public service role, with a commitment to impartial news broadcasting, and a judicious mix of entertainment and education. Many, but not all, of its senior British staff were seconded from the BBC; Hugh Carleton Greene, an important figure in the wartime BBC German Service, was the first Director of the NWDR. Under his guidance, German employees were allowed a remarkable degree of freedom.

The Soviets, as they advanced into Berlin, similarly took care not to damage the radio transmitter in Tegel and the central Radio Berlin studios in Masurenallee. They immediately sent German communists from the 'Ulbricht group' there, with instructions to resume the service as quickly as possible. Hans Mahle and Matthäus Klein, the leaders of the team, set to work, and a few days after the surrender the first broadcast was made, its text written by Fritz Erpenbeck and Wolfgang Leonhardt. They used a copy of *Pravda* to provide the news material, rewording it in what Leonhardt called the 'anti-fascist democratic style'.[11] After this the previous employees of the station provided the material, working under the supervision of Mahle and his comrades. An anonymous diarist in Berlin provides an independent report of their programmes. On Sunday 27 May she wrote:

> The electricity is back on [...] The Berlin station is broadcasting on the radio, generally news reports and disclosures that reek of blood, corpses, and atrocities. They say that millions of people – mostly Jews – were cremated in huge camps and that their ashes were used as fertilizer. On top of that everything was supposedly carefully recorded in thick ledgers – a scrupulous accounting of death. We really are an orderly nation. Late in the evening they played Beethoven, and that brought tears. I turned it off. Who can bear that at the moment?

A few days later she had to switch the radio off again: 'After jazz, more disclosures, some Heinrich Heine and humanity, they started broadcasting tributes to the Red Army, a little too saccharine for my taste.'[12] The British certainly noted the resumption, within only weeks, of 'a full programme' of broadcasting, 'apparently run by two Germans', from Radio Berlin.[13] The BBC announced that Berlin Radio had started broadcasting communist propaganda.[14]

There was an initial understanding amongst the Allies that they would jointly run the central German radio station in Berlin, but having once seized control, the Russians were not going to relinquish this, and slowly the other Allies realised that if they wanted radio stations in Berlin they would have to develop their own. This is an area in which the earliest beginnings of the Cold War can be discerned. The British, who of course were already doing more or less in Hamburg what the Soviets were doing with Berlin Radio, quickly redirected the BBC German Service, which had a huge audience in Germany, specifically into the Soviet Zone.

The Americans did not have the physical advantages of the British or the Soviets, and in the cities of southern and central Germany they occupied in April 1945 they captured no intact stations. Munich was the chosen capital of their zone, and they immediately set about repairing the transmitter there, commencing medium wave broadcasts on 10 June 1945, with a relay of programmes from the American Forces Network.[15] Conscious of the rapid emergence of a new pattern of broadcasting in Hamburg and Berlin, they were quick to emulate this, building their own studios and recruiting staff. They developed stations in Frankfurt, and in Stuttgart, where they broadcast from a radio lorry through 1946.

The fragmentation of radio in Germany after 1945 suited the Allies in two ways. It satisfied the universal desire that nothing resembling the centralised Nazi Propaganda Ministry should exist in Germany, and also allowed them individually to project their chosen self-image into the other parts of Germany. The French started from the most difficult position, inheriting no significant radio facilities in the largely agricultural areas allotted to them. When the idea of a four-Power radio station in Berlin dissolved, the French were left with nothing. They quickly determined to establish a completely new station in the undamaged spa town of Baden-Baden. In the summer of 1945 engineers were sent to construct a new transmitter amongst the hotels and cafés there, and in the autumn the French appointed key civilians to the executive and editorial posts in what became the *Südwestfunk* (South-West Radio or SWF). There were concerns about ex-Nazis amongst both technical and artistic staff at the SWF, and all prospective employees were vetted by the *Sureté*.[16] The station started broadcasting in March 1946, and quickly built its own niche in the German radio world, with a particular anti-Nazism, expressed through a commitment to high intellectual standards and to artistic modernism. As the other Allies had already done, the French combined news and spoken word programmes with carefully considered musical broadcasts. Similarly, they developed the physical infrastructure of the station, building linked transmitters and a local studio in Koblenz.

The NWDR, initially run by the British from Hamburg, was soon transmitting from Cologne, Berlin, Hanover, and Flensburg as well; The Soviets operated three stations, from Berlin and Leipzig; the Americans added stations in Bremen, and one in Berlin, RIAS (Radio in the American Sector), to the three they were already operating. These stations mixed programmes with the most bland titles, like 'Weather', 'Dance Music', and 'News', with more obviously propagandistic broadcasts like 'Voice of the USA'. Quite explicitly, they aimed at populations in other zones. The Soviet-controlled *Deutschlandsender* from Berlin ran programmes like 'From the Soviet Union', 'We Speak for West Germany', and 'Youth Broadcast to West Germany'. RIAS, from the American Sector of Berlin, sent out 'Broadcast for Middle Germany'. The NWDR and SWF confined themselves to cultural propaganda, broadcasting about the arts and the way of life of Britain and France. As German staffs were allowed greater executive and editorial freedom, there were isolated cases where ex-Nazis were discovered and dismissed from work, but only at lower levels. According to a British blacklist, one musician, Hans Doberitz, was 'voted out by the Advisory Council N.W.D.R. as an objectionable Nazi' in July 1946.[17] There were no examples of Nazis infiltrating and actually using an Allied-controlled station for political broadcasts.

All the radio stations in post-Nazi Germany broadcast initially for only limited hours, with long periods off air in between. Gradually they developed continuous programmes, running each day from early in the morning until late at night. All relied on news material supplied from the Allied countries running them, but supplemented this with 'open forum' programmes, where different members of the public were urged to put forward their ideas on current affairs in a new spirit of active democratic citizenship. All broadcast what the Germans called 'serious music', from records or with live performances from their in-house orchestras. By playing international modern music, what the Nazis had called 'degenerate music', they could testify to their anti-fascism. Most broadcast hours were filled up with dance music. Just as the Nazi years had been accompanied by the sentimental dance music of the Goebbels Ministry, the post-war trauma was played out to the strains of sentimental yearnings for *Heimat*. Inevitably a fair amount of jazz was broadcast on Allied stations which transmitted into Germany, and to a lesser extent on the new German stations. This was hugely popular with the young, and with older jazz lovers who had lived through the Nazi persecutions. Many older and more conservative Germans were still horrified by what they perceived as an alien import, and hated it. All stations, regardless of the zone they broadcast from, received numerous complaints, typically framed in racist language, about jazz, and inclined therefore towards more German traditional dance music.

Radio is one of the areas in Germany where the break in 1945 is most evident. The strident propaganda and centralised control of the Nazi era disappeared entirely, and were replaced by a more temperate, pluralistic, regionalised public discourse. The media map of present day Germany still shows the direct influences of the initial days of the Allied occupation.

NEWSPAPERS

Before 1933, Germany had a diverse newspaper culture, with some 4,700 different newspapers and a huge array of magazines and journals. Under the Nazis this was drastically curtailed, and fewer than 1,000 newspapers were still being published in 1944.[18] Most of these were strongly influenced by the Nazi Party and its theories. All were supervised, and restricted to publishing news sanctioned by the Propaganda Ministry. Until the final days of the 'Third Reich', newspapers were still printed on the remaining presses not destroyed by bombing, or seized by the occupying Allies. The main Nazi Party daily, the *Völkischer Beobachter*, was printed in Munich until 30 April 1945, although its final issues took on an increasingly desperate tone. On 24 April, the newspaper reported on Hitler's defence of Berlin: the heroic tenor of the front page was somewhat undermined by its description of Berlin's defenders, civilians and 'party comrades', fighting with 'Panzerfausts, machine pistols, and carbines'.[19] A perceptive reader might have wondered what good these small arms would be against Soviet tanks, artillery, and aircraft.

On 30 April, as the front line approached, the paper reported on the 'Great Battle for Bavaria'; a smaller article on the front page reported that Ulm, Augsburg, and other Bavarian towns were in American hands after 'hard fighting'. Other articles reported on the 'chaos' of the United

Nations' meeting in San Francisco. Here the Soviet Foreign Minister, Molotov, was reportedly trying to establish himself as 'dictator of the conference'.[20] In Berlin itself, a news-sheet for the beleaguered population, the *Panzerbär* (*Armoured Bear*), was printed from the former Ullstein press in Kochstrasse. It alternated between heroic assertions that Berlin would be a 'mass grave for Soviet tanks', and false reassurances of relief from German armies outside the city. The newspaper's masthead showed a bear (the symbol of Berlin) holding a shovel in one hand and a *Panzerfaust* in the other.[21] This was the last gasp of the Nazi press machine.

Well before the surrender the different Allies had been producing small news-sheets for German soldiers and, since January 1945, newspapers for occupied civilians. The first of these was produced by Americans from SHAEF's Psychological Warfare Department (PWD) in Aachen, and was used to develop some of their later strategies, above all a commitment to replacing 'Nazi language' with a more liberal, democratic usage. The first issues of the *Aachener Nachrichten* (published after 24 January 1945) were criticised from all sides, and particularly from SHAEF headquarters in Paris, for the poor quality of their German. The team in Aachen which produced the newspaper, led by the writer Eugene Jolas, defended themselves vigorously. Jolas wrote: 'We have noted the criticism made of the newspaper as well as the praise given to it. [...] our greatest effort is to rid the language of Nazi taint and to infuse it with democratic spirit.'[22] Jolas was soon editing another newspaper from Heidelberg, which started production in mid-April 1945.

Dirk Deissler, who has researched this topic intensively, notes many specific examples of how American Press Control Officers subsequently criticised licensed German newspapers printed in their zone. They were quick to criticise newspapers for anything which presented Hitler or Nazism in a positive light, as for example the description in the *Frankenpost* in November 1945 of Hitler as a 'strong man', and Eva Braun as a 'little courageous woman'. They insisted that specifically Nazi terms like 'Aryan' or 'half-Aryan' should be avoided or only used within quotation marks, and that Gothic script should not be used.[23] Above all they sought to teach a new generation of German journalists and editors that editorial comment should be separated from factual reporting. Until military occupation was formally ended in 1949, American Press Control Officers maintained a vigilant scrutiny of German newspapers in their zone. They were careful not to be seen as censors, but more as educators, and in most instances where German editors published something considered reminiscent of Nazism, they were issued with written or verbal warnings, rather than having their licences revoked.

As German printing presses came to halt in April and May 1945, an extraordinary vacuum was created, in which the surviving population found itself entirely cut off from the rest of the world. People everywhere were desperate for news, and anything printed was eagerly seized upon. That is not to say that the newspapers hastily printed by the new occupiers were universally believed. A population hardened to twelve years of Nazi propaganda, and now living with its consequences, was hardly likely to be over-credulous. Rumours were everywhere, spread by the millions of people, soldiers, civilians, and 'displaced persons' walking from place to place in Germany. There was a great shortage of paper, and the first occupation newspapers were produced in relatively small numbers. Well into the post-war years, paper shortages persisted, and by choosing how to allocate what paper they had available, the different Military Governments were able to exert a decisive influence on the circulation figures of any publication.

There was no significant effort to resume Nazi publishing. Perry Biddiscombe has documented one instance after the surrender in which an Austrian Nazi group smuggled copies of a news-sheet called *The Watch Post* into Germany in September 1946, but this amateurish production was entirely insignificant, as were other clandestine productions of pro-Nazi leaflets.[24] The Allies were able to concentrate on rebuilding the German press in ways they favoured, and on the dissemination of their own propaganda. The first of the significant post-war newspapers to start publication was the Soviet-sponsored *Tägliche Rundschau*, which was first printed on 15 May 1945 and became the principal German-language mouthpiece of the Soviet Military Administration. This was directly run by the Soviets, and was initially edited by Alexander Dymschitz, a highly educated, multilingual officer. Although the *Tägliche Rundschau* was used to disseminate the propaganda of the Soviets in Germany, and to publicise the orders of the nascent Soviet military administration there, it also had literary pretensions, and printed poems, short stories, and commentaries on the arts. Dymschitz, who went on to play a leading role in the arts in the Soviet Zone, enlisted the Expressionist poet Johannes R. Becher, another émigré German communist who was rapidly returned to Berlin, to help tailor the literary content of the newspaper to the needs of a German audience. The Soviets had another advantage – more paper. From the first they were able to publish in greater quantities in post-war Germany, and the *Tägliche Rundschau* was also distributed to large cities outside the Soviet Zone like Munich. Other German-language papers were quickly licensed by the Soviets, including the *Berliner Zeitung* and the *Volkszeitung*, which appeared by the end of May 1945, and *Neues Deutschland*, the daily newspaper of the Communist Party, subsequently the official daily of the German Democratic Republic until 1989.

In the Western zones, apart from small news-sheets printed by army units, there were initially no newspapers, and local commanders soon reported on the dangers of allowing this situation to continue. The British quickly supervised the production of the weekly *Hannoversche Kurier*, in an edition of half a million copies, and of similar newspapers in other large cities, but they were hampered by grave shortages of paper.[25] The British had, along with the Americans, given considerable attention to the evolution of the German language since 1933, and were equally determined to censor Nazi usages. An 'Information Control Policy Directive' of August 1945 explicitly stated that 'Language reminiscent of Nazi terminology should be avoided'.[26] The British and Americans had even, during the war, produced a 132-page dictionary of Nazi terms, and this was used to help occupation staff in post-war Germany.[27] The French had their own linguistic sensibilities, particularly related to their view that post-war Germany should be partitioned. To this end they sought to develop regional feeling in Baden, Pfalz, and the Rhineland, and to encourage this through new local newspapers. Until late in 1946 all newspapers published in the French Zone were subject to pre-production censorship, and the French tried to prevent the use of the word *Reich* to underline the point that the German empire no longer existed. Newspapers and textbooks in the French Zone were not allowed to refer to 'Germans', but had instead to refer specifically to 'Rhinelanders', or 'Badeners'. Instead of a collective 'German' identity, they sought thus to re-create distinctive senses of local identity.[28]

The Americans, as in other areas of information control, were initially divided in their approach to the development of a new German press. The army wanted to produce only basic news-sheets, but the 'psychological warriors' of PWD saw the opportunity to help develop a new journalistic culture. They managed to start production in April 1945 of the *Frankfurter Presse*, and on 31 July 1945 this was licensed as the *Frankfurter Rundschau*.[29] It went on to be one of West Germany's leading liberal voices. During the summer of 1945, the drive and initiative of PWD's Press Section, led by the Hungarian Hans Habe, led to the adoption of an ambitious plan to produce a flagship newspaper to act as a model for a new journalistic and press culture. *Die Neue Zeitung* (*The New Newspaper*) was staffed with distinguished writers and journalists such as Erich Kästner, Stefan Heym, and the music critic Hans-Heinz Stuckenschmidt. It aspired to high standards of journalistic integrity and literary quality. Ironically, Habe convinced the military administration that the old presses of the *Völkischer Beobachter* in Munich were the only ones with the capacity to print *Die Neue Zeitung* in sufficient numbers, and production started there in October 1945. By the end of the year the newspaper had a circulation of over one million. Into the early Cold War period, this newspaper acted as the standard bearer for American values and American culture in West Germany, not without attracting criticism.[30]

With surprising speed, printing presses all over Germany came back into operation. Through 1946 hundreds of licences were given to local newspapers and to an increasing number of journals. Inevitably, although all the occupiers were committed to the exclusion of ex-Nazis from editorial and journalistic positions, a number of these crept back to their former positions. The Allies have been criticised for allowing this, but those ex-Nazis who did work for licensed newspapers did not use them to propagate Nazism; most were keen to display newly acquired 'democratic' credentials.

THE 'DREAM FACTORY'

Even before 1933, Germany had a large and sophisticated film industry, concentrated in the extensive studios at Babelsberg, to the south-west of Berlin. Under the Nazis this industry had been further developed and centralised, producing more than 1,000 feature films between 1933 and 1945. By 1945, all production was in the hands of four companies. Under Goebbels' personal supervision, the weekly newsreel (the *Wochenschau*) had specialised in action photography, produced by propaganda units attached to the front line troops. Although we are accustomed now to the propaganda images endlessly reproduced from films like Leni Riefenstahl's *Triumph of the Will* (1935), the overwhelming bulk of German film production under the Nazis was straightforward entertainment: musicals, love stories, and melodramas. This prosaic fare was produced with the help of the most advanced technology, including the Agfa colour process. This was the famed 'Dream Factory' of Goebbels. Until 1944, more and more cinemas were opened in Germany, and audience figures increased. The last feature film produced under the Nazis, *Kolberg*, was completed in February 1945, and premiered to German troops cut off in La Rochelle, on the Atlantic coast of France. Goebbels had a private screening of the last *Wochenschau* on 26 March, and recorded in his diary that it included 'shattering pictures from the West that we cannot possibly publish'.[31] UFA photographers were still filming a new feature film at Babelsberg in mid-April.

On 24 April 1945, Soviet tanks rolled into Babelsberg, and the era of Nazi cinema came to an end. Most of the directors, technicians, and actors who had worked in the 'Dream Factory' had already dispersed, and many kept a deliberately low profile for the next few years. The equipment and raw materials at Babelsberg, if not already destroyed, were seized by the Soviets as reparations, or smuggled out to the American Sector of Berlin over the next few weeks.[32] All over Germany, those cinemas which were not completely destroyed were closed, their owners strictly forbidden to show any films without a Military Government licence. Thus began what is known in Germany as the *Filmpause*, a period of over a year in which no new films were produced.

Although no films were made, the cinemas were not closed for long. All of the Allies were aware of the enormous role they could play in a struggle for hearts and minds. There was an effort to coordinate British and American policy on film to be shown in occupied Germany. Guidelines were agreed on 12 May for the joint production of a German-language newsreel, *Welt im Film* (*The World in Film*), and the first editions were tested on German audiences in the town of Erlangen in June. The newsreel was accompanied by short documentary films, and the audiences were asked to complete questionnaires after the showing. The first programmes shown in Erlangen reflect the British and American priorities, which were to impress on the Germans the strength of the Allied armed forces, of their cultural and technological achievements, and also to impress on the Germans their responsibility for Nazi crimes. Alongside the *Welt im Film* newsreels the Germans were therefore shown a documentary entitled *The Autobiography of a Jeep*, another on the Tennessee Valley dam, one on Duke Ellington's orchestra, and one entitled *KZ*, the German abbreviation for a concentration camp, with scenes filmed in Buchenwald. At this early stage the British and Americans felt it was inappropriate to show the Germans any film merely for entertainment. The audience reactions were predictably mixed, and many expressed great dislike for the newsreels, which had showed pictures of Germans looting in destroyed cities; others found the items dealing with Germany's defeat 'depressing and humiliating'. Young Germans were particularly critical, and many viewers commented on the unsubtle propaganda techniques used in the films.[33] After these tests, *Welt im Film* was more widely distributed, as cinemas were reopened in the American and British Zones.

The British had by July decided that boredom and apathy were more significant problems amongst the German population than renascent Nazism, and that it would help to reopen cinemas, theatres, and concert halls. Acting independently, Montgomery's headquarters authorised the opening of 370 cinemas in the British Zone, and also advised significant changes to the approach taken by *Welt im Film*. The newsreel, the British argued, should avoid showing too many destroyed German homes, or cultural monuments, and should instead show scenes of reconstruction. Obvious propaganda should be replaced by a more documentary approach. There was at this time still a vague intention to produce a four-Power newsreel for Germany, and *Welt im Film* did include some Soviet footage. Several issues went out of their way to present scenes of Allied harmony and cooperation. These early post-war newsreels consciously presented a harsh message to Germans under occupation: sequences were shown of Germans arrested and executed for offences against Military Government. The issue on 22 June 1945 showed Dutch children receiving food from the Allies, and commented: 'Those who have hungered longest shall be fed first. Germany will have to wait.' The previous week's newsreel was devoted exclusively to coverage of 13 concentration camps, including Bergen-Belsen, Buchenwald, and Ohrdruf. The film of these camps was carefully presented to show the camps in their surroundings, to prevent any accusations that it was faked.[34]

In many places the British and Americans compelled the Germans now under their control to see these pictures. It is impossible to generalise about the impact this had on a population already deeply traumatised by war, but it is reasonable to assume that these images, still shocking today, had a profound effect. Many Germans who had previously closed their eyes and ears were forcibly confronted for the first time with the evidence of cruelty and brutality on a huge scale. Some doubtless tried to dismiss the films as faked, as atrocity propaganda, but it appears that most accepted their veracity. Not all accepted the message coming to them from the soldiers who pushed them into the cinemas, that they were directly responsible, but a period of soul searching was instigated.

The Americans were particularly determined to confront the Germans with film of the concentration camps. In May 1945, only weeks after the surrender, Brigadier-General Robert McClure, head of SHAEF's Psychological Warfare Department, gave a press conference in Paris in which he explained what he called 'the long term task of attempting to reorient the German mind'. Germans would have to wait before they would be allowed to see feature films; in the meantime, an hour-long film of 'German atrocity camps' was being prepared.[35] This film, entitled *Die Todesmühlen* (*The Mills of Death*) was ready in the autumn of 1945 and was widely shown in western Germany. Many Germans stayed away from the film though, and others were repelled by what they saw as heavy-handed propaganda. An American survey reported that it was the least popular of all films shown at this time, and that many Germans said they would not go to the cinema if they knew a film of this kind was being shown. The same survey reported an overwhelming wish to see old German films again.[36] The failure of *Die Todesmühlen* may be seen as the end of Allied efforts to shock and shame the Germans with atrocity film of this kind.

Well before *Die Todesmühlen* was ready, other films were being shown in Germany. The Soviets, quickly followed by the British, took the lead in screening their own films, and allowing German audiences to see them: the anonymous diarist we have previously heard from in Berlin saw a group of people coming out of a cinema on 21 May, 'where, according to the hand-painted signs a Russian film called *Chapaev* was showing. I heard one man's voice, half in a whisper, pronounce the film, "Absolute rubbish!"' Three weeks later she herself saw a Soviet victory film called *At Six p.m. after the War*, apparently made in 1944. Afterwards, she wrote: 'Once again I felt oppressed by our German disaster.'[37] This woman understood some Russian, but quickly the Soviets started to provide subtitles in German, and later to dub German voices onto their films. A German company was established in buildings on the edge of the former UFA studios at Babelsberg, and allowed to synchronise German voices onto *Lenin in October, Lenin in 1918*, and other Soviet films.[38]

The British sent to Germany what were presumably thought to be positive examples of their cinema, *Brief Encounter* and *The Seventh Veil*.[39] The French soon did likewise, and showed their own home newsreel, *Blick in die Welt* (*A View of the World*) with a German voice-over in their zone. The Americans were torn between the Information Control Division of its Military Government in Germany, which wanted to use cinema in the democratic 're-education' of Germany, and the Hollywood industry, which wanted to secure the German market for its own products. The result was that relatively few Hollywood films were shown in the initial period of occupation, despite the vacuum in German film-making. There was no doubt that this vacuum needed filling. As a kind of normality was re-established in Germany, going to the cinema was one of few pleasures or forms of escape open to the population. The *Reichsmark* lost its value dramatically after May 1945, and it became relatively much cheaper to go the cinema. When the weather grew colder in the winter of 1945–1946, fuel was scarce, and the cinema was a warm place to go for a few hours. Occupation troops also provided a large market, and many films were presented in repeat showings, for occupation troops first and German audiences second.

There was no great resurgence in German film-making. Almost everyone in the industry was compromised by collaboration with the Nazis, and there had been no tradition of subversive film making since 1933. The huge emigration to Hollywood after 1933 was not repeated in the opposite direction, and although the émigré filmmaker Billy Wilder came to Germany to write a report on the cinema there for the American Military Government, he did not stay, nor did many other émigrés to Hollywood return. In July 1946 the Americans appointed one of them, the director Erich Pommer, their senior Film Officer, but it was not until 1947 that new German films were made under US supervision.

The Soviets were again first to develop a new German cinema industry. As early as October 1945 they formed a 'film active' in Berlin under the control of communists. This group was composed of six men with expertise in various aspects of the film industry who had spent the Nazi years in Moscow, in Switzerland, or in 'internal exile' in Germany. All were committed anti-fascists, and with Soviet support they formed the kernel of a new film company. This was granted the first post-war licence to produce German films in May 1946, and allowed gradually to re-occupy the former UFA studios in Babelsberg. This company, called DEFA (*Deutsche Film Aktiengesellschaft*) subsequently became the state company of the German Democratic Republic, producing literally thousands of films until 1989. It had the enthusiastic support of the Soviet Military Administration, and was allowed initially to work in a spirit of great freedom and political commitment. The role of the company was to recognise 'the humanistic mission of film', to confront 'the problems of the current period of transition, and to show the way to tomorrow, to a better Germany.' One of it first projects was the production of a weekly newsreel, *Der Augenzeuge* (*The Eye-Witness*).[40]

The Soviets licensed DEFA to produce the first feature film in Germany after 1945, *The Murderers are Amongst Us*, directed by Wolfgang Staudte. He started filming in December, and the film, which engaged directly with the moral dilemmas posed by German involvement in wartime atrocities, was ready to show to audiences in November 1946. Although subsequently much criticised for failing to resolve the moral dilemmas it presented, at the time the film was regarded as 'a serious and courageous film intended less as entertainment than as an appeal to the conscience', and it seemed to herald a new German cinema which would try to confront its past.[41] By the time *The Murderers are Amongst Us* was being shown, two other feature films were in production at Babelsberg; by mid-1947 there were 1,500 people working there. Where the Soviets opted for a centralised cinema industry, the British supported the development of smaller studios. They licensed Karl Hasselbach in Berlin to form the 'Studio 45' in Berlin, and Helmut Käutner in Hamburg to form the 'Camera Film Company'. Both these studios produced films in 1946, although they were not shown until 1947, and achieved nothing like the fame of *The Murderers are Amongst Us*.

These first post-war films, which manifested a desire to think about the Nazi past, were soon eclipsed by many others which did not. Even before these appeared, the signs were there that most cinema goers in post-war Germany were more interested in mindless escapism than in serious historical and moral enquiry. To plug the gap in films available in Germany in 1945 and 1946, the Americans resorted to showing older German films, typically made in the Nazi period. Before they were shown, these musicals and romances, which included films which had been made before 1945 but not shown, were supposedly censored. In fact, from 845 films presented to them virtually none were rejected by the Americans. Although the British rejected 300 films from before 1945, they permitted the showing of some 900. The French equally allowed many films from the Nazi period to be shown;[42] their blend of sentimentality, nostalgia, light music, and escapism was not deemed dangerous. The Dream Factory was back in action.

THE ARTS

It may seem bizarre that in a country shattered by warfare, anybody should be concerned with the arts. Nonetheless, one of the most striking features of post-war Germany is the rapid re-emergence of a thriving artistic culture. Through the occupation period, all over Germany, thousands of bedraggled civilians, often thin, hungry, and in the winter very cold, sought out concerts and theatrical performances, typically in semi-ruined buildings, and found refuge there from their otherwise wretched existence. There were several reasons for this. For the defeated population, high culture, the music of Bach, Mozart, and Beethoven, and the plays of their great classical writers, provided something recognisably 'German' which they were still allowed to celebrate, and which was not associated with the concentration camps and crimes of the Nazis. This was something which the occupiers were happy to permit, and to encourage. They were keen to prove to the Germans that they also were cultured, and therefore competed to sponsor their own high culture in Germany. They also consciously used the arts to re-introduce Germans to currents of international thought which they had been increasingly isolated from since 1933. The arts played a significant role in the 're-education' project. There were more pragmatic factors: the occupiers needed entertainment for their soldiers, administrators, and hangers-on; and the occupied were often glad of somewhere warm to go for a few hours. In the barter economy concert and theatre tickets became, relatively, far cheaper than they were before 1945, or after the currency reforms of 1948. For a brief period, culture flourished in the ruins, a phenomenon which led to this period being described as 'the golden hunger years'.[43]

The Soviets and the French were quickest to re-establish public performances of theatre and music, and both also saw no objection to performances
attended by both occupying troops and German civilians. In the areas
initially occupied by Soviet and French troops, local German artists found
that their services were almost immediately in demand, and that few questions were asked about what they had been doing before the surrender.
In Karlsruhe, the French immediately set about repairing the Baden State
Theatre, and within ten days were staging the first performances there.[44]
Similarly, in Stuttgart, where the opera house was largely undamaged, they
quickly allowed performances by the Philharmonic Orchestra. In Berlin,
the Soviet Commandant, Bersarin, summoned artists to a meeting on
14 May, and instructed them to get back to work. A surviving group of
musicians from the world-famous Berlin Philharmonic Orchestra
performed its first post-war concert on 28 May, and this was rapidly followed by
others. An undamaged cinema in southern Berlin, the Titaniapalast, was
used as a concert hall, and in fact became the home of the Philharmonic
for several years.[45] In other cities occupied by the Soviets, like Dresden,
there was a similarly quick resumption of artistic activity.

There was in Berlin another significant development, which presaged
future Cold War divisions. The Soviets quickly arranged the formation of what was called the *Kulturbund zur demokratischen Erneuerung
Deutschlands* (Cultural League for the Democratic Renewal of
Germany).[46] This was an ostensibly non-party organisation, open to artists and intellectuals all over Germany, and committed to a wide ranging
reconstruction of German cultural life in an anti-Nazi spirit. The official
formation of the *Kulturbund* was marked with a ceremony which in
many ways set the tone for future developments in the Soviet Zone. The
Berlin Philharmonic performed works by Beethoven and Tchaikovsky,
speeches were made in the 'democratic-antifascist' spirit encouraged by
the Soviets, and a number of Germans were appointed to key positions.[47]
A 'manifesto' embodying the new ideas was published. The President of
the *Kulturbund* was Johannes Becher, already working for the Soviet-
licensed daily, the *Tägliche Rundschau*. Local branches of the *Kulturbund*
were quickly formed, not just in the Soviet Zone, and in the first post-
war months and years, it did sponsor a diverse range of cultural activities,
including concerts, theatrical performances, and educational talks. Many
of these struck a decidedly modern and internationalist note, and there
was a freedom which would, after 1947, be greatly circumscribed.

Nonetheless, the British and the Americans were rightly suspicious that the *Kulturbund* was a communist front organisation. It was up and running in Berlin by the time the British and Americans arrived there in July 1945, and they found themselves presented with a *fait accompli*. A Soviet officer, writing in 1959, recalled how a British journalist, newly arrived in Berlin, asked Becher directly whether the *Kulturbund* was a communist organisation. Becher responded, using the jargon of the German communists, that its intention was to bring together 'progressive German artists'.[48] Reluctantly the British allowed the *Kulturbund* to form branches in their zone. Ironically, until its expulsion in November 1947, the headquarters of the *Kulturbund* was in the British Sector of Berlin. The British and Americans had no desire to replace Goebbels' Reich Chamber of Culture with a similarly centralised organisation, and initially discouraged the formation of any but the most local and private artistic bodies. They soon realised that the Soviets had stolen a march on them, and that high culture was an area which the Germans themselves took very seriously. Within a few weeks of arriving, local British commanders in northern Germany were calling upon their superiors to allow concerts, operas, and plays. The demand was supported by Montgomery, and by William Strang, the senior Foreign Office diplomat responsible for Germany.[49] In July 1945, the British issued their first Information Control Directive, announcing that some entertainments would be restarted for German audiences, not for high-flown cultural reasons, but 'to combat idleness, boredom', and 'fear of the future'. 'Music, opera, and ballet', the Directive stated, 'will be given preference over other forms of entertainment, as providing less [sic] opportunities for subversive propaganda.'[50]

The Americans faced a more acute situation. They had demanded that the French relinquish control of Stuttgart and Karlsruhe, but by the time American troops arrived there, unfavourable comparisons were being made. The locals were apparently led to believe that plays and concerts would no longer be allowed, and the Americans had to go to theatrical lengths to persuade them otherwise. When the 100th US Division formally took over command in Stuttgart at midday on 8 July 1945, a prepared licence was immediately presented to a German official, Albert Kehm, and at 12.02 precisely, Schubert's Trout Quintet was performed. This was followed by a symphony concert at 5.00pm that evening.[51] By this time the Americans had already re-formed the

Munich Philharmonic Orchestra and were using this to give public and broadcast concerts. American plans to sponsor high culture were frustrated by the need for troop entertainment. All over Germany, concert halls, theatres, and cinemas, even if only barely useable, were requisitioned by occupying soldiers, but this problem was particularly severe in the American Zone; it would be years before many venues would be fully returned to local German authorities.

Strangely, given their recent experience of Nazi occupation, the French were the most proactive in their cultural programme, and the most willing to overlook potential Nazi affiliations. One might expect that they would favour a harsh occupation, and indeed theirs was in many ways. Food was very short, and much of the limited industrial production of their zone was taken to France in reparations. Nonetheless, the French very quickly developed an ambitious programme to support German artists, and to sponsor tours by French musicians in their zone. They also favoured 'mixed audiences', something the Americans and British were very reluctant to allow. By February 1946 the French could celebrate the success of tours by many of their musicians and ensembles, and their support of German playhouses and orchestras. They had even made available a special train, which could transport a whole opera company or a symphony orchestra, and used this to bring whole ensembles from the American Zone to perform in Baden-Baden.[52]

BLACK LISTS AND THE *FRAGEBOGEN*

The Allies faced a particularly complex problem in trying to 'denazify' the personnel working in the information media. They were concerned here not with prosecuting individuals for carrying out specific crimes, but with excluding from employment in positions of influence those people who had been active Nazis. They were committed to this by the Potsdam Declaration, but the implementation of its principles was very difficult. The most straightforward test which they could apply, whether an individual had been a member of the Nazi Party, was not entirely helpful because millions of Germans were able to claim that they had joined the Party after 1933 not from conviction but from necessity. Although rightly sceptical about these claims, all the Allies in practice tended to use early Party membership to decide who was, or was not, fit for employment in the information services. Anyone who had joined the Party before 1933 was certainly excluded.

In the first weeks and months of Allied occupation, decisions about who to exclude were made locally, and often in haste. The officers with responsibility for different media were reliant on documents captured locally, on denunciations which might or might not be accurate, and on snippets of information gleaned from various other sources. Inevitably they made mistakes. We can get a snapshot of the early denazification of the cultural scene from copies of undated, roughly typed American 'Black, Grey, and White Lists' now in German archives. These list hundreds of individuals from particular institutions which had been investigated. Those on the 'Grey List' were not to be employed in 'policy making' or in a 'creative capacity'; those on the 'Black List' were 'not to be employed at present'. The *Land* Theatre in Coburg had clearly been investigated by the Americans, and dozens of its employees were in these categories, from the conductor down to musicians, singers, stage and lighting technicians, hairdressers, porters, and the 'refreshment room clerk'.[53]

By the autumn of 1945, the occupiers were in a better position to draw together their intelligence, and using captured central records the Americans first published their 'blacklists' in October. In January 1946, the Control Council passed its Directive No. 24, which outlined a common framework for the exclusion of ex-Nazis from 'positions of responsibility'.[54] By this time, the enormous scale of this undertaking had become clear to the occupiers, and all had accepted that they needed the help of German tribunals to screen those working in 'positions of responsibility' in different sectors of society. All over Germany in 1946, committees and tribunals were formed, under Allied supervision, to review these cases. In the American Zone, the 'Law for the Liberation from National Socialism' was passed in March 1946, and provided the framework for these tribunals.[55] It was similarly used in the French and British Zones. All Germans wishing to work in a position of responsibility had to fill in a questionnaire (or *Fragebogen*) and the responses on this were used to judge which of five categories – ranging from 'Major offenders' to 'persons exonerated' – they should be placed in. The Allies were, to a greater or lesser extent, suspicious of these German tribunals, and were not yet prepared to let control of this vital area slip from their grasp. Through 1946 they continued their own investigations, and produced their own lists of people who they felt should be excluded from

responsible positions. Different branches of the four military governments had their own security and intelligence services, and it is hardly
surprising that these were often at cross purposes. Many Germans working in the media or the arts took advantage of this, and if they were
excluded from employment in one zone they moved to another to try
their luck there.

The whole process has been roundly criticised. From the perspective
of Germans trying to eke out a living in the post-war period, the
Allied approach was typically seen as vindictive, bureaucratic, and
arbitrary. A widespread perception was that lesser offenders were
victimised, while those more gravely implicated escaped punishment.
The different approaches taken by the four military governments were
also criticised, and inevitably some were seen as more fair than others.
Broadly, it appears now that the British and French were most lenient,
the Soviets were most arbitrary, and that the Americans were by some
way the most severe and the most consistent. Indeed the Americans,
who argued that higher standards of denazification should apply in the
information services than in other areas of civil society, had constantly
to put pressure on the other occupiers to exclude ex-Nazis who
moved from the American Zone to seek employment elsewhere. The
American 'White, Grey, and Black Lists', which were published and
distributed to the other Allies, grew and grew during 1946, and by the
end of the year those specifically for Germans working in Press, Radio,
Film, and Theatre looked like small telephone directories. They listed
tens of thousands of people, male and female, famous and unknown,
who were excluded from employment.[56] Most controversial were the
cases of artists. Nobody doubted that Nazi journalists or editors should
be excluded, but the British, French, and Soviets, to say nothing of
most Germans, were reluctant to imagine that artists, particularly great
musicians, could be politically compromised.

The most controversial case was that of Wilhelm Furtwängler, still
widely acknowledged as one of the great conductors of the twentieth
century. He had conducted the Berlin Philharmonic throughout the
Nazi years, and in American eyes had therefore been a willing agent for
the Nazi propaganda machine. The Soviets and the French were both
prepared to overlook this and in 1946, when Furtwängler returned from
Switzerland, where he had fled in February 1945, tried to get him to
work in their zones. The British reluctantly followed the American line,

which was clearly enunciated by Robert McClure in a press conference when Furtwängler returned to Berlin in February 1946:

> It is an indisputable fact that through his activities Furtwängler was prominently identified with Nazi Germany. By allowing himself to become a tool of the party, he lent an aura of respectability to the circle of men who are now on trial in Nuremberg for crimes against humanity. [...] It is inconceivable that he should be allowed to occupy a leading position at a time when we are attempting to wipe out every trace of Nazism.[57]

Through 1946, the Americans prevented Furtwängler from conducting in public. There were similarities in the case of the film director Leni Riefenstahl, who was working on a 'mountain film', *Tiefland*, in the Austrian Alps when the war ended. Initially cleared by the Americans, she found herself under French jurisdiction. Some French film officers wanted her to be allowed to complete the film, but the *Sureté* wanted her investigated because of her earlier work with the Nazi Party. McClure intervened personally in May 1946 to demand of the French that she not be allowed to work on films, and after this, she was in fact excluded from work until 1949.[58]

We should think about more than the most famous cases. Through 1945 and 1946, tens of thousands of German writers, actors, musicians, and technicians in all fields of culture and entertainment were excluded from work. In most cases this meant more than financial hardship and damage to public reputation. To be on an Allied blacklist at this time was potentially catastrophic. Artists in employment frequently received better rations and other perks. Those blacklisted might also be turned out of their houses, and were sometimes reduced to manual labour in order to make ends meet. Although most, like Furtwängler and Riefenstahl, were able after 1946 to rebuild their careers to a greater or lesser extent, many suffered permanently. David Monod has researched intensively the American denazification of German musicians. He records how the wartime conductor of the Munich Philharmonic, Oswald Kabasta, reacted to his dismissal in October 1945:

> An impulsive musician with a bad heart and an unsteady temperament, Kabasta was devastated [...] From his hospital room he issued mournful appeals to the Americans and the city for rehabilitation; but ICD remained firm. Four months after his blacklisting, the conductor killed himself.[59]

8

WAR CRIMES TRIALS:
SEPTEMBER 1945–NOVEMBER 1946

There shall be established after consultation with the Control Council
for Germany an International Military Tribunal for the trial of war criminals whose offenses have no particular geographical location whether they
be accused individually or in their capacity as members of organisations or
groups or in both capacities.

*From the London Agreement for the Establishment of an International Military
Tribunal, 8 August 1945.*[1]

On a late September evening in 1945 Albert Speer was delivered to the
prison in Nuremberg in a canvas-covered lorry. He wrote: 'A gate was
opened; I stood for some minutes in the corridor of a block of cells
which I had seen in the newspaper a few weeks earlier. Before I knew
it, I was locked into one of them. Opposite me Goering peeped out
of the opening in his cell door and shook his head. A straw pallet, tattered and filthy old blankets, impassive indifferent guards. Although all
four floors of the building were occupied, an eerie silence prevailed.'[2]
Over the next few days Speer saw several of the other 'major war criminals' now assembled for trial before the International Military Tribunal.
Sauckel, formerly in charge of the slave labour programme, was 'gloomy,
but at the same time rather embarrassed'; Funk, the former President of
the Reich Bank, 'looked extremely worn and downcast'; Keitel, Hitler's
former chief of staff, 'looked shockingly run-down'.

Hjalmar Schacht, Hitler's Minister of Economics before 1937 and Funk's predecessor as President of the Reich Bank, was brought to Nuremberg at the same time as Speer. He too was shocked by the stern treatment and spartan facilities there. The prisoners were kept in strict isolation, and under constant observation. Once a week they were allowed a bath; the food ration was a carefully calculated 1,550 calories per day. The prisoners were not allowed anything which might help them to commit suicide, and wore unkempt clothes. This strict regime was devised and implemented by Colonel Burton Andrus, the American officer in charge of security at the prison and during the subsequent trial. Schacht, who saw no reason why he should be on trial at all, thought Andrus 'a thoroughly unpleasant man'.[3]

By the time Speer and Schacht were transferred to Nuremberg, most of the 'major war criminals' were already there. Erich Raeder, former Grand Admiral of the German Navy, and Hans Fritzsche, a former senior official of the Propaganda Ministry, were delivered by the Soviets in October. Most of them had by this time been in various detention centres for several months, and some were in a very poor mental state, shocked both by their treatment and the charges they now faced. Fritzsche had been roughly interrogated in the Lubyanka prison in Moscow after being captured in Berlin; Hans Frank, the former Governor of Poland, was in a state of abject penitence; Rudolf Hess, who had been held in captivity since his abortive flight to Britain in May 1941, was apathetic and withdrawn, and appeared at times to be insane. Ribbentrop, Hitler's Foreign Minister, was in a particularly poor state, close to breakdown. In contrast Hermann Goering had been weaned off an addiction to painkilling drugs, and was in a better physical and mental state than he had been for some time. On 25 October Robert Ley committed suicide by hanging himself with a towel from the bars of a window set high on the wall of his cell. After this, Andrus tightened his regime further: the prisoners were deprived of shoe laces, ties, or belts, and their previously solid writing tables were changed for insubstantial ones which would not bear their weight. All this was to prevent further suicides, but it added to the misery of the prisoners. Schacht described writing at his flimsy table as 'sheer torment'.[4]

Nuremberg was not initially the preferred site for the trial. The Soviets had wanted to stage the proceedings in Berlin, and the first meetings of the IMT were held there, but all soon agreed that the IMT should sit in Nuremberg, in the American Zone. A large courthouse there, next to the prison, was largely intact, as was the Grand Hotel, which served during the trial as a base for the prosecution teams. Most of the rest of Nuremberg was in ruins, after frequent bombing raids and the street fighting in April 1945. The medieval city once so closely identified with the Nazi Party rallies and the infamous laws denying Jews citizenship was a place of desolation. Major Airey Neave, the British officer selected to serve the indictments on the prisoners, later recorded his first impressions: 'There was a sickening smell of disinfectant. On all sides stood mounds of stone and splintered wood, where the dead civilians lay buried. Some said there were six thousand corpses. It was not possible to drink the local water.'[5]

Through the summer of 1945 the Americans, who at all stages drove the Nuremberg trial, had been preparing the charges and gathering evidence against the accused. Thousands of captured documents were scrutinised and translated. There was no shortage of general evidence about Nazi atrocities, nor could it be denied that Nazi Germany had waged aggressive war. What was difficult was to link the wider patterns of Nazi criminality with the individuals on trial. There were thousands of survivors of the camps, and no shortage of witnesses to individual atrocities, but the defendants before the IMT had not directly taken part in these. Most of them had signed hundreds of documents, some deeply incriminating, but typically they argued that these were invalid, or irrelevant.

Later, as the trial progressed, the prosecution introduced as witnesses a number of Nazi perpetrators who were willing to testify to the direct involvement of some in the dock, but this brought its own problems. There was indeed something bizarre and repugnant about some of these witnesses, self-confessed mass murderers, giving evidence before such a tribunal. Lengthy interrogations of the defendants under oath, before and during the trial, provided some help to the prosecution but also gave an early indication of the strategies that the defendants would employ. Again and again they denied knowledge of the concentration camps, the torture, the medical experiments, the killing of prisoners of war, and the appalling treatment of slave labourers; they rejected the idea of complicity in the plans to invade different countries; and they denied that they were present when critical decisions were made. In some cases they turned on one another. Speer and Sauckel sought thus to shift responsibility for the exploitation of slave labour onto each other; Schacht throughout expressed his low opinion of his fellow defendants; almost all blamed the absent Nazis, Himmler, Goebbels, and Bormann. According to Bradley Smith, the American prosecutors were, before the trial opened, deeply depressed by the difficulties they faced collecting sufficient evidence to prove the charges.[6]

On 19 November, the indictments were served on the individual defendants in their cells by Airey Neave, accompanied by Andrus. These reflected the Tribunal's desire to find those charged guilty both of individual crimes and of complicity with the 'common plan' of Nazi aggression and tyranny. One stated:

> The defendant Kaltenbrunner between 1932–45 was a member of the Nazi Party, a General in the S.S., a member of the Reichstag, a General of the Police, State Secretary for Security in Austria in charge of the Austrian Police, Police Leader of Vienna, Lower and Upper Austria, Head of the Reich Main Security Office.
>
> The defendant Kaltenbrunner used the foregoing positions and his personal influence in such a manner that: he promoted the consolidation of control over Austria seized by the Nazi conspirators; and he authorised, directed and participated in War Crimes and Crimes against Humanity involved in the system of Concentration Camps.[7]

Kaltenbrunner was one of several who wept when they received the indictment. The prisoners were also told at this time of their right to a defence lawyer.

The trial opened on 20 November 1945 with a statement of the charges against the accused. This ran to 24,000 words, and took a whole day to read out. Notoriously, the Soviets had insisted that amongst many other atrocities, the indictment should list the murder of 11,000 Polish officers in the Katyn Forest in 1941.[8] Critics of the IMT have subsequently made much of this, claiming that it displays the hypocrisy of the prosecutors, and the unfairness of the proceedings. As we shall see, it certainly came up at critical points in the trial. The indictment delivered, the defendants were all asked separately to plead innocent or guilty. All pleaded 'not guilty', except Hess, who said 'Nein' when asked to plead. Lord Justice Geoffrey Lawrence, the British President of the Tribunal, entered a plea of 'not guilty' on behalf of Hess. Before presenting detailed evidence, the four Chief Prosecutors spoke about the separate counts under which the defendants were indicted. Robert Jackson, the Chief American Prosecutor, was conscious of the magnitude of the occasion and stressed the huge responsibility of the Tribunal, declaring: 'The wrongs which we seek to condemn and punish have been so calculated, so malignant, and so devastating, that civilization cannot tolerate their being ignored, because it cannot survive their being repeated.'[9] On 4 December the British Prosecutor, Hartley Shawcross, also referred to the larger purpose of the Tribunal, and anticipated the criticism that it represented nothing more than 'victors' justice':

> And so we believe that this Tribunal acting, as we know it will act notwith-
> standing its appointment by the victorious Powers, with complete and judicial
> objectivity, will provide a contemporary touchstone and an authoritative and
> impartial record to which future historians may turn for truth and future
> politicians for warning.[10]

After this, the trial proper got underway, with the detailed exposition of individual charges. As the prosecutors' main strategy was to present an overwhelming mass of documentary evidence, this took many weeks. In Neave's account, this led to 'relentless hours of boredom',[11] but its wider importance should not be overlooked. Systematically, and in great depth, a catalogue of horrors was unfolded and documented. Twenty-seven volumes containing the verbatim transcript of the trial, and many associated documents, were published in 1947 in a conscious effort to provide a secure documentary record of Nazi crimes. To this day, although details have often been questioned, the Nuremberg trial proceedings have provided a remarkably secure evidential base for further study of the 'Third Reich'. Paradigmatic understandings of Nazism were established. Victor Klemperer in Dresden wrote in his diary for January 1946 that he had heard for the first time a new linguistic usage with which we are all now familiar: 'A witness at Nuremberg repeatedly talks of the FINAL SOLUTION, to which Jews were transported, and means by that the gas ovens. Along the lines of human material, items.'[12]

On 29 November 1945 the prosecution showed a film of American and British footage of the concentration camps liberated in April 1945. In an otherwise darkened courtroom, lights were kept on the defendants. Airey Neave, who was watching, noted that 'few of the defendants could bear to watch the whole film'. Funk and Fritzsche wept. Schacht, characteristically and symbolically, 'sat with his back to the screen'.[13] The film doubtless made a particular impact on everyone present, but it highlights the problem the prosecutors faced. They submitted that all the defendants shared responsibility for the scenes shown, but the film itself did not prove that any of them individually had any connection with the concentration camps.

The proceedings of the IMT were extensively publicised around the world, and particularly in Germany. The licensed German press carried long reports, and much of the proceedings were broadcast on Allied radio stations in Germany. The publicity reached most of the German population, and there is no doubt that it was a sombre and sobering experience. Some were alienated by the seemingly endless revelation of horrors, and others simply overloaded. Klemperer recorded in December the view of one acquaintance: 'Reingruber said, it was a mistake on the Allies' part, to spin out the Nürnberg trial so far and so long on the wireless. It made people numb and indifferent. That was also my opinion exactly.'[14] Klemperer's view notwithstanding, it appears from opinion surveys conducted in the American Zone that high percentages of the population there read newspaper accounts of the trial, and perhaps more surprisingly, that typically two thirds or more of respondents thought the newspaper reports were reliable.[15] Nuremberg was the 'hottest topic' of readers' letters to the *Neue Zeitung* in 1946.[16]

As the prosecution case developed, new horrors came to light. The Soviet Prosecutor Colonel Smirnov informed the Tribunal on 27 February 1946 that he wished to present evidence of 'centres for the extermination of people. These cannot even be considered to be concentration camps because the human beings in these places rarely survived more than 10 minutes or 2 hours at the most.' To prove this, Smirnov called to the witness box Samuel Rajzman, one of the few survivors from Treblinka. Rajzman testified that between July 1942 and August 1943 as many as 10,000–12,000 Jews daily had been murdered at Treblinka in gas chambers, most within minutes of arriving at the camp. He estimated that a total of one million people had been killed there. Remarkably, none of the other prosecution or defence lawyers questioned Samuel Rajzman. Perhaps what he said seemed simply unbelievable; perhaps they were stunned by what they had heard. After Rajzman's testimony, Smirnov introduced a document from a Polish magistrate which estimated the total figure of deaths at Treblinka at 781,000.[17] Some abstract knowledge of Treblinka had filtered through to the British and Americans in 1942 and 1943, but the Germans had destroyed the camp after an uprising there, and when the site was overrun by Soviet forces in September 1944, they had given very little publicity to it, preferring to show journalists and photographers the better preserved buildings at Maidanek. If the testimony introduced by Smirnov seemed incredible, it was subsequently confirmed by another witness who had seen the gas chambers at Treblinka in operation.

Rudolf Höss had been working near Flensburg as an agricultural labourer with a false identity after walking out of British custody in 1945. The British meanwhile had found out more about Höss from former guards at Auschwitz, and kept his family, who were living nearby, under surveillance. In March 1946 Höss was arrested by British Military Police; after interrogation he was taken to Nuremberg, where he was questioned by the American prison psychiatrist, and talked remarkably freely. Bizarrely, Höss was called before the IMT as a defence witness by Kaltenbrunner's lawyer, and testified on 15 April. His interrogation reports were also submitted as evidence to the Tribunal. Höss testified that he had visited Treblinka to observe what he thought was a primitive process for mass killing, using carbon monoxide fumes, and gave details of the more sophisticated process, using Zyklon B, a gas developed originally to kill vermin, which he had implemented at Auschwitz. When questioned about the numbers of people killed at Auschwitz, Höss replied that he did not know a precise figure, but referred to another hitherto little-known name that was cropping up with increasing frequency during the trial: Adolf Eichmann. According to Höss, Eichmann had told him that in total two million Jews had been killed at Auschwitz. Höss himself estimated the figure at two and a half million.[18]

This is a good example of the confusion with certain evidential details which has been used to cast doubt on the larger validity of the IMT. Many different estimates have been made of the number killed at Auschwitz, some much higher, others considerably lower. Hartley Shawcross rightly pointed out later in the trial that these various, huge figures should not mask the point that a single murder was an affront to humanity. Arguments about the figures today should in no way obscure the enormity of the crimes tried at Nuremberg.

ZONAL WAR CRIMES TRIALS

As the proceedings at Nuremberg developed in the full spotlight of publicity, hundreds of other war crimes trials were being held, all over Germany and Europe. Most were conducted much more quickly than the IMT, but they shared some of its chief characteristics. Whether these trials were conducted under the authority of Control Council Law No. 10, or under separate military or national jurisdictions, they were not jury trials. Nor was there any right of appeal. Although defendants were allowed to present a defence, and given varying degrees of help with this, war crimes trials held in the immediate aftermath of the German surrender were conducted swiftly, and sentences were carried out even more quickly. In many of the trials held in the Soviet Union, sentences of death were carried out on the day they were pronounced. Although these trials may appear hurried today, there was a widely felt need for swift retribution in 1945. All the occupiers of Germany used the death penalty in their own countries at this time, and differed only in the way they implemented it. The French still used the guillotine, the Americans the electric chair, lethal injection, and hanging, and the Soviets shot those condemned to death in the back of the neck; the British favoured hanging, a form of execution considered deeply shameful in Germany. With the evidence of Nazi atrocities so recently imprinted on public consciousness, those tried as 'war criminals' in 1945 and 1946 were much more likely to face the death penalty than those tried later.

The harshest of the occupiers are those we know least about. The Soviets had been gathering evidence of war crimes committed against them since July 1941, and were determined to take revenge. From the start of the German invasion of the Soviet Union, German prisoners of war were interrogated to establish what route their units had taken in their advance into the Soviet Union, so that they might be linked to the burning of individual villages or to executions in particular places.[19] Detailed documentation of war crimes was collected and published, in Britain and America in translation. The Soviets gathered great numbers of photographs and German documents to support these allegations. These publications are still harrowing today.[20]

By 1945 many captured Germans had already been tried and executed by the Soviets, and we will never know how many were simply done to death without the benefit of any legal process. After the surrender in 1945, many senior German officers who had fled to the west were handed back to the Soviets, who took them back to the site of their crimes for trial. The fate of one group, documented by the War Crimes Commission, illustrates both the kind of German officer the Soviets sought to punish, and how they did it. A special court was established in Riga (now in Latvia) in January 1946, and it processed a number of senior officers including Lieutenant-General Ruff, previously commandant of Riga; Major-General Werther, previously in charge of the coastal district there; Major-General Paul, previously commander of the rear area of the German Fourth Army; and General Kuepper and Lieutenant-General Dejon von Moteton, previously in charge of Saldas and Liepaja, both near Riga. On trial with them was SS General Friedrich Jeckeln, formerly SS and police chief for the whole Baltic region. All were accused of atrocities carried out in the Riga district, and sentenced to death on 3 February 1946. The sentences were carried out on the same day.[21] Before being sent by Himmler to Riga to exterminate the Jews there, Jeckeln had commanded an *Einsatzgruppe* in the Ukraine, where he had personally supervised mass killings. In November and December 1941, Jeckeln organised one of the largest and most public mass executions of the entire Holocaust, when some 30,000 Jews were shot in the Rumbula forest near Riga and buried in mass graves.

Many other senior German officers were taken back to the Soviet Union in 1945 and 1946, and similarly tried and executed for atrocities committed during the war. The Soviets also prosecuted many Germans in their zone of Germany. Richard Evans, working from figures recently released, estimates that a total of 300 death sentences were passed by military tribunals in the Soviet Zone.[22]

Most of the concentration camps liberated by the Allies had been deserted by their guards beforehand, or, as at Mauthausen, turned over by the SS to local police in the last hours before Allied soldiers arrived. At Belsen though, the British had captured the commandant, Josef Kramer, and eighty of his staff, including the camp doctor. Kramer even conducted a senior British officer, Brigadier Glyn-Hughes, on a tour of the camp; during this Kramer appeared 'callous and indifferent'. The British quickly discovered that Kramer and many of the captured SS guards, including female overseers, had previously worked at Auschwitz. Belsen made such an impact on the collective British consciousness in

1945 that it became a matter of the highest importance to stage a public trial of at least some of those directly responsible for the horrors there. Before the IMT opened proceedings in Nuremberg, and before the Control Council passed Law No. 10, a British Military Court was convened in Lüneburg in north Germany under a Royal Warrant to try Kramer and forty-four others on 'war crimes' charges. Kramer and his assistants, including twenty women, were charged with having individually committed murder, and with having knowingly participated in a common plan to operate a system of ill treatment and murder in Belsen and in Auschwitz.

What has gone down in history as the 'Belsen trial' opened on 17 September 1945 and lasted for two months. Twelve defence lawyers were aided by Colonel H.A. Smith, then Professor of International Law at London University, who gave the closing speech for the defence. All the defendants pleaded not guilty. As at Nuremberg, the prosecution presented a mixture of documentary, photographic, and eye-witness evidence. A horrifying catalogue of cruelties was unfolded, ranging from descriptions of the selection procedure at the unloading ramp in Auschwitz, where doctors had decided who was to live and who was to die, to harrowing details of punishments visited on individual prisoners. Many of the images which have since come to define Nazi cruelty were made public at the Belsen trial, like the use of rubber truncheons and of Alsatian dogs to terrify prisoners, or merely for sadistic pleasure. Audiences in and outside Germany, accustomed still to think of women as the gentler sex, were shocked by the allegations of cruelty made against the female guards. A Polish witness, Sophia Litwinska, testified for example that she saw the SS guard Ilse Forster 'beat to death a young girl of 16 or 17 years'. On the more general charges of ill-treatment in Belsen, the court heard from a British officer, Major Berney, that after the liberation of Belsen he had looked for food stocks nearby, and found, only three kilometres away, a *Wehrmacht* camp with hundreds of tons of food of different kinds available, as well as a bakery capable of turning out 60,000 loaves a day.

The defence at the Belsen trial was conducted on behalf both of individual defendants and the whole group, and two main lines of argument were put forward. One suggested that the prosecution case rested on unreliable evidence; many of the incidents alleged by witnesses were simply denied. The defence counsel also argued that the defendants were at a low level in the Nazi apparatus, typically brainwashed by propaganda, and that they were carrying out orders which they did not themselves instigate. Major Winwood asked whether these 'minor characters' should be sentenced to punishments which could not be exceeded by the IMT, then in session in Nuremberg. Technical arguments were advanced about whether the crimes carried out in Auschwitz and Belsen could be termed 'war crimes', and whether if they were, the state, rather than individuals, should be held responsible for breaches of international law.

The court was largely unimpressed by these arguments, and on 17 November 1945, eleven of the defendants, including Kramer and three of the female guards, were sentenced to death. Nineteen others were sentenced to varying periods of imprisonment.[23] Particularly in Britain and in the British Zone, the Belsen trial was given great publicity. An employee of the British-licensed NWDR in Hamburg later recalled the freedom with which Germans presented and commented on the case: 'My colleague Axel Eggebrecht covered the Bergen-Belsen trial in all its gruesome detail every night after the news; on the evening the death sentences were pronounced he argued passionately against capital punishment'.[24] The British official executioner Albert Pierrepoint was brought over to Germany to carry out the sentences using a gallows erected in Hamelin prison. Here, on 13 December 1945, Kramer and his colleagues were hanged; all were then injected with chloroform to make sure that they were dead, and to expedite the process.[25]

Pierrepoint was kept busy in Germany through 1946 and beyond, as British military courts convicted hundreds of Germans and other nationals for war crimes and crimes against humanity. A number of these trials deserve mention. At Hamburg a series of trials were held in 1946 for staff of the Neuengamme concentration camp and its many subsidiaries, liberated by British troops in the last days of the war. Fourteen SS personnel, including the commandant Max Pauly, were sentenced to death, and more imprisoned.[26] British military courts in Wuppertal convicted a number of SS and SD officials for executing British and French prisoners of war. Others who had worked at the Natzweiler concentration camp or its satellite camps in Alsace were sentenced to death in Wuppertal and handed over to the French. Altogether 356 war crimes trials were held by the British in Germany, involving more than 1,000 defendants.[27] Pierrepoint executed some 200 war criminals convicted in

British courts in Germany and Austria after 1945. Others were shot by firing squad. In total the British sentenced 537 war criminals to death, and actually executed 398.[28] The British also delivered many war criminals to other countries for prosecution. Rudolf Höss, after appearing before the IMT in Nuremberg, was delivered to Poland, where he was later tried. He was executed at Auschwitz in April 1947. A group of staff from the Sachsenhausen concentration camp, including its former commandant, was handed over to the Soviets for trial in July 1946. They were lucky that by then the Soviets had abolished the death penalty.

One notorious trial displays the best and the worst aspects of the British attempt to punish Nazi war criminals. In March 1946 a British military court heard charges against three civilians from the firm of Tesch and Stabenow in Hamburg. This firm acted as an agency for the supply of poison gases, and instructed its customers in their use, before 1941 exclusively for destroying vermin and for fumigating different premises. Between 1941 and 1945 the firm had supplied the SS with huge quantities of Zyklon B for use in concentration camps, above all in Auschwitz. Some of this was used for disinfecting clothing and buildings, but by 1944 most of it was being used to kill human beings. The British accused the firm's director, Tesch, and two of his subordinates, Weinbacher and Drosihn, of a 'war crime', that of supplying poison gas 'used for killing allied nationals interned in concentration camps, knowing that it was so to be used'.

Tesch and his colleagues pleaded not guilty, and denied that they had known that the gas was used for killing people, or that they had instructed the SS in how to use Zyklon B to kill people. The trial lasted only eight days. It heard from other employees of the firm that Tesch and Weinbacher had known that the Zyklon B was used for gassing people in Auschwitz. The prosecution further alleged that this was common knowledge in wartime Germany. Although Drosihn was acquitted, Tesch and Weinbacher were found guilty, sentenced to death, and subsequently hanged in Hamelin prison. The evidence today appears less than totally reliable – although it appears highly likely that Tesch and Weinbacher knew that people were being killed with the gas they were supplying to Auschwitz – and the prosecution's charge that four and half million people had been killed at Auschwitz was undoubtedly too high. Tesch and Weinbacher were not the manufacturers of Zyklon B, and there was no clear evidence that they had participated in the gassings at Auschwitz, or elsewhere. The British military authorities were correct though to try to establish responsibility for mass murder, and to assert that this responsibility lay at various levels within the bureaucracy of the death camps.[29]

Running like a thread through almost all American writing on the Second World War in Europe is the idea that the liberation of the concentration camps in April 1945 gave a profound moral purpose to what had hitherto been a distant and rather detached enterprise. Eisenhower subsequently called it a 'crusade in Europe'. Paul Fussell, that most insightful psychological observer, uses the same term, and gives many examples of American officers and soldiers who discovered in April 1945 that they 'had been fighting and suffering for something positive, the sacredness of life itself'.[30] This sense of righteous indignation carried into the post-war period; it underlay the whole conduct of the IMT in Nuremberg, and of military courts in the American Zone.

One such court sat in Dachau, and held in 1945 and 1946 a series of trials of former guards from the camp. In December 1945, thirty-six of these, including a former commandant, Weiss, and a camp doctor, Schilling, were sentenced to death. 116 others were sentenced to terms of imprisonment.[31] Significantly, no proceedings were instituted against those American soldiers who had killed a number of guards at Dachau when they first entered the camp. The American CIC put considerable effort into tracing and capturing former guards from Mauthausen, and in March 1946, sixty-one of these were brought before the military court in Dachau, charged with 'Violations of the Laws and Usages of War'. Fifty-eight were sentenced to death, although some of these sentences were subsequently commuted to life imprisonment.[32]

The Americans also determined to prosecute German civilians involved in medical abuses. At the asylum near Hadamar they had discovered in April 1945 evidence of mass killing using morphine, and in October 1945 several of the perpetrators were brought to trial for the murder of some 400 Polish and Russian nationals there. The court heard that in an earlier phase of the Nazi 'euthanasia' programme, over 10,000 people had been gassed at Hadamar between January and August 1941, but the defendants were not specifically tried for this.[33] The death sentence was passed on Alfons Klein, chief administrator of the asylum, and 'two particularly sadistic orderlies'. They were executed in March 1946 in Bruchsal prison. The American Judge Advocate in this case,

Leon Jaworski, described the Hadamar trial as 'unquestionably the most depressing' of all his experiences in trying war crimes.[34]

The Americans also tried and convicted many German civilians for the murder of more than 1,000 captured airmen. By mid-1946 they had more than 300 Germans awaiting execution at Landsberg prison, and became concerned by the sheer number of executions they had to carry out. Through 1946 Lucius Clay grew more and more alarmed by the number of war crimes trials the Americans were trying to prosecute. He had to accept that these would have to be scaled down, or passed to others, if only because of the number of people needed and the cost. In September 1946 he recommended that American courts should continue to try only 'a comparatively few Nazis selected for notorious and prominent participation in Nazi atrocities'. These should be numbered, he argued, 'in the hundreds and not thousands'.[35]

The French, unlike the Americans and British, had suffered at the hands of the Nazis in their own country, and it was hardly surprising that they wanted both justice and revenge. They had also experienced the 'Germanisation' of two provinces, Alsace and Lorraine, both occupied in 1940 and incorporated within the German 'Reich'. In April 1946 a Military Tribunal was convened in Strasbourg to try eight German officials from the Nazi administration in Alsace. They included Robert Wagner, *Gauleiter* of Alsace between 1940 and 1945, his deputy Hermann Röhn, and others who had run a 'Special Court' in Strasbourg. Wagner and his accomplices were charged with inciting Frenchmen to bear arms against their own country, with the execution of British prisoners of war and French resistance fighters, with carrying out a forced labour programme, running concentration camps in Alsace, and with responsibility for the deportation of Jews to Germany. Wagner and six of the defendants were sentenced to death, but unusually, one of these, Hugo Grüner, former *Kreisleiter* (district leader) of Thann, was acquitted after judicial appeal.[36] The others were shot in Strasbourg in October 1946.

A Military Court was established at Rastatt in the French Zone of Germany, and here in March 1946, thirty-three former guards of the Neubrenne concentration camp, a sub-camp of Ravensbrück, were tried. Fifteen were sentenced to death. The French took longer to prepare the case against former guards of Natzweiler in Alsace, where so many French men and women had suffered, worked to death in the granite quarry, or executed in various ways. After the SS abandoned

Natzweiler in October 1944, many of the guards had been assigned to duty elsewhere and they were well dispersed by the end of the war. Several fell into British custody and were tried by them, or handed over to the French. Werner Rohde, a doctor at Natzweiler, was tried by a British military court at Wuppertal for killing prisoners with lethal injections. He was hanged in October 1946.[37] In February 1947, twenty-one former Natzweiler guards were sentenced to death at Rastatt.[38]

The trials conducted in separate zones referred to here were only the tip of an iceberg. Over 5,000 Nazi war criminals were prosecuted in the three Western zones in 1946 and 1947, and 486 of these were executed.[39] The Americans alone delivered nearly 4,000 more alleged war criminals to other countries for trial, and many of these were executed in places as distant as Yugoslavia and Norway, as well as in France, Poland, and Czechoslovakia.

THE DEFENCE AT NUREMBERG

Few of these trials attracted anything like the media attention that was still focused on the IMT in Nuremberg, where during the summer months of 1946 the defendants had the opportunity to put their defence. They deployed a variety of strategies to try to prove their innocence. Hess successfully persuaded many observers that he was mad, or suffered from amnesia. Hans Frank, who had presided over the Nazi occupation of Poland from his castle in Cracow, was one of several who in a confused way accepted general responsibility for the crimes while denying responsibility for the specific charges brought against them. Frank had reverted to a devout Roman Catholicism since his capture, and his testimony at Nuremberg typified the defence of many of the accused. It was Frank who on 18 April 1946 made the famous and oft-quoted statement that 'a thousand years will pass and this guilt of Germany will not have been erased'. Nonetheless, he maintained that he had known virtually nothing about the extermination camps in Poland, and that these had been the sole responsibility of the SS. Frank had passed his diary to the Americans, and was forced to admit that many statements in it were totally damning, but he insisted that Poland under Nazi occupation had been a place where public health and economic life had been improved, where education, culture, and religion had been safeguarded. He highlighted his own patronage of a symphony orchestra, and his personal protection of monasteries. He alleged that he had only supported Hitler, 'in a most wonderful rise to power, unparalleled in the history of mankind', until 1939: 'I was equally unhappy when in 1939 to my dismay I realised, more and more, that Adolf Hitler appeared to be departing from that course and to be following other methods.' After that he claimed to have repeatedly, but unsuccessfully, tried to resign.[40]

Since his arrest by the British, Speer had made great play of his decision to 'take responsibility' for the crimes of Nazism, and this brought him unpopularity with some of the other defendants at Nuremberg. Through the pre-trial interrogations and during the trial itself, Speer continued to assert this determination: in letters to his wife, and to his defence lawyer (which he knew would be read by prison censors) he stated that he had no concern for himself, and that he thought only of the German people, desiring to lift the burden of collective guilt from them.[41] When he took the witness stand in June 1946 Speer again highlighted his willingness to bear a general responsibility. He had, though, pleaded not guilty to the specific charges against him, and when confronted with details of the exploitation of foreign workers in the German armaments industry, he took refuge in evasions and denial. Wherever possible he likened his approach in increasing armaments production to the methods used in America and Britain.

Early in his cross examination, Speer's lawyer asked him directly whether he shared responsibility for 'the recruiting of foreign labourers and prisoners of war and for taking manpower from concentration camps'. Speer replied: 'Neither I nor my Ministry was responsible for this.' He admitted that he had visited Mauthausen, but claimed that he had seen no cruelty or ill-treatment of prisoners there. His lawyer asked him whether he knew that foreign workers were brought to Germany against their will. Speer replied that he thought they were legally obliged to work for Germany; whether such laws were justified or not, he said, was no concern of his. Cross-examined by Robert Jackson, Speer went into denial. Jackson confronted Speer with numerous examples of ill-treatment of foreign workers at the Krupp works in Essen, including details of a cramped steel cabinet in which individual workers had been locked for up to forty-eight hours. Speer answered: 'I would say that among German people such things do not exist.'

The Soviet prosecutor Raginsky was more aggressive with Speer, and confronted him with his participation in a meeting on 4 January 1944 which had unanimously agreed to deport four million foreign workers to Germany. Speer could not deny that the meeting had taken place, or that he had consented to its decisions, but now said that he could not decide for himself the extent of his responsibility. One of the most damaging points in his testimony had been his confession that he had agreed that idle workers should be threatened with transfer to concentration camps, but Speer claimed that he was not aware of how bad conditions there were. In a final exchange on this subject with his defence lawyer, Speer came out with a statement which paralleled Frank's rosy view of a benevolent German occupation in Poland. While Armaments Minister, Speer testified, he had 'heard only good and calming reports about the concentration camps from official sources'.[42]

Schacht treated his fellow defendants with open contempt. Alone amongst the accused, Schacht had previously been detained by the Gestapo, suspected of involvement in the 20 July 1944 conspiracy against Hitler. Schacht thought it outrageous that he should be indicted with the Nazi leaders before the IMT, since he had resigned his main official positions before the outbreak of war in 1939. He made no secret of his view that his fellow defendants were not only morally corrupt, but coarse and unintelligent. In his testimony at Nuremberg, and subsequently in his memoirs, he made much of their fondness for alcohol, claiming that this blunted their sensibilities. His defence was more sure-footed than Speer's. He admitted freely that he had helped the process of rearmament in Germany in the 1930s, but only, he claimed, so that Germany would be in a better bargaining position with other heavily armed neighbours. He claimed that he had worked under Hitler not to support him, but to restrain him. In his memoirs Schacht made much of how he exposed factual errors in the prosecution case against him, and detailed what he clearly thought were clever and witty replies to various clumsy efforts by Jackson to implicate him in responsibility for the planning of aggressive war in the 1930s.[43]

Eventually, after many weeks of testimony, the defence cases were finished, and the Tribunal moved to the most difficult part of the prosecution, the case against the 'criminal organisations'. Just as the charges against individual defendants had often been bogged down in a mass of differently numbered documents, and in problems of translation, the case against the 'criminal organisations' was enormously complex. Airey Neave was appointed to head a separate Commission to study and summarise the evidence relating to them; he had to consider 136,000 affidavits submitted in defence of the SS alone. Numerous witnesses came forward to testify that the indicted organisations had many different branches, and did not act as concerted bodies. This allowed participants at all levels to slough off responsibility, to assert that it lay higher up, or lower down, or with another office. The defence for the Gestapo argued that it acted quite legally, as an ordinary police force. The defence for the SS stressed its commitment to 'decency' and to 'discussion' with its opponents. German generals called on behalf of the General Staff denied that the *Wehrmacht* had taken part in the extermination of Jews or other civilians in the Soviet Union. Neave, 'sickened by the excuses' he heard and read, was glad to submit his final report to the Tribunal and to finish this work.[44]

THE JUDGEMENT

On 26 July 1946 Robert Jackson began the closing speeches for the prosecution. Although he had often seemed ill at ease in cross examination, his final speech was powerful and for the most part well-argued. Jackson tried to remind the Tribunal of the larger picture of Nazi aggression and criminality which stood behind the mountain of detailed evidence it had been presented with. He argued that civilisation itself demanded that the terrible record of the first half of the twentieth century should be condemned if it was not to be repeated. He tried to link all of the defendants with a larger conspiracy, arguing somewhat implausibly that they had all made 'integral and necessary contributions to the joint undertaking, without any of which the success of the common enterprise would have been in jeopardy.' Using language which at times was unnecessarily colourful, Jackson linked each of the defendants specifically with aspects of this 'common enterprise'.[45]

He was followed by Hartley Shawcross, who gave a long and eloquent presentation, in which he referred specifically to war crimes trials which had already been concluded. If other war criminals, like Kramer, had already 'paid the supreme penalty', Shawcross asked, 'are these men less responsible?' During this closing speech, Shawcross came back and back to the persecution of the Jews, and, given that the IMT has often been charged with understating the significance of the Holocaust, it is worth quoting some of his words specifically on this topic:

> There is one group to which the method of annihilation was applied on a scale so immense that it is my duty to refer separately to the evidence. I mean the extermination of the Jews. If there were no other crime against these men, this one alone, in which all of them were implicated, would suffice. History holds no parallel to these horrors.

Shawcross, like the French and Soviet prosecutors who followed him, dwelt at length on the individual responsibility of the defendants. Of Speer's defence he said: 'It displays once again the complete disregard for the fate of other people which runs like a sordid thread through the evidence in this Trial.' Shawcross also urged the Tribunal to consider its larger responsibility. 'In one way', he said, ' the fate of these men means little: Their personal power for evil lies forever broken; they have convicted and discredited each other and finally destroyed the legend they created round the figure of their leader.' Like Jackson he argued that the Tribunal had to reassert the dignity of the individual, and dispense justice on behalf of the millions of civilians and soldiers killed during the war.[46] The Soviet Prosecutor, Rudenko, brought matters down to earth. He concluded by demanding that all the defendants should receive the death sentence.

On 31 August the defendants made final statements from the dock. Several, like Goering, Hess and Ribbentrop, still proclaimed their loyalty to Hitler. Many admitted that they were deeply shocked by the evidence which had been put before the Tribunal. Hans Frank made a full admission of his own responsibility, but qualified his earlier statement that German guilt would not be erased in a thousand years. It had already been erased, Frank now said, by the crimes committed against Germans since the end of the war. Sauckel stated that he could not recognise the Hitler who had been portrayed before the Tribunal; he only knew a Hitler who was kind to workers, women, and children. Speer cleverly added to his previous defence by arguing that it was modern technology and the mass media which had made Hitler's criminal dictatorship possible, as if somehow the use of radio or telephones absolved individuals from the responsibility for the orders or ideas they passed over these instruments.[47]

After this, there was an interval of four weeks while the members of the Tribunal debated their final judgements in private. On 30 September the court reconvened to hear the judgement. This in itself was a lengthy process, including a review of the Tribunal's formation, of the charges, and of the evidence heard. Finally on 1 October, the verdicts were pronounced: Goering, von Ribbentrop, Keitel, Rosenberg, Jodl, and von Neurath were found guilty on all four counts; Fritzsche, von Papen, and Schacht were completely acquitted. The other defendants were found guilty on at least one count. Of the criminal organisations, only the SS, SD, Gestapo, and Leadership Corps of the Nazi Party were found guilty, and even these verdicts were qualified. The Tribunal ruled that members of these organisations could only be prosecuted if it could be proved that they knew when they joined that the organisation had a criminal purpose. In practice, the idea that a judgement by the IMT would make it possible subsequently to convict many members of these organisations without further proceedings collapsed altogether.

The eighteen individuals found guilty returned to the courtroom on the afternoon of 1 October to hear the sentences. Eleven were sentenced to death by hanging; Hess and Raeder were sentenced to life imprisonment, Speer and von Schirach to twenty years, von Neurath to fifteen years, and Dönitz to ten years. Bormann was sentenced to death *in absentia*.[48] The Soviet judges entered a dissenting verdict, arguing that Fritzsche, von Papen, and Schacht should not have been acquitted, that Hess should have been sentenced to death, and that the Reich Cabinet and the General Staff should also have been declared 'criminal organisations'.[49] There was a grim conclusion to the proceedings at Nuremberg: a gallows was erected in the gymnasium of the prison, and an American executioner was brought in to hang the condemned men. Somehow, Goering managed to kill himself with poison on the night before the executions were carried out. At one o' clock in the morning of 20 October 1946, the others were hanged, in the presence of the prison governor, German witnesses, and a chaplain. Streicher called out 'Heil Hitler' before he died. Keitel screamed 'Deutschland über Alles!' The bodies were taken to Dachau and cremated in the ovens previously used for so many concentration camp prisoners; the ashes were thrown into a nearby river.[50]

There have been many criticisms of the Nuremberg trial. It has been alleged that it was victors' justice; the Allies who sat in judgement were hypocritical, as they had themselves committed similar offences; the defendants were arbitrarily chosen, and they were indicted under charges which did not exist at the time the alleged crimes were committed. The charge of conspiracy or 'common plan' was ill-thought out, as was the attempt to brand whole organisations as criminal. Critics argue that there were many inaccuracies in the evidence presented, and that the sentences handed down were inconsistent. Even the executions were bungled. There is undoubtedly some substance in most of these charges, and the more closely one studies the trial proceedings the easier it is find to find others.

Manifestly this was victors' justice, in the sense that the Tribunal was composed of judges from the Allied countries which had defeated Germany. There was no jury. The Tribunal's Charter, although drawn up in the name of the United Nations, was written by the Allies. Undoubtedly these Allied countries had themselves between 1939 and 1945 committed acts which might be deemed 'war crimes', or 'crimes against humanity'. It was embarrassing to the British and the French that they had planned to occupy Norway before the Germans did so in 1940; and the Soviet invasion of Poland in 1939 was not something the Tribunal in Nuremberg wished to consider. The charge of waging 'aggressive war' was particularly contentious during the trial, and has proved difficult to sustain since. It was equally difficult to prove that the defendants at Nuremberg had been involved in a 'common plan'; many had clearly not taken part in the decision making which led to invasions of different countries, or to the mass murder of the Jews. Who decided when that the so-called 'Final Solution' should be implemented is still contested by the best historians of the subject. 'Intentionalists' and 'functionalists' have debated for decades whether there was a blueprint for the Nazi domination of Europe and the creation of a racial 'New Order'.

It is difficult to believe, as Jackson alleged, that without some of the lesser figures tried at Nuremberg, say Funk or Sauckel, Hitler's conduct of the war, or the persecution of the Jews, would have been 'in jeopardy'. With the benefit of hindsight, the choice of defendants could have been improved upon; most obviously, Heinrich Müller, head of the Gestapo, should have been indicted. There were indeed inaccuracies in the evidence presented at Nuremberg, and the calculated cynicism of the Soviets in maintaining, throughout the trial, that the defendants were responsible for murdering 11,000 Poles in the Katyn Forest was breathtaking. There were inconsistencies in the sentences, most notably between the death penalty meted out to Sauckel, and the term of imprisonment given to Speer, who by any measure had contributed far more to the maintenance of the Nazi war machine, and was more responsible for the suffering of slave labourers in Germany.

None of these criticisms is sufficient to invalidate the trial as a whole, or strong enough to suggest that it should not have taken place. The crimes of the Nazis were too great and too numerous simply to ignore. The idea that Hitler, perhaps with Himmler, Goebbels, and Heydrich, all conveniently dead, should bear total responsibility for these crimes is ludicrous. Recent scholarship, notably the work of Christopher Browning, has made it clear that 'ordinary Germans' who took part in atrocities were not forced to do so on pain of death or imprisonment. The more we learn about the 'Third Reich', the more we find evidence of moral corruption and indifference (the 'sordid thread' identified by Shawcross) running through broad strata of German society between 1933 and 1945. The fact that the Allies might themselves not have lived up to the high moral standards re-asserted at Nuremberg, before or since, was not in itself a reason to ignore the crimes of the Nazis. Furthermore, the IMT was not a show trial, as the Soviets had wished. Their effort to pin the blame for the Katyn forest massacre on the Germans manifestly failed, after cross-examination of defence witnesses. Similarly the Tribunal recognised that not all charges against all defendants could be sustained. The final ruling on 'criminal organisations' did not lead to thousands of innocent people being convicted. As for the sentences, few have argued that Speer should have been let off more lightly; if anything there has been criticism of the British, American, and French judges for allowing him to mislead them. It is instructive to note that as soon as Schacht was acquitted by the Allies at Nuremberg and released, he was tried before a German denazification court and sentenced to eight years' hard labour.[51]

The Americans brought, along with many aspects of their culture, the developing science of public opinion research to Germany after 1945, and from the start of their occupation they conducted extensive surveys amongst the German population of their zone. One of the most disturbing aspects of the surveys was that they revealed a strong residual loyalty to Nazism: throughout the Nuremberg trial an average of 47% of respondents still thought that Nazism had been 'a good idea, badly carried out'. The answers given to questions about the Nuremberg trial itself though are revealing. As many as 87% of Germans surveyed said that they had learnt from the trial; 60% felt that the indictment of 'criminal organisations' was justified; after the trial, 60% believed that none of the verdicts was too harsh. Throughout the trial, more than three quarters of those surveyed thought that the IMT was conducted fairly. In October 1946, 72% of Germans surveyed in the American Zone said that they would have liked to have seen Hitler brought before the IMT.[52] Of course these figures can be challenged and subjected to varying interpretations. Nonetheless, they provide some evidence that even amongst the defeated German population there was a broad acceptance of the Nuremberg process as justified, fair, and informative.

There were no further proceedings before the IMT in occupied Germany. The difficulties of cooperation between the Allies had been so great that all subsequent war crimes trials in Germany were conducted separately in individual zones, or increasingly after 1946 by German courts. The Americans, who had been most committed to the principles of the Tribunal's Charter, did stage eleven more trials in the Nuremberg courthouse between 1947 and 1949 under the authority of Control council Order No. 10. These followed the pattern set by the IMT in that they indicted groups of alleged war criminals, thus doctors, generals, SS administrators, and industrialists, but they were conducted by the Americans alone. Not until the International Criminal Tribunal for the former Yugoslavia opened its hearings in 1995 was the precedent set by the IMT at Nuremberg followed. It might be argued from this fifty-year delay, and the occurrence of numerous aggressive wars and associated crimes since 1946, that the Nuremberg trial was misconceived or pointless, but this is to overlook its obvious successes. The idea of 'crimes against humanity' has since been widely adopted, and has been used in notable cases, like that against Adolf Eichmann in 1961. At the time of writing, Saddam Hussein is being tried on this charge before an Iraqi court. Above all, Nuremberg re-asserted the principle of individual responsibility. It explicitly rejected the defence that a criminal was only following orders, and that the 'state', the 'Party', or some other impersonal bureaucratic organisation could supersede the responsibility of individuals for their own acts.

CONCLUSION

The judgement of the IMT in November 1946, and the execution or imprisonment of the last surviving senior Nazi leaders, marked the end of the first phase of denazification in post-war Germany. After this, an increasing number of war crimes trials were turned over to German courts, now functioning again in all four zones. At the same time, the whole denazification of civil society, which had reached its high point, was similarly derogated to German tribunals. All over Germany, 'nominal Nazis', previously excluded from responsible positions in the economy, the professions, and the arts, were gradually allowed to return to their former positions. Although the Soviets and their communist protégés in East Germany bitterly criticised the western Allies for allowing this, arguing that there was a 'restoration' of former Nazi elites in the western zones, they pursued a similar policy. Order No. 201 of the Soviet Military Administration in August 1947 allowed ex-Nazis to enter many previously restricted occupations in the Soviet Zone. In a symbolic moment, Wilhelm Furtwängler conducted the Berlin Philharmonic for the first time since the war on 25 May 1947. His return to the podium, although accompanied by gritted teeth in the American military government, was acclaimed by a German public which wanted now to turn its back on the Nazi past, and to get on with reconstruction. Although Furtwängler conducted the same music as he had in the last days of the 'Third Reich' – Beethoven's Fifth and Sixth symphonies – the American Music Control Officer in Berlin, John Bitter, reported that 'it was an honest musical success, no political demonstration, and the Philharmonic played beautifully'.[1]

By this time it was absolutely clear that there was no Nazi resistance in Germany. On the contrary, in every field the Allies had discovered a willingness to cooperate with them in the larger task of building a post-Nazi society. As we have seen, this cooperation was evident in education, the media, and in the arts, but it extended also to areas which might have been much more controversial. As well as the existing apparatus of German courts, the Allies had established thousands of local German tribunals to denazify their fellow countrymen and women, and these continued their work, in some cases, into the early 1950s. In certain rare instances, Germans working on these tribunals, or appearing before them as witnesses, were subjected to intimidation, but this was extremely rare, and did not at any stage threaten the larger process of denazification. A far more serious problem was the tendency of all these tribunals to err on the side of leniency, declaring up to 90% of those who came before them as 'exonerated'. When the different Allies permitted regular German courts to operate again after 1945, they were initially concerned that these courts might revert to the excessive cruelty of the Nazi period, and therefore stipulated that any death sentences passed by them must be ratified by their own military governments.

In fact, despite the high numbers of ex-Nazis who continued to work in the judiciary, these courts also tended to treat war criminals who came before them with leniency. In many cases, this was taken to disturbing extremes. Eric Johnson has researched the treatment of former Gestapo officials in the Rhineland, and notes how the state prosecuting authority in Cologne investigated over one hundred former Gestapo officers involved in the persecution, deportation and murder of the city's Jewish population. Only three of these officers were finally brought to trial, in 1954. Emanuel Schäfer, former head of the Gestapo in Cologne, who had also committed 'many misdeeds of the rankest order both in Germany and abroad during his prolific career', was sentenced to six years and nine months imprisonment. Although Schäfer was also wanted in Poland, Yugoslavia, and the Soviet Union, where he was accused of responsibility in the deaths of thousands of citizens, he was not deported. Franz Sprinz, who had succeeded Schäfer as head of the Cologne Gestapo, was sentenced to three years in prison. Kurt Matschke, head of the Jewish affairs section of the Cologne Gestapo from 1943, 'received only a two-year sentence'. According to Johnson, the treatment given to Gestapo officers in the Rhineland 'would prove to be similar in the rest of Germany'.[2]

By the end of 1946 it was also clear that the abolition of the Nazi Party had been entirely successful. By this time, new political parties, and older parties previously suppressed by the Nazis, were operating in all parts of Germany, standing for elections at local and regional level, and increasingly playing a part in the administration of public affairs. As in so many fields, the Soviets had stolen a march on the other Allies by allowing German political parties to operate in areas they occupied very soon after the collapse of the 'Third Reich'. It was perhaps no surprise that they allowed the German Communist Party to operate, but on 26 May 1945 they also established three other 'anti-fascist' parties.[3] Following this, the British and Americans had felt compelled to allow political parties like the Social Democrats and the newly formed Christian Democratic Union to operate in their zones from September 1945. The French allowed the formation of 'democratic and anti-Nazi parties' in their zone from December 1945.[4] Naturally all the occupiers maintained a close watch on the developing political scene in Germany, and were suspicious of anything which smacked of resurgent Nazism. From time to time in the occupation period, and subsequently in the early 1950s, concerns were raised about the nationalist orientation of certain groups, particularly when they involved former Nazis. Thus the British 'Political Division' in Berlin in 1949 reported to the Foreign Office in London that the *Deutsche Partei* (German Party) – which had nationalist tendencies, and sang the *Deutschlandlied* (the German national anthem) at its meetings – had won 13% of the vote in Hamburg in the recent elections for a new Federal Government.[5] None of these small right-wing parties ever played more than a marginal role in politics in either East or West Germany. The Americans, British, and French soon became more concerned about the activities of communists in their zones than those of former Nazis.

The end of the Nuremberg trial certainly did not mark the end of Allied war crimes trials. These continued until 1948, and for longer outside Germany. Slowly, and as we have seen, inadequately, German courts prosecuted some war criminals into the 1950s. Most significantly, under the authority of Control Council Law No. 10, the Americans staged a further eleven large trials in the Nuremberg courthouse between December 1946 and April 1949. As with the IMT, they indicted here groups of people who stood as representatives of some of the worst aspects of Nazi tyranny, thus doctors, judges, industrialists, the SS men who had administered the concentration camps, and those who had led the *Einsatzgruppen* in mass killings in the Soviet Union in 1941. Separately they held a trial of thirty-one Buchenwald guards in 1947. Significantly, the sentences passed by Allied military courts in 1947 and after became increasingly less harsh. The Soviets abolished the death penalty in their zone – as they did in the Soviet Union itself – in 1947, and as a result only terms of imprisonment were given to the Sachsenhausen guards tried in November 1947. Lucius Clay commuted the death sentences of a number of convicted war criminals in the American Zone in the summer of 1948, and pardoned others who had been sentenced to long terms of imprisonment. These included some very high profile cases with the public, like Ilse Koch, the wife of a former Buchenwald Commandant, and Clay's decision was bitterly criticised by many in America.[6]

Cynics, then and since, argued that the prosecution of war criminals had been sacrificed to the demands of Cold War politics, and that both the Americans and the Soviets were now more interested in getting the Germans on their side than in dispensing justice. This, it has been suggested, chimed with the German desire to forget about Nazism, and to overlook its crimes. While there is some truth in these allegations, there were also more pressing practical concerns, and, inevitably, a degree of weariness which set in as the immediacy of these crimes receded. Even after Clay's intervention in 1948, the Americans were still left with hundreds of convicted war criminals in Landsberg prison, including some sentenced to death. The newly elected Federal German Government abolished the death penalty in 1949, but the Americans reserved the right to carry out further death sentences in Germany during the early years of the Federal Republic, despite numerous protests from the Adenauer government, the churches, and the general public. In January 1951, the American High Commissioner John McCloy commuted all but five of the death penalties, and reduced the terms of imprisonment of the remaining prisoners in Landsberg.[7] The last American death sentences in Germany were carried out in June 1951. Those executed included Otto Ohlendorf, former head of *Einsatzgruppe* D, who had earlier testified before the IMT in 1946, and Paul Blobel, commander of *Sonderkommando* 4a, which had massacred more than 33,000 Jews at Babi Yar in Kiev in 1941.

The Allied Control Council continued to operate until March 1948, and its Laws and Directives did include further measures of denazification and demilitarisation. As the division between East and West became more pronounced in 1946 and 1947, it became increasingly difficult for the Western Allies to agree with the Soviets about the management of the German economy and the development of new institutions. In 1947 the Americans and British fused their zones to create the 'Bizonia', and in 1948 the French added theirs to make 'Trizonia', the future Federal Republic of Germany. The Soviets had already created central administrations for their zone, some run still by members of the émigré groups flown in at *Stunde Null*. The mood in the Control Council became more fractious, and the Soviets finally walked out in March 1948, shortly before closing the road and rail links between West Berlin and the western zones. Denazification was one area where there was, almost until the end, still some agreement. Significantly, the penultimate Law of the Control Council, passed on 19 December 1947, repealed 'Nazi Legislation on Motion Pictures'.[8] The Control Council for Germany remains a unique historical phenomenon, a remarkable experiment in the application of military law to reconstruct civil society, largely unknown to the general public.

The military occupation of Germany continued well after 1946, although there has been no military action since 1945. Formally, the separate military occupations in Germany ended in October 1949, with the formation of a Federal Republic in the West, and of the German Democratic Republic in the East. At the same time, the separate Military Governments were dissolved and replaced by 'High Commissions'. Germany was by 1949 a particularly tense front line in the Cold War, and large military forces had been there for years. Around the military bases of the Soviets, Americans, British, and French, whole settlements had been established to cater for their needs. Although the Russians finally pulled out of eastern Germany in 1994, there are still extensive American and British military establishments in Germany today.

It is very easy to find fault with the Allied occupation and denazification of Germany, and much of the historical writing on these topics does precisely this. Of course the occupiers lived in better material conditions than the occupied, in all zones. The British and Americans, like the Soviets, requisitioned the best surviving buildings in Germany for their own occupying forces, and similarly took advantage of other facilities, from opera houses to swimming pools. They had the commodities, notably cigarettes, alcohol and food, with the greatest value in the barter economy that flourished between 1945 and 1948. The fact that these were often traded for sex in post-war Germany was naturally a source of enormous resentment amongst the occupied population. At the political level, the paradox of 'democracy' being imposed by occupying armies has often been remarked on. The Germans themselves were acutely aware of this at the time, combining the words *Demokratie* and *Diktatur* to make the new label *Demokratur*. We should go further though, and not be coy about it: the Allies introduced multi-party democracy into Germany, or rather two forms of multi-party democracy in East and West, but they did not allow all parties to take part. The Nazi Party was expressly and finally made illegal. Nor was any similar party operating under a different name tolerated. By 1949, separate parties were operating in the GDR and in the Federal Republic, and lest we fall into the trap of assuming that somehow the West was 'free' and the East was not, we should remember that the Communist Party was outlawed in the Federal Republic in 1956.

Denazification has been seen as a part of this critical view of allied occupation. It is of course true that many alleged war criminals escaped. The well-known ones – Eichmann, Mengele, Stangl – are only the tip of an enormous iceberg. Many others, as we have seen, got away lightly, and many more still went unpunished. Some, like Werner von Braun and the other rocket scientists, were taken away by the Allies and given new lives. Of the minority who were prosecuted and punished by the Allies, one can say that their sentences were inconsistent, and in some cases unjust. Since the end of the occupation, and particularly since 1958, there has been a ceaseless procession of ex-Nazis tracked down, exposed, and prosecuted all over the world. Inevitably they have been entrapped in Cold War politics, or in the internal and external political affairs of the countries they have fled to, or where their crimes are alleged to have been committed. As their stories become public, it is all too often obvious that they got away from Germany and Austria – or elsewhere in Europe – very easily at the end of the war and during the occupation period. The various Allies appear often to have been negligent, inconsistent, and indifferent in dealing with these people.

The same can be said of the wider denazification: most areas of civil society, the professions, and the institutions of both the Federal Republic and the GDR – to say nothing of Austria – contained huge numbers of people whose background, affiliation, and activities before 1945 ought to have been debarred them from such public roles. Scholars have pointed to the most shocking examples, such as doctors who had practised 'euthanasia' who continued in medical practice, and judges who had convicted many to death under the Nazis who presided over various courts in the 1950s.[9] The figure of the Nazi doctor or dentist still working in a post-war medical environment has taken a strong hold on popular consciousness through endless embodiment in literature and cinema. One thinks here as much of the sinister Dr Emmenberger in Dürrenmatt's novel *Das Verdacht*[10] as of the dentist in the film *Marathon Man*. Escaping SS men and 'Nazi hunters' have provided material for whole literary and cinematic genres. Undoubtedly, many – too many – Nazis got away.

We must balance these critical views with an appreciation of what the Allies actually did, and with some of the effects of denazification. As we have seen, they arrested thousands of suspected 'war criminals'; they instituted cumbersome legal proceedings against them; they sentenced thousands to imprisonment, and executed hundreds. Should they have executed more? H.N. Brailsford, in a study commissioned by the Fabian Society in Britain, considered precisely this question in 1944. He wrote: 'The number of Germans guilty of war crimes, in one degree or another, may run into hundreds of thousands. We do not want a blood-bath. [...] To suggest life long imprisonment on such a scale is equally impossible: it would amount to a return to slavery'.[11] All we have learnt about Nazism since Brailsford wrote this suggests that the numbers implicated in serious crimes were even greater than he realised. Similarly, the Allies conducted huge screening processes in most areas of employment in Germany, looking to filter out people who had been active Nazis. By the end of 1946, in total the Allies had excluded some 300,000 people from positions of responsibility. Out of a total population of 65 million, this is a very high figure. They could have excluded more. There was a very fine balance to be struck between enforcing on the German people an absolutely rigorous denazification which would punish each and every ex-Nazi, but at the same time alienate most of the defeated population and produce martyrs amongst them, and a more pragmatic programme, which in its severity nonetheless made an incredibly forceful point.

From a purely material point of view, there were important considerations. Even the Americans struggled to finance their occupation in

Germany. Telford Taylor estimated in September 1946 that the prosecution of between two and four hundred more alleged war criminals in the American Zone would cost 'in excess of 4 million dollars'. Partly on these grounds Clay argued that the trials should be scaled down to a level at which, he recognised, they would play a symbolic role, looking to make an example of the most notorious Nazis, and not to punish them all.[12] What hope was there that the poverty-stricken British, or the Soviets and French – both devastated by war and occupation themselves – could afford more? None of them could for any length of time sustain their zone in Germany as an economic dependency and they therefore had to get the economy functioning again. This was impossible without the involvement of ex-Nazis in key administrations and professions. The German population lived, after May 1945, for the most part in abject poverty. Food rapidly became very scarce and by the winter of 1947 malnutrition was widespread. Children and the elderly suffered particularly. Clothing was so limited that many children went to school barefoot. Fuel was very scarce, and cold and damp took a toll. Diseases like tuberculosis were prevalent. Much of the work which did go on in factories and workshops involved dismantling the machinery for transport to the Soviet Union, France, or Britain.

The Allies could have been more rigorous, but only at the expense of sacrificing what judicial objectivity there was in their systems, and of further impoverishing the German people. Undoubtedly they would have generated much more unpopularity and discontent. They had to be conscious of the mood of the occupied people, and had to win their trust and to work with them. They also had to try to restore a decent material standard of life. A French officer noted grimly in 1947 that 'democracy was no replacement for calories'.[13] Indeed, the more we know about the severity of conditions in post-war Germany, the more remarkable it seems that there was so much cooperation and goodwill between occupiers and occupied.

Denazification was successful to the extent that a great number of the most guilty were punished. Nazism was very largely excluded from public life and discourse; most ex-Nazis who did continue in positions of responsibility had to present themselves as respectable 'democrats'. In politics, education, the press, and the arts, strongly anti-Nazi cultures were established. The public staging of war crimes trials did generate and enforce a confrontation with the most ghastly aspects of Nazism, one which has continued, in different forms, to the present day. It is a commonplace that Germany – particularly West Germany – developed a collective amnesia about Nazism after 1945, that it was swept under the carpet, and became a taboo subject. In fact, particularly in the early post-war years there was a great deal of discussion of Nazism, much of it, but by no means all, generated by the occupiers. We have seen how the various war crimes trials were publicised, and how cinema audiences were confronted with evidence of Nazi crimes. Newspapers and journals in 1946 and 1947 carried many articles examining these issues, and there was further discussion in letters they published. As German courts took on the burden of prosecuting war crimes after 1948, reports of proceedings against former Gestapo, SS, and *Wehrmacht* officers were a frequent occurrence.[14]

In fact, the taboo subjects in post-war Germany were not the crimes of the Nazis, but those of the Allies, and this is in itself an eloquent testimony to the extent of the wider German acceptance of wrong-doing. W.G. Sebald has noted how there was an extraordinary silence in Germany after 1945 about the bombing of German cities, and this is paralleled by the silence about rape. When German communists convened public meetings in the Soviet Zone after *Stunde Null*, this was the crime that dared not speak its name. Even though hospitals and doctors changed their rules to allow abortions for women with what were euphemistically termed 'war-related pregnancies', often, bizarrely with reference to Nazi regulations which permitted this,[15] the mass rape in Soviet and French Zones was not a subject for public discussion. Of course German victimhood was discussed in private, within families, but it was only later in the 1950s that these memories became more public, and were legitimised by publication. In a round table discussion published in the journal *German History* on the 60th anniversary of 1945, one commentator said that '1945 had the peculiar effect that the overwhelming majority began to think of defeat as the best thing that could possibly have happened to them.'[16] Undoubtedly this conviction played a huge part in the willingness of Germans after 1945 to accept the punishment of war criminals, the denazification of society, and the often striking material inequalities between occupiers and occupied.

Clausewitz, whose ideas have enormous relevance to the Second World War even though they were developed more than a century earlier, wrote in another of his famous aphorisms: 'In war the result is never final.' If one accepts his definition of war as the continuation of policy by other means, there is an indisputable logic here. Once war finishes, it is replaced by policy, and the negotiation between different policies. Clausewitz went further though, stating: 'Lastly, even the ultimate outcome of a war is not always to be regarded as final. The defeated state often considers the outcome merely as a transitory evil, for which a remedy may still be found in political conditions at some later date.'[17] Clearly he had in mind here the continued relationship between states which had engaged in a more 'limited war', perhaps exchanging a province or a few fortresses, or where the victor had extracted a war indemnity from the defeated party.

His idea certainly holds for 1918, when after the Treaty of Versailles, Nazism emerged as a political movement dedicated to the overthrow of the Treaty. 1945 was very different. It would be possible to argue that, after 1949, 'political conditions' in both the GDR and the Federal Republic were such as to allow for a return of some kind of normality within the two superpower blocs of the Cold War. Both states sought what might be called 'remedies' for some of the problems brought about by the war, but the decisive outcome of the war – the destruction of Nazism – was not regarded by either as a 'transitory evil'. In both states the central elements of the Nazi 'racial state' were explicitly rejected. A culture of human rights, and strong protection for individual freedoms was enshrined in the West. In the East, although a confrontational, class-based model of society was imposed, the GDR was based on an ideal of equality which was in complete opposition to Nazism. Even that most contentious aspect of the 1945 settlement, Stalin's *de facto* enforcement of the revised frontier between Germany and Poland along the Oder-Neisse line, has now been formally accepted, and appears unchallenged.

Of course there has been a recent resurgence of neo-Nazism, and it is tragic that it should have developed particularly strongly in parts of the former GDR. Without minimising the significance of this phenomenon, it should be placed in context. When, in 2003, the first neo-Nazi demonstration was allowed in the former West Berlin, the 2,000 or so skinheads marching with pre-1919 insignia (the swastika and other Nazi insignia are still not permitted in public in Germany) were greatly outnumbered by anti-Nazi demonstrators, and to a lesser extent, by police. Some counter-demonstrators held banners referring to Control Council Laws, showing that their continuing relevance, if not known outside Germany, is appreciated there. There is a separate argument over whether these 'neo-Nazis' are more properly understood as part of wider European right-wing racism than as a resurgence of the philosophy of Nazism.

Germany now is a state committed to human rights, at the heart of the European Union. Not without its own particular problems, it is like all other states in the globalised world coming to terms with multi-culturalism and multi-ethnicism. Since 1945, no German state has taken part in a war of aggression. A strong tradition of pacifism has become entrenched there. The culture of human rights is one which arises directly from the Second World War. First considered as a guiding principle at the United Nations conference in San Francisco in 1945, it was not until 1948 that the Universal Declaration of Human Rights was adopted by the United Nations. Since then more and more countries have signed the two International Covenants which enshrine these rights in law. It is of course well known that the victorious Allies in the Second World War were not places of racial equality. The 'colour bar' in America was still very real, and Britain in 1945 had yet to face the issues opened up by large-scale immigration from former colonies. The Soviet Union, although a multi-ethnic federation, still embodied a strong strand of anti-Semitism.

It is all the more notable that the Allied Control Council was using the language of 'discrimination' and of individual equality before the law, and enshrining these in its legislation for Germany immediately after the defeat of the 'Third Reich', well before the countries represented in it came around to that position. Article I of Control Council Law No. 1 repealed twenty-six 'Nazi Laws'. Article II applied to all other German laws, 'however or whenever enacted'. It stipulated that no law was to be applied in a way which would 'cause injustice or inequality [...] by discriminating against any person by reason of his race, nationality, religious beliefs, or opposition to the National Socialist German Party or its doctrines'.[18] In this fundamental sense, the settlement of 1945 has held up remarkably well. It has been challenged, and it has not eradicated wars of aggression, 'ethnic cleansing', or attempts to create societies based on segregation of one form or another. The equality of all individuals before the law is, however, still the ethical foundation of the western democracies and the many states which now emulate them.

The relative success of the occupation of Germany may also be judged in comparison with that going on today in Iraq. Here, three years after a complete military defeat, occupation forces appear all too often to be in conflict with the occupied population, or with large elements of it. A sustained and aggressive resistance has largely confined occupation troops and their civilian administrators to fortified zones and the protection of barracks in urban centres. Vicious attacks on other elements of the indigenous population continue to undermine all efforts to reconstruct civil society. Essential services have not been successfully restored. The efforts by occupation forces to empower new elites in different areas of society have met with considerably less success than they did in Germany in 1945. The trial of Saddam Hussein, perhaps unwisely, has not been held before an international tribunal, and the difficulties which have arisen in the course of his indictment before an Iraqi court similarly point to the relative success of the Nuremberg trial in 1945–1946. The trial of Saddam Hussein has dragged on, and appears some way from any resolution. The strain of conducting the trial, and the systematic intimidation of prosecution lawyers and witnesses by insurgents, have seriously undermined proceedings, and it appears not to be having any significant effect on the wider effort to move Iraq from dictatorship to some kind of functioning democracy. At the time of writing, Saddam Hussein and his fellow defendants have embarked on a hunger strike, bringing proceedings altogether to a halt. The Nuremberg trial appears orderly, expeditious, and just in comparison.

Of course there are huge differences between the occupation of Iraq after 2003 and the occupation of Germany after 1945. This is not the place to explore them. Suffice to say here that Germany in 1945 had actually suffered far greater physical destruction than Iraq in 2003, and suffered much greater human losses. The hostility between occupiers and occupied might with good reason have been far greater. The difficulties still faced in Iraq – to say nothing of Kosovo or Afghanistan – may serve, though, to place the occupation and denazification of Germany after 1945 in some perspective.

What of the purely military side of the equation? Eisenhower in particular has been criticised for his cautious handling of the campaign in north-west Europe, and his failure to adhere to key principles, notably that which dictates that the destruction of the enemy's forces is the central objective in war. His commitment to the 'broad front', and his reluctance to risk any broad strategic strokes which might have led to the encirclement and destruction of the German armies in the west, have been roundly condemned. The faltering conduct of the actual fighting by reluctant British and American soldiers has been added to the charges against Eisenhower, and the wider Anglo-American military leadership. Russell Weigley has considered these charges, and his intimate knowledge of the American military campaign, coupled with his understanding of American military tradition and its relationship with wider American history, lend his views lasting authority. Reluctantly, and having considered the charges from many angles, he concludes that the victory in Europe in the Second World War 'was more expensive and more often postponed than it might have been, because American military skills were not as formidable as they could have been'. A 'bolder generalship', he argues, 'might have shortened the war'.[19]

This is of course to enter the realm of speculation. Eisenhower, with more justification than Haig in 1918, can claim that he despatched his mission, having fully achieved its aims. In his final message to the troops who served under him he said simply: 'The task which we set ourselves is finished'.[20] In the course of his campaign, he did destroy huge German forces, particularly at Falaise, during the chase through France and Belgium, and in the final weeks of the war. He faced an enemy which produced huge numbers of new troops and new weapons, and which, like most defenders, counted on an improving strategic position with a contracting front line to defend and shortening routes of supply. The hopes some had – not Eisenhower, we should note – that the 'Third Reich' would collapse in August and September of 1944 now appear totally misplaced. The residual strength of Hitler's armed forces was much too great.

Soviet military policy in the east has been similarly criticised, as we have seen, from within. According to Chuikov, Stalin could have taken Berlin in February 1945 and ended the war then. From outside, this criticism has been more muted, mainly from recognition that the Red Army fought across much greater distances than did the western Allies, and faced a greater proportion of the German armed forces. In fact, there is greater substance to these charges. Through 1944 and 1945, more and more of the declining German military strength was diverted to the west. Virtually all its air power was deployed there by the end of the war. By allowing the remnants of Hitler's once formidable army some eight weeks to regroup outside Berlin, Stalin made the eventual attack in April 1945 considerably more difficult than it would have been in February.

Like Eisenhower and his political masters, Stalin and his generals had by the closing stages of the war an ever increasing material preponderance on their side. They could only possibly lose the war by making enormous errors of judgement. In both the East and West, the Allies had every incentive to act with caution. If they had other political objectives which lie outside the scope of this book – in Stalin's case the establishment of satellite states in Eastern Europe – there was every incentive to take the small amount of time to further them. In contrast, Hitler, facing a cumulatively worsening situation, could not afford to play for time. His many errors are notorious: his inability to countenance strategic withdrawals; his commitment to grand offensives which were in reality beyond his grasp, like the Ardennes in December 1944, and towards Budapest in 1945; and his unhelpful interference with the development of potentially decisive new weapons like the ME-262 jet fighter. Hitler's unwillingness to accept the advice of his generals has been frequently contrasted with Stalin's increasing trust in his. It has less frequently been compared with the situation in Britain. Churchill interfered every day with the conduct of the war, and was the source of a constant stream of ideas, great and small, realistic and unrealistic. Some were brilliant, others ludicrously bad. Churchill always deferred, even if after protracted arguments, to the judgement of his Chiefs of Staff, and many of his more foolish ideas never got beyond the drawing board.

In contrast, Hitler was indeed ill-served. Particularly after the failure of the bomb plot on 20 July 1944 – which in any case involved only a relatively few members of the officer corps – there was no one amongst his generals, or indeed his civilian subordinates, to stand up to him. Most, of course, were, as Eisenhower had noted, far too steeped in blood to turn back. There was no significant civilian resistance movement in Germany, and a stronger civil society which might have debated the conduct of the war, or its likely outcomes, had long ago disappeared. Hitler at least saw with clarity that there would be no place for him in any post-war dispensation, and – fortunately – was resolved to avoid what he saw as the indignity of a trial. Here the Allied commitment to unconditional surrender, so often criticised, was enormously helpful. At no stage after the Casablanca declaration did the Allies, separately or collectively, lend any credence to the idea that they would negotiate the future of a Nazi government of any colour, or under any leadership, in a post-war Germany.

In comparison with other great settlements in European history, 1945 indeed looks so remarkably durable in different ways that the Second World War in Europe has been described 'in the public, national versions of the past' as 'a war with no losers'.[21] If by this it is suggested that the Second World War in Europe appears, particularly after 1989, to have ended without any one country feeling the sense of injustice and consequent resentment that has followed so many other wars (and, as Clausewitz noted, the desire to remedy this situation), this is indeed a valid statement. Seen from the perspective of individuals who were involved, it can of course be challenged. The Allied victory and the German defeat of 1945 brought to an end a conflict in Europe that took the lives of untold millions, amongst the victors, amongst the Jews and other minorities persecuted so viciously during the war, and amongst the Germans themselves. It has become fashionable to organise hierarchies of victimhood, to claim that the sufferings of some were greater or more significant than the sufferings of others, but for individuals who were killed, it matters little if they were soldiers or civilians, young or old, male or female, from Kiev, Hamburg, London, or Minnesota.

The human losses, the trauma of survivors, and the enormous material destruction which all came to a head in the early months of 1945 are indeed only conceivably justifiable in terms of the subsequent achievement, the success of denazification, of the occupation of Germany, and the astonishing recovery of Europe in the post-war era. This has been over-exaggerated, and romanticised, perhaps partly as a necessary and understandable reaction to the sacrifice involved. The Second World War has been immortalised in America as 'the good war', in Britain as 'the people's war', and in the former Soviet Union as 'the Great Patriotic War'. De Gaulle in France portrayed it as part of a longer heroic struggle which reached back to 1914. Most recently the Americans who fought and lived through the war have been cast as 'the great generation'. All these claims have become tangled up in the disputes over history and memory which have developed in individual nation-states, and in the trans-national movements towards a globalised, post-Cold War world. We can still with straightforward certainty assert that the Allies in 1944 and 1945 fought a just war.

NOTES

Every effort has been made to keep the notes here to a minimum. Published sources are given in full on the first occasion they are referred to, and subsequently abbreviated. The following abbreviations have been used for archival sources:

TNA PRO	The National Archive (formerly Public Record Office), London
SoGM	Soldiers of Gloucestershire Museum, Gloucester
IfZ OMGUS	Institut für Zeitgeschichte, Munich, records of the Office of Military Government (United States)
BAK OMGUS	Bundesarchiv, Koblenz, records of the Office of Military Government (United States)
BHA OMGB	Bayerisches Hauptstaatsarchiv, Munich, records of the Office of Military Government (United States), Bavaria
GLAK OMGWB	Generallandesarchiv, Karlsruhe, records of the Office of Military Government (United States), Würtemmberg-Baden
AOFC	Centre des Archives de l'Occupation française en Autriche et en Allemagne, Colmar
SAPMO-BArch	Stiftung Archiv der Parteien und Massenorganisationen der DDR im Bundesarchiv, Außenstelle Berlin

INTRODUCTION

1   SoGM, Letter by the Commander-in-Chief on Non-Fraternisation, March 1945.
2   In recent years historians in Germany have become more aware that the term 'Third Reich' is a Nazi usage, an example of what Victor Klemperer, well before 1939, was calling the *Lingua tertii imperii* – the 'language of the Third Empire'. Increasingly these historians are putting phrases like 'Third Reich' or 'Final Solution' in inverted commas to display this recognition and to distance themselves from these usages. I have followed this convention here. See Victor Klemperer, *The Language of the Third Reich: A Philologist's Notebook* (trans.

Brady, New York and London: Continuum, 2002).

3 See Carl von Clausewitz, *On War* (trans. and ed. Howard and Paret, Princeton: Princeton University Press, 1989), pp. 86–87.

4 See for example John Grigg, *1943: The victory that never was* (London: Methuen, 1985), pp. 75–78. He quotes here Roosevelt's 'unconditional surrender' statement.

5 Cited in Grigg, *1943*, p. 75.

6 Cited in Cordell Hull, *The Memoirs of Cordell Hull*, Vol. II, (London: Hodder and Stoughton, 1948), p. 1291. See also pp. 1570–1582.

7 Hull, *Memoirs*, Vol. II, p. 1617.

8 'Plans Nazis pour la Guerre clandestine', *Mission Militaire pour les Affaires Allemandes, Bulletin d'Information*, No. 2, pp. 29–30.

CHAPTER 1: THE PRELUDE: JANUARY–SEPTEMBER 1944

1 Directive to Supreme Commander Allied Expeditionary Force, 12 February 1944, cited in *Report by the Supreme Commander to the Combined Chiefs of Staff on the Operations in Europe of the Allied Expeditionary Force, 6 June 1944 to 8 May 1945* (London: HMSO, 1946), vii.

2 Victor Klemperer, *To the Bitter End: The Diaries of Victor Klemperer 1942–45* (trans. Chalmers, London: BCA, 1998), p. 273.

3 See Richard Overy, *Why the Allies Won* (London: Pimlico, 1996), pp. 282ff.

4 Mihail Sebastian, *Journal 1935–1944* (London: Pimlico, 2003), p. 599.

5 F.W. von Mellenthin, *Panzer Battles* (London: Futura, 1977), pp. 332, 349.

6 Cited in Guenther Blumentritt, *Von Rundstedt: The Soldier and the Man* (trans. Reavely, London: Odhams, 1952), p. 244.

7 Harry Butcher, *Three Years with Eisenhower: The Personal Diary of Captain Harry C. Butcher, USNR, Naval Aide to General Eisenhower, 1942–1945* (London: Heinemann, 1946), p. 524.

8 Sybil Bannister, *I lived under Hitler: An Englishwoman's Story* (London: Rockliff, 1957), p. 172.

9 Cited in Arthur Bryant (ed.), *The Alanbrooke War Diaries 1939–43: The Turn of the Tide* (London: Collins, 1965), p. 381.

10 Earl Ziemke, *Stalingrad to Berlin: The German Defeat in the East* (Washington: Dorset Press, 1968), p. 214.

11 Butcher, *Three Years with Eisenhower*, p. 567.

12 See the 'documentary novel' by Anatoly Kuznetsov, *Babi Yar* (trans. Guralsky, London: Sphere, 1969).

13 Ziemke, *Stalingrad to Berlin*, pp. 293–295.

14 See Antony Beevor and Luba Vinogradova (eds), *A Writer at War: Vasily Grossman with the Red Army, 1941–1945* (New York: Pantheon, 2005), pp. 254–256.

15 H.R. Trevor-Roper (ed.), *Hitler's War Directives 1939–1945* (London: Pan, 1966), p. 218.

16 Butcher, *Three Years with Eisenhower*, p. 445.

17 John Colville, *The Fringes of Power: 10 Downing Street Diaries 1939–1955* (New York and London: Norton, 1985), pp. 497–498.

18 *Report by the Supreme Commander*, p. 42.

19 Butcher, *Three Years with Eisenhower*, p. 537.

20 Dwight Eisenhower, *Crusade in Europe* (New York: Doubleday, 1948), p. 279.

21 Sebastian, *Journal 1935–1944*, pp. 611, 614, 617.

22 Both cited in Omer Bartov, *Hitler's Army: Soldiers, Nazis, and War in the Third Reich* (New York and Oxford: Oxford University Press, 1992), p. 171.

23 Sebastian, *Journal 1935–1944*, p. 603.

24 Mellenthin, *Panzer Battles*, p. 343.

25 Colville, *The Fringes of Power*, pp. 502, 508.

26 Bernard Montgomery, *El Alamein to the River Sangro; Normandy to the Baltic* (London: BCA, 1973), p. 290.

27 Alan Adelson and Robert Lapides (eds), *Łódź Ghetto: Inside a Community under Siege* (New York: Penguin, 1989), xvii.

28 The entries from this diary are cited in Adelson and Lapides, *Łódź Ghetto*, pp. 419–439. See also pp. 495–496.

29 Albert Speer, *Inside the Third Reich* (New York: Avon, 1971), pp. 699, 697.

30 Angus Calder, *The People's War: Britain 1939–1945* (London: Panther, 1971), p. 648.

31 Butcher, *Three Years with Eisenhower*, p. 503.

32 Speer, *Inside the Third Reich*, p. 524, footnote.

33 Blumentritt, *Von Rundstedt*, p. 247.

34 Butcher, *Three Years with Eisenhower*, p. 578.

35 *Report by the Supreme Commander*, p. 64.

36 Bartov, *Hitler's Army*, pp. 6, 95–96.

37 Max Hastings, *Armageddon: The Battle for Germany 1944–45* (London: Pan, 2005), pp. 27–28.

38 See Beevor and Vinogradova (eds), *A Writer at War*, p. 311.

39 Klemperer, *To the Bitter End*, p. 340.

CHAPTER 2: HOPES AND FEARS: SEPTEMBER 1944–JANUARY 1945

1   *Evangelisches Feldgesangbuch* (Berlin: Mittler und Sohn, no date), p. 9. This was a tiny pocket book with hymns and prayers distributed free to German soldiers from the start of the war.

2   Butcher, *Three Years with Eisenhower*, p. 568.

3   See Cornelius Ryan, *A Bridge Too Far* (London: Hodder and Stoughton, 1975), pp. 63–96.

4   Montgomery, *El Alamein to the River Sangro; Normandy to the Baltic*, p. 312.

5   See Ryan, *A Bridge Too Far*, p. 7.

6   Speer, *Inside the Third Reich*, p. 509.

7   Blumentritt, *Von Rundstedt*, p. 258.

8   Mellenthin, *Panzer Battles*, p. 372.

9   Klemperer, *To the Bitter End*, pp. 346–347.

10 Montgomery, *El Alamein to the River Sangro; Normandy to the Baltic*, pp. 324–325.

11 See Bernard Montgomery, *The Memoirs of Field-Marshal the Viscount Montgomery of Alamein, K.G.* (London: Collins, 1958), pp. 296–298.

12 See Weigley, *Eisenhower's Lieutenants*, pp. 283–286, 385–389.

13 Andrew Cunningham, *A Sailor's Odyssey: The Autobiography of Admiral of the Fleet Viscount Cunningham of Hyndhope* (London: Hutchinson, 1951), pp. 609–610.

14 Paul Fussell, *The Boys' Crusade: American G.I.s in Europe: Chaos and Fear in World War Two* (London: Weidenfeld and Nicolson, 2004), xi, xv.

15 See Colville, *The Fringes of Power*, pp. 512–516.

16 Hull, *Memoirs*, Vol. II, pp. 1602–1622.

17 See Clemens Zimmerman, 'From Propaganda to Modernization: Media Policy and Media Audiences under National Socialism', *German History*, 24:3 (2006), pp. 431–454, p. 454.

18 Although Morgenthau remained bitterly critical of Hull's 'utopian' approach to foreign policy, it is interesting to note that within a few years he was a strong advocate of West German re-armament. See Hans Morgenthau, *American Foreign Policy: A Critical Examination* (London: Methuen, 1952), especially pp. 95–99, 186–187.

19 Ziemke, *Stalingrad to Berlin*, p. 388.

20 See Ziemke, *Stalingrad to Berlin*, pp. 387–403.

21 Edith Hahn, *The Nazi Officer's Wife: How One Jewish Woman Survived the Holocaust* (London: Abacus, 2001), p. 245.

22 Klemperer, *To the Bitter End*, p. 355.

23 Rudolf Hoess, *Commandant of Auschwitz: The Autobiography of Rudolf Hoess* (London: Phoenix Press, 2000), pp. 166, 168.

24 Speer, *Inside the Third Reich*, p. 527.

25 Heinz Guderian, *Panzer Leader* (London: Futura, 1974), p. 380.

26 Guderian, *Panzer Leader*, p. 381.

27 A sign erected at the German frontier by the Red Army. See Anthony Beevor, *Berlin: The Downfall 1945* (London: Penguin, 2002), p. 66.

28 Ziemke, *Stalingrad to Berlin*, p. 417.

29 Vasili Chuikov, *The Fall of Berlin* (trans. Kisch, New York: Ballantyne, 1969), pp. 83–86.

30 Cited in Adelson and Lapides (eds), *Łódź Ghetto*, p. 487.

31 See the reproduction and translation of *Nachrichten für die Truppe* (a British and American propaganda leaflet for German troops), 12 February 1945, in Karl Friedrich Gau, *Silesian Inferno: War Crimes of the Red Army on its March into Silesia in 1945* (trans. Schlosser, Cologne: Informations- und Dokumentationszentrum West, 1970), pp. 175, 189–191.

32 Colville, *The Fringes of Power*, p. 556.

33 See Ilya Ehrenburg, *Men, Years – Life*, Vol. V, *The War 1941–45* (trans. Shebunina, London: Macgibbon and Kee, 1964), pp. 162–172.

34 Bannister, *I lived under Hitler*, pp. 182–183, 199.

35 Speer, *Inside the Third Reich*, p. 537.

36 Hoess, *Commandant of Auschwitz*, pp. 169–170.

37 Many writers, following Höss' post-war testimony, have given a figure of two and a half or three million killed at Auschwitz. In a detailed documentation published in Communist Poland, Jósef Buszko gave a figure of 3.5 million gassed in Birkenau and an additional 340,000 who died of hunger and disease in Auschwitz ('Vorwort', *Auschwitz: faschistisches Vernichtungslager* (Warsaw: Interpress, 1988), pp. 5–9, p. 6).

38 Jósef Buszko, 'Vorwort', *Auschwitz: faschistisches Vernichtungslager*, pp. 5–9.

39 Danuta Czech, 'Konzentrationslager Auschwitz. Abriss der Geschichte', *Auschwitz: faschistisches Vernichtungslager*, pp. 11–37, p. 30.

40 Czech, 'Konzentrationslager Auschwitz. Abriss der Geschichte', p. 32.

41 Andrzej Strzelecki, 'Die Befreiung des KZ Auschwitz und die Hilfsaktion für die befreiten Häftlinge', *Auschwitz: faschistisches Vernichtungslager*, pp. 145–156, p. 148.

42 See Henry Świebocki, 'Aufdeckung und Entlarvung von SS-Verbrechen', *Auschwitz: faschistisches Vernichtungslager*, pp. 135–144, p. 143.

43 Klemperer, *To the Bitter End*, 381.

44 See Hahn, *The Nazi Officer's Wife*, pp. 250–252.

CHAPTER 3: NEMESIS: JANUARY–APRIL 1945

1 *Bomber Command Continues* (London: HMSO, 1942), p. 45.

2 Klemperer, *To the Bitter End*, pp. 381, 389, 393.

3 Any serious student of the evolution of British policy should see the official history, Charles Webster and Noble Frankland, *The Strategic Air Offensive against Germany 1939–1945*

(London: HMSO, 1961), particularly Vol. IV, *Annexes and Appendices*, which contains many of the most important documents relating to this. See here Vol. IV, pp. 144, 148.

4   Webster and Frankland, *The Strategic Air Offensive*, Vol. IV, p. 200.

5   Webster and Frankland, *The Strategic Air Offensive*, Vol. IV, p. 195. On the adoption of area bombing, see Max Hastings, *Bomber Command* (London: Pan, 1981), pp. 144–164.

6   All casualty figures in the bombing of Germany are disputed. Hans Rumpf, *The Bombing of Germany* (trans. Fitzgerald, London: Frederick Muller, 1963), gives a figure of 30,482 killed in Hamburg in 1943 (p. 82).

7   Speer, *Inside the Third Reich*, p. 370.

8   See Leon Wolff, *Low Level Mission* (London: Panther, 1960).

9   See Martin Middlebrook, *The Nuremberg Raid 30–31 March 1944* (Glasgow: Fontana, 1975).

10   Hastings, *Bomber Command*, p. 306.

11   See W.G. Sebald, *On the Natural History of Destruction* (London: Penguin, 2004), p. 14.

12   Bannister, *I lived under Hitler*, pp. 203ff.

13   See William Manchester, *The Arms of Krupp 1587–1968* (London: Michael Joseph, 1969), p. 525.

14   Manchester, *The Arms of Krupp*, pp. 557–558.

15   See Hastings, *Bomber Command*, pp. 394ff.

16   Hastings, *Bomber Command*, p. 368.

17   Frederick Taylor, *Dresden, Tuesday 13 February 1945* (London: Bloomsbury, 2004), p. 6.

18   Colville, *The Fringes of Power*, p. 559.

19   Hastings, *Bomber Command*, pp. 426–427.

20   Rumpf, *The Bombing of Germany*, p. 115.

21   See Robin Neillands, *The Bomber War: Arthur Harris and the Allied Bomber Offensive 1939–1945* (London: John Murray, 2001), pp. 372–373; and Winston Churchill, *The Second World War*, Vol. VI, *Triumph and Tragedy* (London: Cassell, 1954), pp. 470–471.

22   Webster and Frankland, *The Strategic Air Offensive*, Vol. IV, pp. 183–184.

23   Calder, *The People's War*, p. 652.

24   Directive of 5 May 1942, cited in Webster and Frankland, *The Strategic Air Offensive*, Vol. IV, p. 148.

25   Combined Chiefs of Staff Directive for the Bomber Offensive from The United Kingdom, 21 January 1943, cited in Webster and Frankland, *The Strategic Air Offensive*, Vol. IV, pp. 153–154.

26   Bottomley to Harris, 27 January 1945, cited in Webster and Frankland, *The Strategic Air Offensive*, Vol. IV, p. 301.

27   Cited in Hastings, *Bomber Command*, p. 155.

28   Hastings, *Bomber Command*, pp. 291–292.

29   Colville, *The Fringes of Power*, p. 562.

30   Sebald, *On the Natural History of Destruction*, p. 19.

31   Cited in Hastings, *Bomber Command*, p. 159.

32   Cited in David MacIsaac, *Strategic Bombing in World War Two: The Story of the United States Strategic Bombing Survey* (New York and London: Garland, 1976), pp. 78–79.

33   See MacIsaac, *Strategic Bombing in World War Two*, pp. 79, 196.

34   *Target Germany: The U.S. Army Air Forces' Official Story of the VIII Bomber Command's First Year over Europe* (London: HMSO, 1944), p. 116.

35   Cited in Taylor, *Dresden*, p. 367.

36   Cited in H.R. Trevor-Roper (ed.), *The Goebbels Diaries: The Last Days* (trans. Barry, London: BCA, 1978), p. 174.

37   See Neillands, *The Bomber War*, pp. 141–144.

38   Jeffrey Herf, *Divided Memory: The Nazi Past in the two Germanys* (Cambridge, Massachusetts and London: Harvard University Press, 1997), p. 206.

39   Colville, *The Fringes of Power*, p. 564. See also Churchill's note to General Ismay, reproduced in Churchill, *The Second World War*, Vol. VI, Appendix C, p. 640.

40   Bannister, *I lived under Hitler*, p. 218.

41   Klemperer, *To the Bitter End*, pp. 398, 400, 404, 405. *Freiheitskampf* was the Nazi Party newspaper in Saxony.

42   'Report of the Crimea Conference', 11 February 1945, cited in United States Department of State (ed.), *The Conferences at Malta and Yalta, 1945* (Westport: Greenwood Press, 1976), pp. 970–971.

43   *Report by the Supreme Commander*, p. 107.

44   Montgomery, *El Alamein to the River Sangro; Normandy to the Baltic*, p. 372.

45   Diary entry for 5 March 1945, Trevor-Roper (ed.), *The Goebbels Diaries: The Last Days*, p. 49.

46   Weigley, *Eisenhower's Lieutenants*, p. 627.

47   Cited in Desmond Hawkins (ed.), *War Report D-Day to VE-Day: Dispatches by the BBC's War Correspondents with the Allied Expeditionary Force 6 June 1944–5 May 1945* (London: BBC, 1985), pp. 279–280.

48   See Speer, *Inside the Third Reich*, pp. 549–557, and Guderian, *Panzer Leader*, pp. 422–424.

49   Cited in Speer, *Inside the Third Reich*, p. 557.

50   Trevor-Roper (ed.), *The Goebbels Diaries: The Last Days*, pp. 94–95, 105, 258.

51   Klemperer, *To the Bitter End*, p. 417.

CHAPTER 4: THE LIBERATION OF THE CAMPS

1   William Rust, 'The Death Camps', *Daily Worker*, 21 April 1945

2   Cited in Weigley, *Eisenhower's Lieutenants*, p. 682.

3   *Report by the Supreme Commander*, p. 131.

4   Churchill, *The Second World War*, Vol. VI, p. 446.

5   See Weigley, *Eisenhower's Lieutenants*, pp. 697–698.

6   Eisenhower, *Crusade in Europe*, p. 407.

7   Truman Library – Ken Hechler Oral History Interview, November 29, 1985, <http://www.trumanlibrary.org>.

8   See Cornelius Ryan, *The Last Battle* (London: New English Library, 1967), pp. 198–238.

9   See Eisenhower to Marshall, 15 April 1945, <http://www.eisenhower.archives.gov>.

10   See Butcher, *Three Years with Eisenhower*, p. 673.

11   See Bernard Montgomery, *The Memoirs of Field-Marshal the Viscount Montgomery of Alamein, K.G.* (London: Collins, 1958), pp. 331–333.

12   Montgomery, *El Alamein to the River Sangro; Normandy to the Baltic*, pp. 386–389.

13   Matthew Halton, 12 April 1945, cited in Hawkins, *War Report*, pp. 286–287.

14   See Eisenhower, *Crusade in Europe*, pp. 408–409.

15   Mel Mermelstein, *By Bread Alone: The Story of A-4685* (Cracow: Poligrafia Inspektoratu, 1993), pp. 169–226.

16   See Eugen Kogon, *The Theory and Practice of Hell: The German Concentration Camps and the System Behind Them* (trans. Norden, London: World Distributors, 1958), pp. 8–10.

17   See Speer, *Inside the Third Reich*, pp. 472–480.

18   Cited in Eberhard Kolb (ed.), *Bergen-Belsen: From "Detention Camp" to Concentration Camp, 1943–1945* (trans. Claeys and Lattek, Göttingen: Vandenhoeck & Ruprecht, 1986), pp. 47–48.

19   See the accounts cited in Tom Pocock, *1945: The Dawn Came Up Like Thunder* (London: Collins, 1983), pp. 79–86.

20   See the account by Rudolf Küstermeier, 'The Last Weeks before the Liberation of the

Camp', in Kolb (ed.), *Bergen-Belsen*, pp. 91–99.

21 See Daniel Jonah Goldhagen, *Hitler's Willing Executioners: Ordinary Germans and the Holocaust* (London: Little, Brown and Company, 1996), p. 367.

22 See <http://www.holocaustforgotten.com>.

23 Kolb (ed.), *Bergen-Belsen*, p. 40.

24 See Goldhagen, *Hitler's Willing Executioners*, pp. 327–330.

25 Cited in Fussell, *The Boys' Crusade*, p. 154.

26 See *Law Reports of Trials of War Criminals, The United Nations War Crimes Commission*, Vol. I (London, HMSO, 1947), p. 47.

27 Cited in Fussell, *The Boys' Crusade*, p. 155.

28 Quoted in Robin Neillands, *The Conquest of the Reich: D-Day to VE Day – A Soldiers' History* (London: Weidenfeld and Nicholson, 1995), p. 273.

29 Fussell, *The Boys' Crusade*, p. 153.

30 See Stanislaw Ozimek, 'The Polish Newsreel in 1945: The Bitter Victory', in K.R.M. Short and Stephan Dolezel (eds), *Hitler's Fall: The Newsreel Witness* (London: Croom Helm, 1988), pp. 70–79.

31 See Barbie Zelizer, *Remembering to Forget: Holocaust Memory through the Camera's Eye* (Chicago and London: University of Chicago Press, 1998), pp. 49–61.

32 See Beevor and Vinogradova (eds), *A Writer at War*, pp. 280–306.

33 *The German Occupation of Poland: Extract of Note Addressed to the Governments of the Allied and Neutral Powers on May 3, 1941* (London: Cornwall Press, 1941), p. 12.

34 See Richard Breitman, *Official Secrets: What the Nazis Planned, What the British and Americans Knew* (London: Penguin, 2000).

35 *What Buchenwald Really Means* (London: Victor Gollancz Ltd, 1945)

36 Cited in Zelizer, *Remembering to Forget*, p. 62.

37 Cited in Ulrike Jordan (ed.), *Conditions of Surrender: Britons and Germans Witness the End of the War* (London: Taurus, 1997), p. 98.

38 Cited in *Buchenwald Camp: The Report of a Parliamentary Delegation* (London: His Majesty's Stationery Office, 1945), p. 3.

39 Chuikov, *The Fall of Berlin*, p. 118.

40 Chuikov, *The Fall of Berlin*, p. 114.

41 Chuikov, *The Fall of Berlin*, pp. 121–128.

42 See the details on <http://www.deepimage.co.uk>.

43 Speer, *Inside the Third Reich*, pp. 595–596.

44 Trevor-Roper (ed.), *The Goebbels Diaries*, pp. 79–82.

45 See David Welch, 'Goebbels, Götterdämmerung, and the Deutsche Wochenschauen', in Short and Dolezel (eds), *Hitler's Fall*, pp. 80–99.

46 Ziemke, *Stalingrad to Berlin*, p. 470.

47 Trevor-Roper (ed.), *Hitler's War Directives*, pp. 300–301.

48 Ziemke, *Stalingrad to Berlin*, p. 475.

49 H.R. Trevor-Roper, *The Last Days of Hitler* (London: Pan, 1952), p. 124.

50 Ziemke, *Stalingrad to Berlin*, p. 481.

51 Speer, *Inside the Third Reich*, pp. 605–613.

CHAPTER 5: OCCUPATION AND PARTITION: APRIL–JULY 1945

1 Colonel Fedorov, *The Red Army: An Army of the People* (London: Cobbett, 1944), p. 34.

2 Traudl Junge (with Melissa Müller), *Until the Final Hour: Hitler's Last Secretary* (trans. Bell,

London: Phoenix, 2005), p. 186.

3 For the full text of the broadcast, see Jordan (ed.), *Conditions of Surrender*, pp. 139–140.

4 See Ryan, *The Last Battle*, pp. 376–377.

5 Cited in Owen and Walters (eds), *Voices of War*, p. 573.

6 Cited in Christoph Studt (ed.), *Das Dritte Reich: Ein Lesebuch zur deutschen Geschichte 1933–1945* (Munich: Beck, 1995), p. 300.

7 Trevor-Roper, *The Last Days of Hitler*, p. 182.

8 See Part III of Jack Taylor's Report, 'Concentration Camp Mauthausen', 30 May 1945, reproduced in *Zeitgeschichte*, 22 (September/October, 1995), pp. 322–341; also Evelyn Le Chêne, *Mauthausen: The History of a Death Camp* (London: Methuen, 1971).

9 See Charles de Gaulle, *Mémoires de Guerre: Le Salut 1944–1946* (Paris: Plon, 1959), p. 422.

10 See Reinhard Rürup (ed.), *Topography of Terror: Gestapo, SS and Reichssicherheitshauptamt on the 'Prinz-Albrecht-Terrain' – A Documentation* (trans. Angress, Berlin: Arenhövel, 1989), p. 186.

11 Ryan, *The Last Battle*, p. 376.

12 Cited in Beevor and Vinogradova (eds), *A Writer at War*, pp. 324–343.

13 Wolfgang Leonhardt, *Die Revolution entläßt ihre Kinder* (Frankfurt am Main and Berlin: Ullstein, 1974), p. 286.

14 Montgomery, *Memoirs*, p. 335.

15 The document is reproduced in Montgomery, *Memoirs*, facing p. 344.

16 Butcher, *Three Years with Eisenhower*, p. 702.

17 Cited in de Gaulle, *Mémoires de Guerre: Le Salut*, p. 208.

18 See Cunningham, *A Sailor's Odyssey*, pp. 643–644.

19 Hastings, *Armageddon*, p. 566.

20 Hoess, *Commandant of Auschwitz*, pp. 172–173.

21 Anonymous, *A Woman in Berlin: Diary 20 April 1945 to 22 June 1945* (trans. Boehm, London: Virago, 2005), p. 85.

22 See Alison Owings, *Frauen: German Women Recall the Third Reich* (London: Penguin, 2001), p. 30.

23 The Reverend Cecil Cullingford, cited in Jordan (ed.), *Conditions of Surrender*, p. 97.

24 Bannister, *I lived under Hitler*, pp. 232–233.

25 Cited in Montgomery, *Memoirs*, pp. 370–371.

26 Montgomery, *Memoirs*, p. 357.

27 Butcher, *Three Years with Eisenhower*, pp. 715–716.

28 Cunningham, *A Sailor's Odyssey*, p. 647.

29 Hahn, *The Nazi Officer's Wife*, p. 257.

30 Cited in Russell Miller and Renate Miller, *Ten Days in May: The People's Story of VE Day* (London: Michael Joseph, 1995), pp. 224–225.

31 Cited in Jordan (ed.), *Conditions of Surrender*, p. 81.

32 Adolf Galland, *The First and the Last: The Rise and Fall of the German Fighter Forces 1938–1945* (London: Fontana, 1970), p. 286.

33 Cunningham, *A Sailor's Odyssey*, p. 647.

34 'Conditions in Germany', 5 July 1945, in Jean Edward Smith (ed.), *The Papers of General Lucius D. Clay*, Vol. I, *Germany 1945–1949* (Bloomington: Indiana University Press, 1974), pp. 46–49, p. 47.

35 Rüdiger Overmanns, 'Die Rheinwiesenlager 1945', in Hans-Erich Volkmann (ed.), *Ende das Dritten Reiches – Ende des Zweiten Weltkrieges. Eine Perspektive Rückschau* (Munich: Piper, 1995), pp. 259–291, p. 277.

36 Cited in Jordan (ed.), *Conditions of Surrender*, p. 91.

37 Gareth Pritchard, *The making of the GDR 1945–53* (Manchester: Manchester University Press, 2000), p. 35.

38 Klemperer, *To the Bitter End*, pp. 448, 450–451.

39 Konrad Adenauer, *Memoirs, 1945–53* (trans. von Oppen, London: Weidenfeld and Nicolson, 1966), pp. 19–21.

40 See Jordan (ed.), *Conditions of Surrender*, pp. 105–110.

41 See Pocock, *1945*, pp. 132–136.

42 *Official Gazette of the Control Council for Germany*, Supplement No. 1 (Berlin: Allied Secretariat, 1945), pp. 7–9.

43 'Clay for Joint Chiefs of Staff, 6 June 1945', in Smith (ed.), *The Papers of General Lucius D. Clay*, Vol. I, pp. 18–20.

44 Otto Winzer, *Zwölf Jahre Kampf gegen Faschismus und Krieg* (Berlin: Dietz, 1955), p. 259.

45 See de Gaulle, *Mémoires de Guerre: Le Salut*, pp. 447–448.

46 *Official Gazette of the Control Council for Germany*, No. 1, 29 October 1945, pp. 4–8.

47 Clausewitz, *On War*, p. 90.

CHAPTER 6: DENAZIFICATION: MAY–SEPTEMBER 1945

1 Robert Vansittart, *Roots of the Trouble* (London: Hutchinson, 1943), p. 29.

2 Cited in Herbert Feis, *Between War and Peace: The Potsdam Conference* (Princeton: Princeton University Press, 1960), p. 341.

3 *Official Gazette of the Control Council for Germany*, No. 1, 29 October 1945, pp. 8–21.

4 See George Clare, *Berlin Days* (London: Macmillan, 1989), p. 52.

5 See the report from the US Mission Berlin to the Department of State, Washington, 9 January 1956, National Archives and Records Administration, Record Group 407, Entry 360, Box 3794, 1951–52, Decimal 314.4. I am grateful to Astrid Eckert for sending me a copy of this document.

6 Ulf Schmidt, '"The Scars of Ravensbrück": Medical Experiments and British War Crimes Policy, 1945–1950', *German History*, 23:1 (2005), pp. 20–49, fn. 37.

7 *History of the United Nations War Crimes Commission and the Development of the Laws of War. United Nations War Crimes Commission* (London: HMSO, 1948), p. 541.

8 See Le Chêne, *Mauthausen*, pp. 170–176.

9 Le Chêne, *Mauthausen*, pp. 260–285. To put this in perspective, Le Chêne lists a total of 818 persons known to have been on the staff of Mauthausen and its sub-camps.

10 'Concentration Camp Mauthausen', 30 May 1945, *Zeitgeschichte*, 22 (September/October, 1995), p. 340.

11 Speer, *Inside the Third Reich*, p. 632.

12 See Airey Neave, *Nuremberg: A Personal Record of the Trial of the Major Nazi War Criminals* (London: Hodder and Stoughton, 1980), pp. 29–40.

13 Manchester, *The Arms of Krupp*, p. 682.

14 'Conditions in Germany', 5 July 1945, cited in Smith (ed.), *The Papers of General Lucius D. Clay*, Vol. I, pp. 46–49, p. 46.

15 Epuration, Enonce des Principes de Potsdam, 1er Stade, *Zone Française d'Occupation. Résultats de six Mois d'Activité*, March 1946, p. 52.

16 See Laffon's order of 25 October 1945, reprinted in Reinhard Grohnert, *Die Entnazifizierung in Baden 1945–1949* (Stuttgart: Kohlhammer, 1991), pp. 252–253.

17 See *Notice sur le Gouvernement Militaire*, November 1945, p. 9.

18 See the discussion in Naimark, *The Russians in Germany*, pp. 376–378.

19 See Siegfried Knappe and Ted Brusaw, *Soldat: Reflection of a German Soldier, 1936–1949* (London: BCA, 1993), pp. 291–352.

20 See Hull, *Memoirs*, Vol. II, p. 1289.

21 Harry Truman, *The Memoirs of Harry S. Truman*, Vol. I, *Year of Decisions 1945* (London: Hodder and Stoughton, 1955), p. 206.

22 Cited in Truman, *Memoirs*, Vol. I, pp. 236–237.

23 See the Protocol of Proceedings of the Berlin Conference, July 17–August 2, 1945, in Feis, *Between War and Peace*, pp. 338–354, p. 341.

24 Richard Overy, *Interrogations: Inside the Mind of the Nazi Elite* (London: Penguin, 2002), p. 22.

25 See Bradley Smith, *The Road to Nuremberg* (New York: Basic Books, 1981), pp. 50–52.

26 Overy, *Interrogations*, pp. 37, 41.

27 See Directive No. 18, 'For Disbandment and Dissolution of the German Armed Forces', 12 November 1945, *Enactments and Approved Papers of the Allied Control Council and Coordinating Authority for the Year 1945*, Vol. 1, p. 188.

28 See Proclamation No. 2, Section 3, 8 (a), *Official Gazette of the Control Council for Germany*, No. 1, 29 October 1945, pp. 8–19, p. 10.

29 'Law No. 10: Punishment of Persons guilty of War Crimes, Crimes against Peace and against Humanity', *Official Gazette of the Control Council for Germany*, No. 3, pp. 50–55.

30 'Conditions in Germany', 18 August 1945, in Smith (ed.), *The Papers of General Lucius D. Clay*, Vol. I, pp. 59–61, p. 61.

31 *Official Gazette of the Control Council for Germany*, No. 2, pp. 33–34.

32 *Gazette of the Office of Military Government for Würtemmberg-Baden for the year of 1946* (Stuttgart, 1946), p. 69.

33 See his diary entry for 10 May 1945, in Klemperer, *To the Bitter End*, p. 457.

34 Diary entry for 28 April 1945, cited in Studt (ed.), *Das Dritte Reich*, p. 298.

35 Eveline B., diary entry for 6 May 1945, cited in Jordan (ed.), *Conditions of Surrender*, p. 103.

36 *Enactments and Approved Papers of the Allied Control Council and Coordinating Authority for the Year 1946*, Vol. III, p. 133.

37 IfZ OMGUS 5/310–3/6, Report on Textbook Evaluation, Education Branch, Office of U.S. High Commissioner, September 1950

38 Preface to *Deutsches Lesebuch – Prosa* ([Breslau 1926] Emergency Edition, no date)

39 Naimark, *The Russians in Germany*, p. 455.

40 Robert Birley, 'Potsdam in Practice', in Brian Rees (ed.), *History and Idealism: Essays, Addresses and Letters* (London: John Murray, 1990), pp. 75–93, p. 82.

41 Frank Willis, *The French in Germany* (Stanford: Stanford University Press, 1962), p. 155.

42 *Zone Française d'Occupation en Allemagne. Résultats de Six Mois d'Activité*, March 1946, p. 52.

43 Naimark, *The Russians in Germany*, p. 455.

44 Edmond Vermeil, 'Notes sur la Rééducation en Zone Française', in Helen Liddell (ed.), *Education in Occupied Germany* (Paris: M. Rivière, 1949), p. 57.

45 See Max Weinreich, *Hitler's Professors: The Part Played by Scholarship in Germany's Crimes Against the Jewish People* ([1946] New Haven and London: Yale University Press, 1999).

46 See the handwritten notes in TNA PRO FO 1050/1370, and also *Christian-Albrechts-Universität Kiel. Personal- und Vorlesungsverzeichnis. Sommersemester 1945* (Kiel, 1945).

47 Kurt Jürgensen, 'Towards Occupation: First Encounters in Northern Germany', in Jordan (ed.), *Conditions of Surrender*, pp. 53–66, p. 62.

48 See Heuss' letter to Military Government Stuttgart, 12 December 1945, and the attached report on the 'State School for Music in Stuttgart', IfZ OMGUS 5/301–3/9.

49 See Klaus Schölzel, 'Die Entlastung des Geistes', in Hermann Glaser, Lutz von Pufendorf, and Michael Schöneich (eds), *So viel Anfang war nie: Deutsche Städte 1945–1949* (Berlin: Siedler, 1989), pp. 310–315.

50 See Richard J. Evans, *Rituals of Retribution: Capital Punishment in Germany 1600–1987* (New York and Oxford: Oxford University Press, 1996), p. 747.

51 F.S.V. Donnison, *Civil Affairs and Military Government North-West Europe 1944–1946* (London: HMSO, 1961), p. 388.

CHAPTER 7: RE-SHAPING THE MASS MEDIA

1 From Proclamation No. 2, Section IV, *Official Gazette of the Control Council for Germany*, No. 1, 29 October 1945, p. 10.

2 IfZ OMGUS 5/243–2/8, Militärregierung – Deutschland, Nachrichtenkontrolle Anweisung Nr. 1.

3 See Order No. 51 of the Soviet Military Administration, September 1945, cited in Ministerium für Auswärtige Angelegenheiten (ed.), *Um ein antifaschistisch-demokratisches Deutschland. Dokumente aus den Jahren 1945–1949* (Berlin: Staatsverlag der DDR, 1968), pp. 145–148.

4 *Manual for the Control of German Information Services. Restricted. 12 May 1945*, pp. 143–145.

5 TNA PRO FO 898/401, RH BL to Harvey, 10 July 1945.

6 TNA PRO FO 1005/1803, Bishop to IC Services, CCG(BE), 22 July 1945.

7 See Perry Biddiscombe, *The Last Nazis: SS Werewolf Guerrilla Resistance in Europe 1944–1947* (Stroud: Tempus, 2004), pp. 36–39.

8 Hans Bausch (ed.), *Rundfunk in Deutschland, Band 3, Rundfunkpolitik nach 1945. Erster Teil 1945–1962* (Munich, 1980), p. 43.

9 TNA PRO FO 936/125, Proposal for Broadcasting Control Unit Cologne, 10 August 1945.

10 TNA PRO FO, Respective Functions of B.B.C. German Service and N.W.D.R. Statement of Policy, 24 November 1945.

11 Leonhardt, *Die Revolution*, p. 306.

12 Anonymous, *A Woman in Berlin*, pp. 260–261, 278–279.

13 TNA PRO FO 898/401, Russian Policy in Occupied Germany, 18 June 1945.

14 Leonhardt, *Die Revolution*, p. 307.

15 IfZ OMGUS 5/243–2/8, SHAEF, PWD, Semi-monthly Progress Report, 15 June 1945, p. 8.

16 AOFC AC 594/6, L'Administrateur Général à les Délégués Supérieures pour la Gouvernement Militaire, 18 February 1946.

17 IfZ OMGUS 5/244–1/11, Addendum No. 2 to ISC/2043 of 1st March 1946, 20 July 1946.

18 Joseph Wulf, *Presse und Funk im Dritten Reich: Eine Dokumentation* (Frankfurt am Main and Berlin: Ullstein, 1989), p. 7.

19 Cited in Wulf, *Presse und Funk im Dritten Reich*, p. 272.

20 See the reproduction in Wulf, *Presse und Funk im Dritten Reich*, pp. 246–247.

21 See the reproduction in Trevor-Roper (ed.), *The Goebbels Diaries: The Last Days*, between pp. 243–244.

22 Cited in Dirk Deissler, *Die entnazifizierte Sprache: Sprachpolitik und Sprachregelung in der Besatzungszeit* (Frankfurt am Main: Peter Lang, 2004), p. 156.

23 See Deissler, *Die entnazifizierte Sprache*, p. 161.

24 See Biddiscombe, *The Last Nazis*, pp. 219–222.

25 Donnison, *Civil Affairs and Military Government*, p. 240.

26 Cited in Deissler, *Die entnazifizierte Sprache*, p. 136.

27 *German-English Dictionary of Administrative Terms* (Washington: War Department, 1944)

28 See Deissler, *Die entnazifizierte Sprache*, pp. 189ff.

29 See Manfred Malzahn, *Germany 1945–1949: A Sourcebook* (London and New York: Routledge, 1991), pp. 171–173.

30 On the *Neue Zeitung*, see Jessica Gienow-Hecht, *Transmission Impossible: American Journalism as Cultural Diplomacy in Postwar Germany* (Baton Rouge: Louisiana State University Press, 1999).

31 Trevor-Roper (ed.), *The Goebbels Diaries: The Last Days*, p. 236.

32 Klaus Kreimeier, *The UFA Story: A History of Germany's Greatest Film Company, 1918–1945* (trans. Kimber and Kimber, New York: Hill and Wang, 1996), pp. 362–363.

33 See Heinrich Bodensieck, '*Welt im Film*: Origins and Message', in Short and Dolezel (eds), *Hitler's Fall: The Newsreel Witness*, pp. 119–147.

34 See Stephan Dolezel, '*Welt im Film* 1945 and the Re-education of Occupied Germany', in Short and Dolezel (eds), *Hitler's Fall: The Newsreel Witness*, pp. 148–157.

35 IfZ OMGUS 5/243–2/17, Text of Press release, Brig. Gen Robert A McClure, 25 May 1945, pp. 5–6.

36 Anna Merritt and Richard Merritt (eds), *Public Opinion in Occupied Germany: The OMGUS Surveys, 1945–1949* (Urbana, Chicago, and London: University of Illinois Press, 1970), pp. 100–101.

37 Anonymous, *A Woman in Berlin*, pp. 237, 300.

38 Kreimeier, *The UFA Story*, p. 247.

39 H.H. Wollenberg, *Fifty Years of German Cinema* (London; Falcon Press, 1948), p. 47.

40 See for the early days of DEFA the essay by Dieter Wolf, 'Gesellschaft mit beschränkter Haftung', in Wolfgang Jacobsen (ed.), *Babelsberg: Ein Filmstudio 1912–1992* (Berlin: Argon Verlag, 1992), pp. 247–270, here p. 249.

41 Wollenberg, *Fifty Years of German Cinema*, p. 47.

42 Robert Shandley, *Rubble Films: German Cinema in the Shadow of the Third Reich* (Philadelphia: Temple University Press, 2001), p. 17.

43 The phrase was coined by the journalist Hans Borgelt. See Elizabeth Koch, '"The Golden Hunger Years": Music and Superpower Rivalry in Occupied Berlin', *German History*, 22:1 (2004), pp. 76–100.

44 BHA OMGB 10/48–1/5, Annex to Weekly Situation Report, Film, Theater, and Music Control Section, 6871st DISCC, 7 August 1945.

45 The best account of developments in post-war Berlin is still Brewster Chamberlin, *Kultur auf Trümmern. Berliner Berichte des amerikanischen Information Control Section Juli–Dezember 1945* (Stuttgart: Deutsche Verlags Anstalt, 1979).

46 See the letters from Jelissarov to Becher, 25 June 1945, and from Becher and Willman to Zhukov, July 1945, in SAPMO DY 27/841.

47 *Berliner Zeitung*, 5 July 1945

48 Grigori Weiss, 'Auf der Suche nach der versunkenen Glocke', in Johannes-R.-Becher-Archiv der Deutschen Akademie der Künste (ed.), *Erinnerungen an Johannes R. Becher* (Leipzig: Philipp Reclam, 1968), p. 215.

49 TNA PRO FO 898/401, Strang to Eden, 11 July 1945, p. 4.

50 TNA PRO FO 1056/20, ISCB Directive No. 1, 20 July 1945.

51 GLAK OMGWB 12/91–1/7, Weekly Situation Report of the Film, Theater, and Music Control Section, 14 July 1945.

52 'Esquisse d'un bilan des spectacles en Allemagne', *La Revue de la Zone Française*, No. 4,

February 1946, pp. 16–17.

53 IfZ OMGUS 11/47–3/24, List No. 3. Black, Grey, and White Lists for IC Purposes [undated]

54 *Official Gazette of the Control Council for Germany*, No. 5, 31 March 1946, pp. 98–115.

55 For the full text of the law see *Germany, Office of Military Government, Report of the Military Governor*, No. 34, 1 April 1947–30 April 1948, pp. 52–97.

56 See IfZ OMGUS 11/47–3/26, White, Grey, and Black List for Information Control Purposes, 1 August 1946; and IfZ OMGUS 5/242–1/48, White, Grey, and Black List for Information Control Purposes, 1 November 1946, Supplement 1 to list of 1 August 1946.

57 IfZ OMGUS 5/270–3/4, For Release 21 February, 0900 Hours, 20 February 1946.

58 Leni Riefenstahl's account of her denazification should be treated with caution. See *The Sieve of Time* (London: Quartet Books, 1992), pp. 306ff. See also AOFC GFCC Berlin, 131/5, McClure to Hoffet, Chef de la Section de l'Information, 17 May 1946.

59 David Monod, *Settling Scores: German Music, Denazification, and the Americans, 1945–1953* (Chapel Hill and London: University of North Carolina Press, 2005), p. 59.

CHAPTER 8: WAR CRIMES TRIALS: SEPTEMBER 1945–NOVEMBER 1946

1 Article 1, London Agreement for the Establishment of an International Military Tribunal, 8 August 1945, <http://www.trumanlibrary.org>.

2 Speer, *Inside the Third Reich*, pp. 638–639.

3 Hjalmar Schacht, *My First Seventy-six Years: The Autobiography of Hjalmar Schacht* (trans. Pike, London: Allan Wingate, 1955), p. 450.

4 Schacht, *My First Seventy-six Years*, p. 451.

5 Neave, *Nuremberg*, p. 42.

6 See Smith, *The Road to Nuremberg*, p. 239.

7 Cited in Neave, *Nuremberg*, p. 138.

8 *Trial of the Major War Criminals before the International Military Tribunal, Nuremberg, 14 November 1945 – 1 October 1946*, Vol. 2 (Nuremberg: International Military Tribunal, 1947), p. 65.

9 *Trial of the Major War Criminals*, Vol. 2, p. 99.

10 Cited in Lord Russell of Liverpool, *The Scourge of the Swastika: A Short History of Nazi War Crimes* (London: Cassell, 1954), vii.

11 Neave, *Nuremberg*, p. 260.

12 Victor Klemperer, *The Lesser Evil: The Diaries of Victor Klemperer 1945–1949* (trans. Chalmers, London: Weidenfeld and Nicolson, 2003), p. 87.

13 Neave, *Nuremberg*, p. 270.

14 Klemperer, *The Lesser Evil*, p. 78.

15 Merritt and Merritt (eds), *Public Opinion in Occupied Germany*, p. 34.

16 Gienow-Hecht, *Transmission Impossible*, p. 83.

17 *Trial of the Major War Criminals*, Vol. 8, pp. 321–330.

18 *Trial of the Major War Criminals*, Vol. 11, pp. 396–422.

19 See Beevor and Vinogradova (eds), *A Writer at War*, p. 43, fn. 4.

20 See for example *Soviet Documents on Nazi Atrocities: Illustrated by some 200 Original Photographs* (London: Hutchinson, 1942).

21 *History of the United Nations War Crimes Commission*, pp. 526–531.

22 Evans, *Rituals of Retribution*, p. 806.

23 For the 'Belsen Trial', see *Law Reports of Trials of War Criminals, The United Nations War Crimes Commission*, Vol. II (London: HMSO, 1947), pp. 1–125. Quotations here are from pp. 1, 12, 10, 122.

24 Cited in Jordan (ed.), *Conditions of Surrender*, p. 84.

25 Evans, *Rituals of Retribution*, p. 767.

26 *History of the United Nations War Crimes Commission*, p. 542.

27 Russell, *The Scourge of the Swastika*, vii, fn. 1.

28 See Evans, *Rituals of Retribution*, pp. 767, 805.

29 For a summary of the trial, see *Law Reports of Trials of War Criminals, The United Nations War Crimes Commission*, Vol. I (London: HMSO, 1947), pp. 93–103.

30 Fussell, *The Boys' Crusade*, p. 157.

31 *History of the United Nations War Crimes Commission*, p. 541.

32 See Le Chêne, *Mauthausen*, Appendix II.

33 *Law Reports of Trials of War Criminals*, Vol. I, pp. 47–54.

34 Cited in Michael Burleigh, *Death and Deliverance: 'Euthanasia' in Germany, 1900–1945* (Cambridge: Cambridge University Press, 1994), pp. 271–272.

35 Smith (ed.), *The Papers of General Lucius D. Clay*, Vol. I, pp. 267–268.

36 *Law Reports of Trials of War Criminals*, Vol. III, pp. 24ff.

37 *History of the United Nations War Crimes Commission*, p. 535.

38 *History of the United Nations War Crimes Commission*, p. 542.

39 Herf, *Divided Memory*, p. 206.

40 See Frank's testimony in *Trial of the Major War Criminals*, Vol. 12, pp. 1–25.

41 See Speer, *Inside the Third Reich*, p. 649.

42 Speer's testimony is in *Trial of the Major War Criminals*, Vol. 16, pp. 436–586.

43 See Schacht, *My First Seventy-six Years*, pp. 463–501.

44 See Neave, *Nuremberg*, pp. 300–323.

45 See *Trial of the Major War Criminals*, Vol. 19, pp. 395–430, here 413.

46 See *Trial of the Major War Criminals*, Vol. 19, pp. 431–527, here 433, 499, 526.

47 *Trial of the Major War Criminals*, Vol. 22, pp. 364–408.

48 For the judgment, see *Trial of the Major War Criminals*, Vol. 22, pp. 522–585; for the sentences, see pp. 586–587.

49 The dissenting Soviet opinion has been reprinted in *The World War II Collection* (London: The Stationery Office, 2001), pp. 566–587.

50 Neave, *Nuremberg*, pp. 348–349.

51 See Schacht, *My First Seventy-six Years*, pp. 506–513.

52 Merritt and Merritt (eds), *Public Opinion in Occupied Germany*, pp. 32–33, 93, 94, 122, 161, 31.

CONCLUSION

1 Cited in Monod, *Settling Scores*, p. 165.

2 See Eric Johnson, *The Nazi Terror: Gestapo, Jews and Ordinary Germans* (London: John Murray, 2000), pp. 3–8.

3 See Pritchard, *The making of the GDR*, pp. 36–37.

4 See Ordonnance No. 22 and No. 23, *Journal Officiel du Commandement en Chef français en Allemagne*, 21 December 1945, pp. 54–58.

5 TNA PRO FO 371/76525, Report from Political Division, Berlin to German Political Dept., FO, 10 October 1949.

6 For a sensitive discussion of perceptions of Ilse Koch and others, and the way these changed in the post-war period, see Alexandra Przyrembel, 'Transfixed by an Image: Ilse Koch, the "Kommandeuse of Buchenwald"', *German History*, 19:3 (2001), pp. 369–399.

7 Herf, *Divided Memory*, pp. 294–295.

8 *Official Gazette of the Control Council for Germany*, No. 18, 31 October 1948, p. 308.

9 See, for prominent and scandalous examples, Simon Wiesenthal, *Justice not Vengeance* (trans. Osers, London: Weidenfeld and Nicolson, 1989).

10 Published in English as *The Quarry*. See Friedrich Dürrenmatt, *His Five Novels* (London: Pan, 1985).

11 H.N. Brailsford, *Our Settlement with Germany* (Harmondsworth: Penguin, 1944), pp. 70–71.

12 See Smith (ed.), *The Papers of General Lucius D. Clay*, Vol. I, pp. 266–268.

13 *La France en Allemagne, Numéro Special: Information et Action Culturelle*, August 1947, p. 61.

14 See, for a discussion of this neglected area, Alaric Searle, 'The Tolsdorff Trials in Traunstein: Public and Judicial Attitudes to the Wehrmacht in the Federal Republic, 1954–1960', *German History*, 23:1 (2005), pp. 50–78.

15 See Maria Mesner, 'Gender and abortion after the Second World War: the Austrian case in a comparative perspective', in Eleonore Bruening, Jill Lewis, and Gareth Pritchard (eds), *Power and the People: A Social History of Central European Politics, 1945–56* (Manchester: Manchester University Press, 2005), pp. 252–265.

16 See 'The Changing Legacy of 1945 in Germany: A Round-Table Discussion', *German History*, 23:4 (2005), pp. 519–543, p. 527.

17 Clausewitz, *On War*, p. 80.

18 *Official Gazette of the Control Council for Germany*, No. 1, 29 October 1945, pp. 6–7.

19 Weigley, *Eisenhower's Lieutenants*, pp. 730, 729.

20 See his message from Supreme Headquarters Allied Expeditionary Force, reproduced here as illustration 38.

21 Doris Bergen, in 'The Changing Legacy of 1945 in Germany: A Round-Table Discussion', p. 522.

BIBLIOGRAPHY

ARCHIVAL SOURCES

The archives of the British Occupation of Germany, 1949-1955, are now available for consultation in the National Archive (formerly the Public Record Office) in London. Those referred to here are all in the files of Foreign Office correspondence. They are preceded in the notes by the abbreviation TNA PRO FO. I have also used a number of documents from the Soldiers of Gloucestershire Museum (preceded here by the abbreviation SoGM).

The files of the Office of Military Government for Germany (United States), known to historians as the OMGUS files, are now in the American National Archives at College Park in Maryland. A large proportion of them were put on microfilm by teams of German and American scholars in the 1970s, and these copies are now distributed in several German archives. There are central collections at the Institut für Zeitgeschichte in Munich (preceded in the notes here by the abbreviation IfZ OMGUS), and at the Bundesarchiv in Koblenz (preceded here by the abbreviation BAK OMGUS). In addition, the files of American military governments in the separate states of their zone are available on microfilm in the *Land* archives today. Thus the files for Bavaria are in the Bayerisches Hauptstaatsarchiv in Munich (preceded in the notes here by the abbreviation BHA OMGB); those for Baden-Württemberg are in the Generallandesarchiv in Karlsruhe (preceded here by the abbreviation GLAK OMGWB).

The files of the French military occupation of Germany are now open at the Centre des Archives de l'Occupation française en Autriche et en Allemagne in Colmar. Those I have referred to here are mainly from the section on Affaires Culturelles (preceded by the abbreviation AOFC AC). I have also referred to a few from the section Berlin, G.F.C.C., Sous-série Division de l'Information (preceded in the notes here by the abbreviation AOFC Berlin G.F.C.C.).

The files of the Socialist Unity Party (SED) of the German Democratic Republic and its 'mass organisations' are now open at the Stiftung Archiv der Parteien und Massenorganisationen der DDR im Bundesarchiv, Außenstelle Berlin. When referring to these I have used the customary abbreviation SAPMO-BArch.

These archives also hold copies of the publications of the separate military governments, many of which are listed below. Readers should be aware that in these British, French, and German

259

archives there are whole record groups which are not open to historians except on special request. Many of these are documents relating to individuals, as in the case of denazification proceedings.

PUBLISHED PRIMARY SOURCES

Most of these were published only in small numbers and are therefore only available today in specialist libraries and archives.

Bomber Command Continues: The Air Ministry Account of the Rising Offensive against Germany, July 1941–June 1942 (London: HMSO, 1942)

Buchenwald Camp: The Report of a Parliamentary Delegation (London: HMSO, 1945)

Christian-Albrechts-Universität Kiel. Personal- und Vorlesungsverzeichnis. Sommersemester 1945 (Kiel, 1945)

Enactments and Approved Papers of the Allied Control Council and Coordinating Authority for the Year 1945 [Berlin]

Evangelisches Feldgesangbuch (Berlin: Mittler und Sohn, no date)

Gazette of the Office of Military Government for Würtemmberg-Baden for the year of 1946 (Stuttgart, 1946)

German-English Dictionary of Administrative Terms (Washington: War Department, 1944)

Germany, Office of Military Government, Report of the Military Governor, No. 34, 1 April 1947–30 April 1948

History of the United Nations War Crimes Commission and the Development of the Laws of War (London: HMSO, 1948)

Journal Officiel du Commandement en Chef français en Allemagne, 21 December 1945

La France en Allemagne, Numéro Special: Information et Action Culturelle, August 1947

La Revue de la Zone Française

Law-Reports of Trials of War Criminals, The United Nations War Crimes Commission (London: HMSO, 1947)

Manual for the Control of German Information Services. Restricted. 12 May 1945

Mission Militaire pour les Affaires Allemandes, Bulletin d'Information, No. 2 [1945]

Notice sur le Gouvernement Militaire, November 1945

Official Gazette of the Control Council for Germany

Report by the Supreme Commander to the Combined Chiefs of Staff on the Operations in Europe of the Allied Expeditionary Force, 6 June 1944 to 8 May 1945 (London: HMSO, 1946)

Soviet Documents on Nazi Atrocities: Illustrated by some 200 Original Photographs (London: Hutchinson, 1942)

Target Germany: The U.S. Army Air Forces' Official Story of the VIII Bomber Command's First Year over Europe (London: HMSO, 1944)

The German Occupation of Poland: Extract of Note Addressed to the Governments of the Allied and Neutral Powers on May 3, 1941 (London: Cornwall Press, 1941)

The World War II Collection (London: The Stationery Office, 2001)

Trial of the Major War Criminals before the International Military Tribunal, Nuremberg 14 November 1945 - 1 October 1946 (Nuremberg: International Military Tribunal, 1947)

What Buchenwald Really Means (London: Victor Gollancz Ltd, 1945)

Zone Française d'Occupation en Allemagne. Résultats de Six Mois d'Activité, March 1946

BIBLIOGRAPHY

SECONDARY SOURCES AND CONTEMPORARY ACCOUNTS PUBLISHED AFTER 1945

Since many of these books have been published several times in different editions and in different languages, I have indicated in square brackets the date of first publication. In many cases English-language editions which are more readily available today are listed here. To help the reader interested in going further I have added a brief note on each title.

Adelson, Alan, and Lapides, Robert (eds), *Łódź Ghetto: Inside a Community under Siege* (New York: Penguin, 1989). A large and harrowing collection of contemporary documents and writings from the second largest ghetto in Europe.

Adenauer, Konrad, *Memoirs, 1945–53* ([1965] trans. von Oppen, London: Weidenfeld and Nicolson, 1966). Informative but dull memoirs of the Federal German Republic's first post-war Chancellor.

Annan, Noel, *Changing Enemies: The Defeat and Regeneration of Germany* (London: HarperCollins, 1995). Annan was a senior official in the British administration in Germany; his account focuses mainly on politics in the British Zone.

Anonymous, *A Woman in Berlin: Diary 20 April 1945 to 22 June 1945* (trans. Boehm, London: Virago, 2005). An extraordinarily candid first hand account of a civilian woman in the transition from war to peace in Berlin.

Auf der richtigen Seite: Nationalkomitee Freies Deutschland (Berlin: Militärverlag der Deutschen Demokratischen Republik, 1985). Propagandistic account of the Soviet-sponsored communist organisation of German POWs.

Auschwitz: faschistisches Vernichtungslager (Warsaw: Interpress, 1988). Although this is very much the official Communist version, this collection of essays is an invaluable source.

Bannister, Sybil, *I lived under Hitler: An Englishwoman's Story* (London: Rockliff, 1957). A heart-warming account by an Englishwoman living in the 'Third Reich' and in post-war Germany.

Bartov, Omer, *Hitler's Army: Soldiers, Nazis, and War in the Third Reich* ([1991] New York and Oxford: Oxford University Press, 1992). This book, based largely on German soldiers' correspondence, established several of the current understandings of the nature of Hitler's army, particularly on the Eastern Front.

Bausch, Hans (ed.), *Rundfunk in Deutschland, Band 3, Rundfunkpolitik nach 1945. Erster Teil 1945–1962* (Munich, 1980). This is the standard German-language history of radio in Germany. Volume 3 deals with the critical post-war period.

Johannes-R.-Becher-Archiv der Deutschen Akademie der Künste (ed.), *Erinnerungen an Johannes R. Becher* (Leipzig: Philipp Reclam, 1968). Propagandistic accounts of the leading cultural official of the GDR and his role there.

Beevor, Anthony, *Berlin: The Downfall 1945* (London: Penguin, 2002). A dramatic account of the Soviet capture of Berlin which includes much first-hand testimony.

Beevor, Antony and Vinogradova, Luba (eds), *A Writer at War: Vasily Grossman with the Red Army, 1941–1945* (New York: Pantheon, 2005). Probably the best account available in English of the Red Army at war between 1941 and 1945; includes Grossman's remarkable essay on Treblinka.

Biddiscombe, Perry, *The Last Nazis: SS Werewolf Guerrilla Resistance in Europe 1944–1947* ([2000] Stroud: Tempus, 2004). A detailed study of the failed Nazi resistance effort.

Birley, Robert, 'Potsdam in Practice', in Brian Rees (ed.), *History and Idealism: Essays, Addresses and Letters* (London: John Murray, 1990), pp. 75–93. An interesting summary of education policy in the British Zone by the ex-public school headmaster in charge of Education Branch.

Blumentritt, Guenther, *Von Rundstedt: The Soldier and the Man* (trans. Reavely, London: Odhams, 1952). Rundstedt is presented here as the archetypal 'honourable', apolitical, professional soldier.

Brailsford, H.N., *Our Settlement with Germany* (Harmondsworth: Penguin, 1944). A fascinating gaze into the future by a decent and humane liberal socialist.

Breitman, Richard, *Official Secrets: What the Nazis Planned, What the British and Americans Knew* (London: Penguin, 2000). An excellent and sympathetic account of Allied wartime knowledge of the Holocaust.

Bruce, George, *The Warsaw Uprising* ([1972] London: Pan, 1974). Good account, from the Western perspective, of the doomed uprising of the Home Army.

Bryant, Arthur (ed.), *The Alanbrooke War Diaries 1939–43: The Turn of the Tide* ([1957] London: Collins, 1965). Full of revealing insights into the British conduct of the war, and into Churchill's leadership.

Burleigh, Michael, *Death and Deliverance: 'Euthanasia' in Germany, 1900–1945* (Cambridge: Cambridge University Press, 1994). Charts in shocking detail how the 'euthanasia' programme in Nazi Germany grew from pre-1933 developments in German psychiatry.

Butcher, Harry, *Three Years with Eisenhower: The Personal Diary of Captain Harry C. Butcher, USNR, Naval Aide to General Eisenhower, 1942–1945* (London: Heinemann, 1946). This detailed diary written by a loyal aide to Eisenhower is full of interesting anecdotes and insights.

Calder, Angus, *The People's War: Britain 1939–1945* ([1969] London: Panther, 1971). Still invaluable for any study of the 'home front' in Britain.

Chamberlin, Brewster, *Kultur auf Trümmern. Berliner Berichte des amerikanischen Information Control Section Juli–Dezember 1945* (Stuttgart: Deutsche Verlags Anstalt, 1979). Still the best primary account of cultural developments in post-war Berlin, from the American perspective.

Le Chêne, Evelyn, *Mauthausen: The History of a Death Camp* (London: Methuen, 1971). A detailed and engaged account of the evolution of Mauthausen and its many sub-camps.

Chuikov, Vasili, *The Fall of Berlin* ([1965] trans. Kisch, New York: Ballantyne, 1969). Although Chuikov writes from a Communist Cold War perspective, he is occasionally critical of Soviet policy in the final stages of the war.

Churchill, Winston, *The Second World War* (London: Cassell, 1954). Churchill's multi-volume history is still worth reading, and includes many valuable primary documents.

Clare, George, *Berlin Days* (London: Macmillan, 1989). A frustratingly vague memoir by an émigré working in the Intelligence Branch of the British Information Control Service.

Clausewitz, Carl von, *On War* (trans. and ed. Howard and Paret, Princeton: Princeton University Press, 1989). Although at times contradictory, Clausewitz is still invaluable for any study of war.

Colville, John, *The Fringes of Power: 10 Downing Street Diaries 1939–1955* (New York and London: Norton, 1985). Colville's gossipy recollection of working as Churchill's secretary gains depth from his periods of active service as an RAF pilot.

Cunningham, Andrew, *A Sailor's Odyssey: The Autobiography of Admiral of the Fleet Viscount Cunningham of Hyndhope* (London: Hutchinson, 1951). Much of the detail here is on the campaigns in the Mediterranean, but Cunningham also offers an interesting perspective on Allied strategy at the highest level.

Deissler, Dirk, *Die entnazifizierte Sprache: Sprachpolitik und Sprachregelung in der Besatzungszeit* (Frankfurt am Main: Peter Lang, 2004). This recent study of language reform in post-war Germany is unusual in its focus on the American and French Zones.

Donnison, F.S.V., *Civil Affairs and Military Government North-West Europe 1944–1946* (London: HMSO, 1961). Although written in the slightly stodgy style of 'official history', this is still a valuable study.

Ehrenburg, Ilya, *Men, Years – Life*, Vol. V, *The War 1941–45* (trans. Shebunina, London: Macgibbon and Kee, 1964). Ehrenburg presents himself here as a civilised and cosmopolitan observer, but his memoir is still trapped within the confines of orthodox Soviet historiography.

Eisenhower, Dwight, *Crusade in Europe* (New York: Doubleday, 1948). A personal account of the American and British campaign in north-west Europe by a fundamentally decent man.

Evans, Richard J., *Rituals of Retribution: Capital Punishment in Germany 1600–1987* (New York and Oxford: Oxford University Press, 1996). A remarkable book, despite its macabre focus; full of shocking details.

Fedorov, Colonel, *The Red Army: An Army of the People* (London: Cobbett, 1944). A war-time propaganda account of the heroic Red Army and its great leader for consumption in Britain.

Feis, Herbert, *Between War and Peace: The Potsdam Conference* (Princeton: Princeton University Press, 1960). Good analysis of the Potsdam conference.

Ferrell, Robert (ed.), *The Eisenhower Diaries* (London and New York: Norton, 1981). Eisenhower was not a consistent diarist, and regrettably he did not keep a detailed record of the period 1944–1946.

Franzel, Emil, *Die Vertreibung. Sudetenland 1945–1946* (Landshut: Aufstieg, 1967). A passionate and resentful account of the expulsion of the Germans from Bohemia in 1945.

Fussell, Paul, *The Boys' Crusade: American G.I.s in Europe: Chaos and Fear in World War Two* ([2003] London: Weidenfeld and Nicolson, 2004). This is a new kind of military history, concerned with the psychological impact of the experience of war. Fussell is best known for his superb writing on the First World War.

Galland, Adolf, *The First and the Last: The Rise and Fall of the German Fighter Forces 1938–1945* ([1953] London: Fontana, 1970). A blinkered account of the *Luftwaffe*'s fighter arm by one of its leading aces.

Gau, Karl Friedrich, *Silesian Inferno: War Crimes of the Red Army on its March into Silesia in 1945* (trans. Schlosser, Cologne: Informations- und Dokumentationszentrum West, 1970). A disturbingly detailed documentation of the atrocities visited on the German population of Silesia in early 1945 by the Red Army.

De Gaulle, Charles, *Mémoires de Guerre: Le Salut 1944–1946* (Paris: Plon, 1959). Good for a French perspective, and includes valuable documents reprinted after de Gaulle's narrative.

Gienow-Hecht, Jessica, *Transmission Impossible: American Journalism as Cultural Diplomacy in Postwar Germany* (Baton Rouge: Louisiana State University Press, 1999). A detailed analysis of the American flagship newspaper in post-war Germany.

Glaser, Hermann, Von Pufendorf, Lutz, and Schöneich, Michael (eds), *So viel Anfang war nie: Deutsche Städte 1945–1949* (Berlin: Siedler, 1989). A really excellent collection of articles on different subjects and different towns of Western Germany after 1945.

Goldhagen, Daniel Jonah, *Hitler's Willing Executioners: Ordinary Germans and the Holocaust* (London: Little, Brown and Company, 1996). Goldhagen's much maligned book has a useful section on the 'death marches'.

Grigg, John, *1943: The victory that never was* ([1980] London: Methuen, 1985). A controversial criticism of the Allies for making grave strategic errors in 1943.

Grohnert, Reinhard, *Die Entnazifizierung in Baden 1945–1949. Konzeptionen und Praxis der "Epuration" am Beispiel eines Landes der französischen Besatzungszone* (Stuttgart: Kohlhammer, 1991). One of the new studies now emerging, based on archival material relating to the French Zone.

Guderian, Heinz, *Panzer Leader* ([1952] London: Futura, 1974). An appallingly complacent account by Hitler's leading tank commander.

Hahn, Edith, *The Nazi Officer's Wife: How One Jewish Woman Survived the Holocaust*

([1999] London: Abacus, 2001). A remarkable story of Jewish survival in the 'Third Reich'.

Hastings, Max, *Bomber Command* ([1979] London: Pan, 1981). Judicious, balanced, and informative.

Hastings, Max, *Armageddon: The Battle for Germany 1944–45* ([2004] London: Pan, 2005). Hastings has breathed new life into the narrative history format, and includes here much new eyewitness material.

Hawkins, Desmond (ed.), *War Report D-Day to VE-Day: Dispatches by the BBC's War Correspondents with the Allied Expeditionary Force 6 June 1944–5 May 1945* ([1946] London: BBC, 1985). Invaluable for gaining a flavour of the BBC's war-time reporting.

Herf, Jeffrey, *Divided Memory: The Nazi Past in the two Germanys* (Cambridge, Massachusetts and London: Harvard University Press, 1997). A critical text for understanding how attitudes towards Nazism diverged in Germany after 1945.

Hoess, Rudolf, *Commandant of Auschwitz: The Autobiography of Rudolf Hoess* ([1959] London: Phoenix Press, 2000). This horrifying book reveals much about the mindset of the SS man.

Hull, Cordell, *The Memoirs of Cordell Hull* (London: Hodder and Stoughton, 1948). An invaluable primary source, which also shows how many non-European matters American statesmen had to deal with during the war.

Jacobsen, Wolfgang (ed.), *Babelsberg: Ein Filmstudio 1912–1992* (Berlin: Argon Verlag, 1992). An interesting history of the 'German Hollywood' in changing political circumstances.

Johnson, Eric, *The Nazi Terror: Gestapo, Jews and Ordinary Germans* (London: John Murray, 2000). Absolutely vital for an understanding of how the Gestapo functioned in the 'Third Reich'.

Jordan, Ulrike (ed.), *Conditions of Surrender: Britons and Germans Witness the End of the War* (London: Taurus, 1997). Good collection of writings about the first confrontations between British and Germans in 1945, with some fascinating primary recollections.

Junge, Traudl (with Melissa Müller), *Until the final hour: Hitler's last secretary* ([2002] trans. Bell, London: Phoenix, 2005). This memoir, which provided a starting point for the controversial film *Der Untergang*, is actually very disappointing, and depicts the extraordinary moral vacuum in which Hitler's entourage worked.

Klemperer, Victor, *To the Bitter End: The Diaries of Victor Klemperer 1942–45* ([1995] trans. Chalmers, London: BCA, 1998). Klemperer's diaries stand head and shoulders above any other memoir to come out of the 'Third Reich'.

Klemperer, Victor, *The Lesser Evil: The Diaries of Victor Klemperer 1945–1949* ([1999] trans. Chalmers, London: Weidenfeld and Nicolson, 2003). Similarly, Klemperer's post-war diaries are easily the best to emerge from the Soviet Zone and GDR.

Klemperer, Victor, *The Language of the Third Reich: A Philologist's Notebook* ([1957] trans. Brady, New York and London: Continuum, 2002). More than just an analysis of 'Nazi language', this is also a fascinating set of recollections drawn from everyday life in the 'Third Reich'.

Knappe, Siegfried, and Brusaw, Ted, *Soldat: Reflections of a German Soldier, 1936–1949* (London: BCA, 1993). Formulaic recollections of a German soldier on the Eastern Front.

Koch, Elizabeth, '"The Golden Hunger Years": Music and Superpower Rivalry in Occupied Berlin', *German History*, 22:1 (2004), pp. 76–100. This article provides some insights into the cultural scene in post-war Berlin, but neglects the British and French presence there.

Kogon, Eugen, *The Theory and Practice of Hell: The German Concentration Camps and the System Behind Them* ([1950] trans. Norden, London: World Distributors, 1958). Kogon was a prisoner at Buchenwald, and his post-war writings played an important role in shaping public understanding of the concentration camps.

Kolb, Eberhard (ed.), *Bergen-Belsen: From "Detention Camp" to Concentration Camp, 1943–1945* (trans. Claeys and Lattek, Göttingen: Vandenhoeck & Ruprecht, 1986). A superb anthology, containing historical essays, some documents, and eye-witness recollections.

Kreimeier, Klaus, *The UFA Story: A History of Germany's Greatest Film Company, 1918–1945* ([1992] trans. Kimber and Kimber, New York: Hill and Wang, 1996). Provides interesting insights into Goebbels' 'Dream Factory'.

Leonhardt, Wolfgang, *Die Revolution entläßt ihre Kinder* ([1955] Frankfurt am Main and Berlin: Ullstein, 1974). The classic exposé of Stalinist methods, from the youngest member of the 'Ulbricht Group' sent to Berlin in 1945.

Liddell, Helen (ed.), *Education in Occupied Germany* (Paris: M. Rivière, 1949). Good collection of essays on different aspects of education in post-war Germany, with contributions from a number of those centrally involved.

Lucas, James, *The Last Days of the Reich: The Collapse of Nazi Germany, May 1945* (London: BCA, 1986). Packed with interesting narrative detail.

MacIsaac, David, *Strategic Bombing in World War Two: The Story of the United States Strategic Bombing Survey* (New York and London: Garland, 1976). A balanced and critical analysis of American strategic bombing.

Malzahn, Manfred, *Germany 1945–1949: A sourcebook* (London and New York: Routledge, 1991). Good collection of primary documents from post-war Germany on many varied topics.

Manchester, William, *The Arms of Krupp 1587–1968* (London: Michael Joseph, 1969). This is old-fashioned narrative history at its best, thoroughly researched, and with much illuminating detail.

Mawdsley, Evan, *Thunder in the East: The Nazi-Soviet War 1941–1945* (London: Hodder Arnold, 2005). A recent account drawing on German and Soviet archival material.

Von Mellenthin, F.W., *Panzer Battles* ([1955] London: Futura, 1977). Another complacent account of a supposedly 'honourable' war by a German general.

Merritt, Anna, and Merritt, Richard (eds), *Public Opinion in Occupied Germany: The OMGUS Surveys, 1945–1949* (Urbana, Chicago, and London: University of Illinois Press, 1970). Contains much raw material in statistical form.

Mermelstein, Mel, *By Bread Alone: The Story of A-4685* ([1979] Cracow: Poligrafia Inspektoratu, 1993). A harrowing Holocaust memoir; Mermelstein was in Buchenwald at the end of the war.

Mesner, Maria, 'Gender and abortion after the Second World War: the Austrian case in a comparative perspective', in Eleonore Bruening, Jill Lewis, and Gareth Pritchard (eds), *Power and the People: A Social History of Central European Politics, 1945–56* (Manchester: Manchester University Press, 2005), pp. 252–265. This essay also contains important material about rape and abortion in Germany at the end of the war.

Middlebrook, Martin, *The Nuremberg Raid 30–31 March 1944* ([1973] Glasgow: Fontana, 1975)

Middlebrook, Martin, *The Berlin Raids: RAF Bomber Command, Winter 1943–44* ([1988] London: Cassell, 2000). Middlebrook skilfully balances narrative detail with fair-minded analysis; his books are invaluable for any study of 'area bombing'.

Miller, Russell, and Miller, Renate, *Ten Days in May: The People's Story of VE Day* (London: Michael Joseph, 1995). An anthology of British recollections.

Ministerium für Auswärtige Angelegenheiten (ed.), *Um ein antifaschistisch-demokratisches Deutschland. Dokumente aus den Jahren 1945–1949* (Berlin: Staatsverlag der DDR, 1968). An official GDR publication which nonetheless contains many valuable documents.

Minott, Rodney, *The Fortress that never was: The Myth of the Nazi Alpine Redoubt* (London: Longmans, 1964). A still-relevant pointer to the dangers of basing strategy on mistaken 'intelligence'.

Monod, David, *Settling Scores: German Music, Denazification, and the Americans, 1945–1953* (Chapel

Hill and London: University of North Carolina Press, 2005). Detailed recent study of this controversial topic.

Montgomery, Bernard, *El Alamein to the River Sangro; Normandy to the Baltic* ([1947–1948] London: Book Club Associates, 1973). Montgomery's first post-war memoirs are still an invaluable source for these campaigns.

Montgomery, Bernard, *The Memoirs of Field-Marshal the Viscount Montgomery of Alamein, K.G.* (London: Collins, 1958). This later memoir includes more critical material on the Americans, and also includes some detail on Montgomery's role in post-war Germany.

Morgenthau, Hans, *American Foreign Policy: A Critical Examination* (London: Methuen, 1952). A series of lectures mainly relevant to the early Cold War.

Naimark, Norman, *The Russians in Germany: A History of the Soviet Zone of Occupation, 1945–1949* (Cambridge, Massachusetts and London: Harvard University Press, 1995). The authoritative study of the Soviet Zone, with an excellent, if disturbing, chapter on rape there.

Neave, Airey, *Nuremberg: A Personal Record of the Trial of the Major Nazi War Criminals* ([1978] London: Hodder and Stoughton, 1980). Good personal memoir.

Neillands, Robin, *The Bomber War: Arthur Harris and the Allied Bomber Offensive 1939–1945* (London: John Murray, 2001). A straightforward and balanced account.

Overy, Richard, *Why the Allies Won* ([1995] London: Pimlico, 1996). Overy steps away from the military detail to analyse the underlying reasons for the Allied victory.

Overy, Richard, *Interrogations: Inside the Mind of the Nazi Elite* (London: Penguin, 2002). Interesting material drawn from the pre-trial interrogations of the 'major war criminals' tried at Nuremberg.

Owen, James, and Walters, Guy (eds), *Voices of War: The Second World War Told by Those Who Fought It* ([2004] London: Penguin, 2005). A good collection, with contributions by participants on all sides and at every level of the conflict.

Owings, Alison, *Frauen: German Women Recall the Third Reich* ([1993] London: Penguin, 2001). An important contribution to the growing, and controversial, literature on women in the 'Third Reich'.

Pocock, Tom, *1945: The Dawn Came Up Like Thunder* (London: Collins, 1983). There are some interesting details in this eye-witness account from a Fleet Street correspondent.

Pritchard, Gareth, *The making of the GDR 1945–53* (Manchester: Manchester University Press, 2000). An invaluable guide to the foundational years of the GDR.

Przyrembel, Alexandra, 'Transfixed by an Image: Ilse Koch, the "Kommandeuse of Buchenwald"', *German History*, 19:3 (2001), pp. 369–399. Although at times difficult to follow, this is a valuable analysis of the post-war fascination with female perpetrators.

Riefenstahl, Leni, *The Sieve of Time: The Memoirs of Leni Riefenstahl* ([1978] London: Quartet Books, 1992). A bland account, in which Riefenstahl denies that she was a Nazi propagandist.

Rumpf, Hans, *The Bombing of Germany* ([1961] trans. Fitzgerald, London: Frederick Muller, 1963). One of the first accounts from the German side; the author was a senior fire-fighter during the war.

Rürup, Reinhard (ed.), *Topography of Terror: Gestapo, SS and Reichssicherheitshauptamt on the "Prinz-Albrecht-Terrain" – A Documentation* (trans. Angress, Berlin: Arenhövel, 1989). An excellent documentation of the headquarters of the Nazi apparatus of terror.

Lord Russell of Liverpool, *The Scourge of the Swastika: A Short History of Nazi War Crimes* (London: Cassell, 1954). Although this account by the former legal adviser on war crimes trials in the British Zone is now dated, it still speaks volumes.

Ryan, Cornelius, *The Last Battle* ([1966] London: New English Library, 1967)

Ryan, Cornelius, *A Bridge Too Far* ([1974] London: Hodder and Stoughton, 1975). Ryan's books are old-fashioned narrative history of the best kind; readable, and based on many primary sources and eye-witness accounts.

Schacht, Hjalmar, *My First Seventy-six Years: The Autobiography of Hjalmar Schacht* (trans. Pike, London: Allan Wingate, 1955). A revealing, if disingenuous memoir, in which Schacht denies any responsibility for aiding Hitler.

Schmidt, Ulf, '"The Scars of Ravensbrück": Medical Experiments and British War Crimes Policy, 1945–1950', *German History*, 23:1 (2005), pp. 20–49. A revealing analysis, with useful details of wider British policy on war crimes.

Searle, Alaric, 'The Tolsdorff Trials in Traunstein: Public and Judicial Attitudes to the Wehrmacht in the Federal Republic, 1954–1960', *German History*, 23:1 (2005), pp. 50–78. A useful article which challenges conventional views on attitudes to the *Wehrmacht* in the Federal Republic in the 1950s.

Sebald, W.G., *On the Natural History of Destruction* ([1999] London: Penguin, 2004). An important reflection on the British bombing of Germany.

Sebastian, Mihail, *Journal 1935–1944* ([1996] London: Pimlico, 2003). Sebastian, who was killed in an accident in 1945, might have been the Romanian Klemperer; his journal provides a fascinating view of one of Germany's satellite states from the inside.

Shandley, Robert, *Rubble Films: German Cinema in the Shadow of the Third Reich* (Philadelphia: Temple University Press, 2001). Useful as an introduction to post-war German cinema.

Short, K.R.M., and Dolezel, Stephan (eds), *Hitler's Fall: The Newsreel Witness* (London: Croom Helm, 1988). A good collection, with essays on some less well-known newsreel productions.

Smith, Bradley, *The Road to Nuremberg* (New York: Basic Books, 1981). Although some have questioned Smith's judgement, this is an invaluable study of the evolution of plans for the International Military Tribunal, solidly based on archival material.

Smith, Jean Edward (ed.), *The Papers of General Lucius D. Clay*, Vol. I, *Germany 1945–1949* (Bloomington: Indiana University Press, 1974). Excellent primary material on the American occupation; the editor is also Clay's biographer.

Speer, Albert, *Inside the Third Reich* ([1969] New York: Avon, 1971). Speer's bestseller needs to be treated with caution; he leaves out far too much!

Studt, Christoph (ed.), *Das Dritte Reich: Ein Lesebuch zur deutschen Geschichte 1933–1945* (Munich: Beck, 1995). A good collection of first hand accounts from the 'Third Reich'.

Taylor, Frederick, *Dresden, Tuesday 13 February 1945* (London: Bloomsbury, 2004). A detailed recent study of the most controversial RAF attack of the war.

'The Changing Legacy of 1945 in Germany: A Round-Table Discussion', *German History*, 23:4 (2005), pp. 519–543. An interesting series of overviews from some distinguished German historians.

Trevor-Roper, H.R., *The Last Days of Hitler* ([1947] London: Pan, 1952). Still the classic account, much imitated.

Trevor-Roper, H.R. (ed.), *Hitler's War Directives 1939–1945* ([1964] London: Pan, 1966). Valuable primary material which provides insights into Hitler's military thinking.

Trevor-Roper, H.R. (ed.), *The Goebbels Diaries: The Last Days* ([1945] trans. Barry, London: Book Club Associates, 1978). A detailed and candid commentary by one of Hitler's most loyal supporters.

Truman, Harry S., *The Memoirs of Harry S. Truman*, Vol. I, *Year of Decisions 1945* (London: Hodder and Stoughton, 1955). Truman's memoir demonstrates how Germany was not the only topic on his agenda on becoming President in 1945.

United States Department of State (ed.), *The Conferences at Malta and Yalta, 1945* ([1955] Westport: Greenwood Press, 1976). Contains long verbatim transcripts of the discussions, as well as related documents.

Vansittart, Robert, *Roots of the Trouble* (London: Hutchinson, 1943). This, and Vansittart's other wartime writings illuminate certain British perceptions of Nazism and the German 'national character'.

Volkmann, Hans-Erich (ed.), *Ende das Dritten Reiches – Ende des Zweiten Weltkrieges. Eine Perspektive Rückschau* (Munich: Piper, 1995). A substantial collection of essays by international historians on diverse aspects of the collapse of the 'Third Reich'.

Webster, Charles, and Frankland, Noble, *The Strategic Air Offensive against Germany 1939–1945* (London: HMSO, 1961). This four-volume official history is still compulsory reading for the serious student.

Weigley, Russell F., *Eisenhower's Lieutenants: The Campaign of France and Germany, 1944–1945* (Bloomington: Indiana University Press, 1990). The best account of the American land campaign against Germany.

Weinreich, Max, *Hitler's Professors: The Part Played by Scholarship in Germany's Crimes Against the Jewish People* ([1946] New Haven and London: Yale University Press, 1999). Passionate, engaged, and critical; essential for an understanding of Nazism.

Wiesenthal, Simon, *Justice not Vengeance* (trans. Osers, London: Weidenfeld and Nicolson, 1989). The classic account of post-war Nazi hunting.

Willis, Frank, *The French in Germany* (Stanford: Stanford University Press, 1962). Still the only English-language history of the French occupation of Germany.

Wilmot, Chester, *The Struggle for Europe* (London: Collins, 1952). This early post-war account by a former war correspondent is still worth reading.

Winzer, Otto, *Zwölf Jahre Kampf gegen Faschismus und Krieg* (Berlin: Dietz, 1955). This is the heroic Communist version of their resistance to Nazism; nonetheless revealing.

Wolff, Leon, *Low Level Mission* ([1958] London: Panther, 1960). Good account by the distinguished historian of the First World War of the ill-fated raid on Ploesti in 1943.

Wollenberg, H.H., *Fifty Years of German Cinema* (London; Falcon Press, 1948). An interesting survey written soon after 1945.

Wulf, Joseph, *Presse und Funk im Dritten Reich: Eine Dokumentation* (Frankfurt am Main and Berlin: Ullstein, 1989). This, and Wulf's other documentations on the media and arts in the 'Third Reich', are invaluable starting points.

Ziemke, Earl F., *Stalingrad to Berlin: The German Defeat in the East* (Washington: Dorset Press, 1968). A compelling narrative from the German perspective, based firmly on captured German archives.

Zimmerman, Clemens, 'From Propaganda to Modernization: Media Policy and Media Audiences under National Socialism', *German History*, 24:3 (2006), pp. 431–454. A good recent summary which challenges traditional views of the all-pervasive nature of Nazi propaganda.

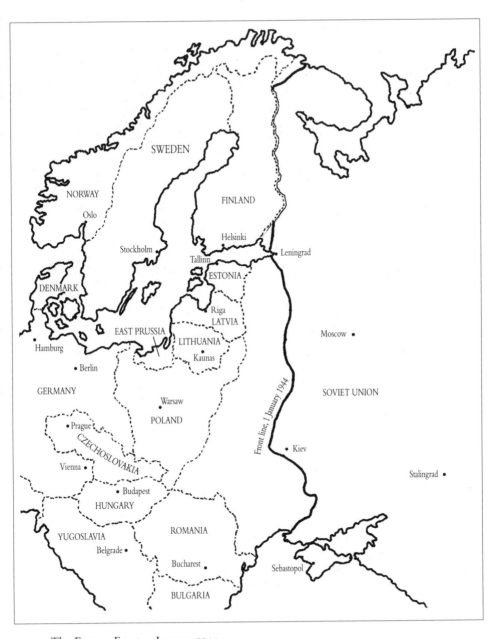

1 The Eastern Front, 1 January 1944.

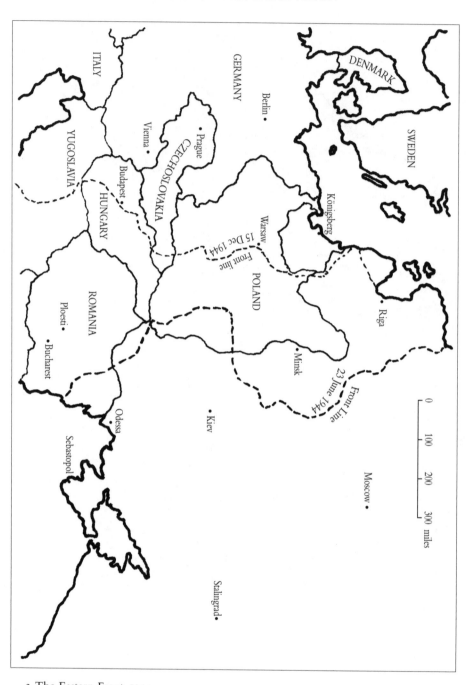

2 The Eastern Front, 1944.

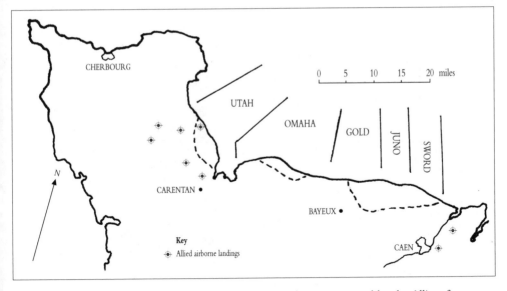

3 The invasion of Normandy, June 1944, showing the areas secured by the Allies after the first day.

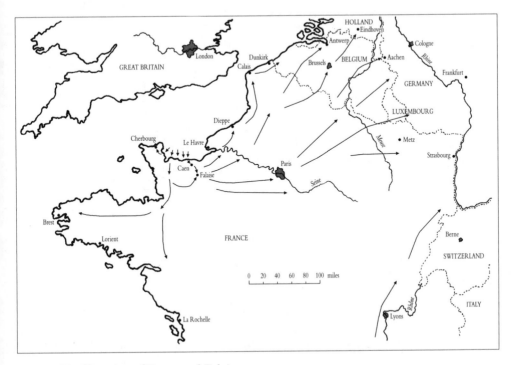

4 The liberation of France and Belgium.

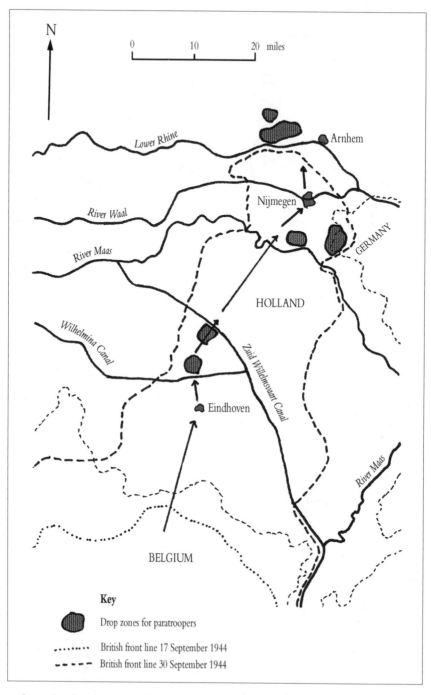

5 Operation 'Market-Garden', showing the major waterways the attack was intended to secure.

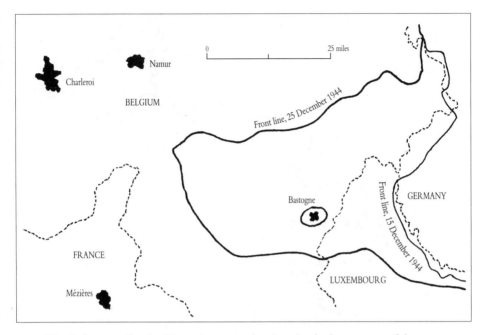

6 The Ardennes offensive, December 1944, showing the furthest extent of the German advance.

7 Eisenhower's 'broad front' approaches the Rhine, March 1945.

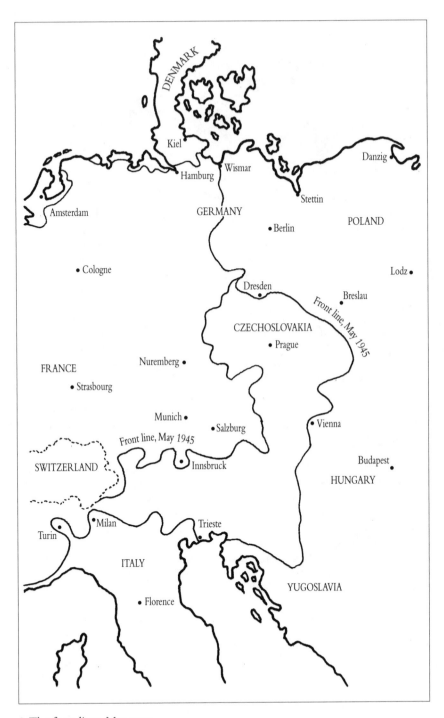

8 The front lines, May 1945.

9 Occupied Germany, 1945–1949.

INDEX

TEMPUS – REVEALING HISTORY

Britannia's Empire
A Short History of the British Empire
BILL NASSON

'Crisp, economical and witty' *TLS*
'An excellent introduction the subject' *THES*

£12.99   0 7524 3808 5

Madmen
A Social History of Madhouses,
Mad-Doctors & Lunatics
ROY PORTER

'Fascinating'
The Observer

£12.99   0 7524 3730 5

Born to be Gay
A History of Homosexuality
WILLIAM NAPHY

'Fascinating' *The Financial Times*
'Excellent' *Gay Times*

£9.99   0 7524 3694 5

William II
Rufus, the Red King
EMMA MASON

'A thoroughly new reappraisal of a much
maligned king. The dramatic story of his life is
told with great pace and insight'
John Gillingham

£25   0 7524 3528 0

To Kill Rasputin
The Life and Death of Grigori Rasputin
ANDREW COOK

'Andrew Cook is a brilliant investigative historian'
Andrew Roberts
'Astonishing' *The Daily Mail*

£9.99   0 7524 3906 5

The Unwritten Order
Hitler's Role in the Final Solution
PETER LONGERICH

'Compelling' *Richard Evans*
'The finest account to date of the many twists
and turns in Adolf Hitler's anti-semitic obsession'
Richard Overy

£12.99   0 7524 3328 8

Private 12768
Memoir of a Tommy
JOHN JACKSON
FOREWORD BY HEW STRACHAN

'A refreshing new perspective' *The Sunday Times*
'At last we have John Jackson's intensely
personal and heartfelt little book to remind us
there was a view of the Great War other than
Wilfred Owen's' *The Daily Mail*

£9.99   0 7524 3531 0

The Vikings
MAGNUS MAGNUSSON

'Serious, engaging history'
BBC History Magazine

£9.99   0 7524 2699 0

If you are interested in purchasing other books published by Tempus, or in case you have difficulty finding any
Tempus books in your local bookshop, you can also place orders directly through our website

www.tempus-publishing.com

TEMPUS – REVEALING HISTORY

D-Day The First 72 Hours
WILLIAM F. BUCKINGHAM

'A compelling narrative' *The Observer*

A *BBC History Magazine* Book of the Year 2004

£9.99   0 7524 2842 X

The London Monster
Terror on the Streets in 1790

JAN BONDESON

'Gripping' *The Guardian*

'Excellent... monster-mania brought a reign of terror to the ill-lit streets of the capital'
The Independent

£9.99   0 7524 3327 X

London
A Historical Companion

KENNETH PANTON

'A readable and reliable work of reference that deserves a place on every Londoner's bookshelf'
Stephen Inwood

£20   0 7524 3434 9

M: MI5's First Spymaster
ANDREW COOK

'Serious spook history' *Andrew Roberts*
'Groundbreaking' *The Sunday Telegraph*
'Brilliantly researched' *Dame Stella Rimington*

£20   0 7524 2896 9

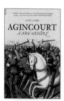   

Agincourt A New History
ANNE CURRY

'A highly distinguished and convincing account'
Christopher Hibbert
'A *tour de force*' *Alison Weir*
'*The* book on the battle' *Richard Holmes*
A *BBC History Magazine* Book of the Year 2005

£25   0 7524 2828 4

Battle of the Atlantic
MARC MILNER

'The most comprehensive short survey of the U-boat battles' *Sir John Keegan*

'Some events are fortunate in their historian, none more so than the Battle of the Atlantic. Marc Milner is *the* historian of the Atlantic campaign... a compelling narrative' *Andrew Lambert*

£12.99   0 7524 3332 6

The English Resistance
The Underground War Against the Normans

PETER REX

'An invaluable rehabilitation of an ignored resistance movement' *The Sunday Times*

'Peter Rex's scholarship is remarkable'
The Sunday Express

£12.99   0 7524 3733 X

Elizabeth Wydeville: The Slandered Queen
ARLENE OKERLUND

'A penetrating, thorough and wholly convincing vindication of this unlucky queen'
Sarah Gristwood

'A gripping tale of lust, loss and tragedy'
Alison Weir

A *BBC History Magazine* Book of the Year 2005

£18.99   0 7524 3384 9

If you are interested in purchasing other books published by Tempus, or in case you have difficulty finding any Tempus books in your local bookshop, you can also place orders directly through our website

www.tempus-publishing.com

TEMPUS – REVEALING HISTORY

Quacks Fakers and Charlatans in Medicine
ROY PORTER

'A delightful book' *The Daily Telegraph*
'Hugely entertaining' *BBC History Magazine*

£12.99   0 7524 2590 0

The Tudors
RICHARD REX

'Up-to-date, readable and reliable. The best introduction to England's most important dynasty' *David Starkey*
'Vivid, entertaining... quite simply the best short introduction' *Eamon Duffy*
'Told with enviable narrative skill... a delight for any reader' *THES*

£9.99   0 7524 3333 4

The Kings & Queens of England
MARK ORMROD

'Of the numerous books on the kings and queens of England, this is the best'
Alison Weir

£9.99   0 7524 2598 6

The Covent Garden Ladies
Pimp General Jack & the Extraordinary Story of Harris's List
HALLIE RUBENHOLD

'Sex toys, porn... forget Ann Summers, Miss Love was at it 250 years ago' *The Times*
'Compelling' *The Independent on Sunday*
'Marvellous' *Leonie Frieda*
'Filthy' *The Guardian*

£9.99   0 7524 3739 9

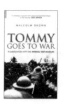

Okinawa 1945
GEORGE FEIFER

'A great book... Feifer's account of the three sides and their experiences far surpasses most books about war'
Stephen Ambrose

£17.99   0 7524 3324 5

Tommy Goes To War
MALCOLM BROWN

'A remarkably vivid and frank account of the British soldier in the trenches'
Max Arthur
'The fury, fear, mud, blood, boredom and bravery that made up life on the Western Front are vividly presented and illustrated'
The Sunday Telegraph

£12.99   0 7524 2980 4

Ace of Spies The True Story of Sidney Reilly
ANDREW COOK

'The most definitive biography of the spying ace yet written... both a compelling narrative and a myth-shattering *tour de force*'
Simon Sebag Montefiore
'The absolute last word on the subject' *Nigel West*
'Makes poor 007 look like a bit of a wuss'
The Mail on Sunday

£12.99   0 7524 2959 0

Sex Crimes
From Renaissance to Enlightenment
W.M. NAPHY

'Wonderfully scandalous'
Diarmaid MacCulloch

£10.99   0 7524 2977 9

If you are interested in purchasing other books published by Tempus, or in case you have difficulty finding any Tempus books in your local bookshop, you can also place orders directly through our website

www.tempus-publishing.com